CLASSICAL MEMORIES/MODERN IDENTITIES
Paul Allen Miller and Richard H. Armstrong, Series Editors

Philology and Its Histories

edited by
Sean Gurd

 THE OHIO STATE UNIVERSITY PRESS / COLUMBUS

Copyright © 2010 by The Ohio State University.
All rights reserved.

Library of Congress Cataloging-in-Publication Data

Philology and its histories / edited by Sean Gurd.
    p. cm. — (Classical memories/modern identities)
Includes bibliographical references and index.
ISBN-13: 978-0-8142-1130-4 (cloth : alk. paper)
ISBN-10: 0-8142-1130-5 (cloth : alk. paper)
ISBN-13: 978-0-8142-9229-7 (cd-rom)
 1. Philology—History. 2. Criticism, Textual—History. I. Gurd, Sean Alexander, 1973– II. Series: Classical memories/modern identities.
P61.P56 2010
400—dc22
                            2010016087

This book is available in the following editions:
Cloth (ISBN 978-0-8142-1130-4)
CD-ROM (ISBN 978-0-8142-9229-7)

Cover design by Juliet Williams
Type set in Adobe Garamond Pro
Text design by Juliet Williams

∞ The paper used in this publication meets the minimum requirements of the American National Standard for Information Sciences—Permanence of Paper for Printed Library Materials. ANSI Z.39.48-1992.

CONTENTS

Acknowledgments   vii

Introduction
    SEAN GURD   1

1 Reading Outside the Library
    KATHLEEN McNAMEE   20

2 Philologizing Philologists: A Case Study.
    Philological History and the Text of Rutilius Namatianus' *De Reditu Suo*
    CRAIG MAYNES   47

3 Angelo Poliziano's *Lamia:*
    "Philology" and "Philosophy" at the University of Florence
    CHRISTOPHER S. CELENZA   75

4 Philology and the Emblem
    BRADLEY J. NELSON   107

5 On the Road: Travel, Antiquarianism, Philology
    JONATHAN SACHS   127

6 What Is Philology? Cultural Studies and Ecdotics
    NADIA ALTSCHUL   148

7 Nietzsche, Rhetoric, Philology
    JAMES I. PORTER   164

8 The Philosophy of Philology and the Crisis of Reading:
    Schlegel, Benjamin, de Man
    IAN BALFOUR   192

Works Cited   213
Contributors   229
Index   231

ACKNOWLEDGMENTS

The essays in this volume were first discussed at a workshop in Montréal in the fall of 2006, generously funded by the Social Sciences and Humanities Research Council of Canada and by Concordia University. For their help in the initial planning for that event and in the subsequent production of this volume, I owe thanks to Daniel Anderson and Julija Šukys. Eugene O'Connor and Paul Allen Miller have been generous and very helpful overseers of the production of the book. But above all I wish to thank the authors of the essays that follow. They did the real work and deserve to be read slowly and with celebration.

INTRODUCTION

Sean Gurd

The essays in this volume discuss moments in the history of philology, a history of the ever-changing regulation, disciplining, and interpreting of texts. When philologists take up the tools of textual criticism, they contribute to the very form of texts, and when they adopt articulate protocols to define correct interpretation, they become the legislators of reading practice. In philology, in other words, literature is both produced and received; philology is where literature happens, and we do well to attend to its permutations through time.[1]

But what is philology? Much more than it appears at any given moment. These essays are largely unconcerned with the nineteenth-century German university, where *Philologie* was synonymous with the study of language and literature. That epoch's apparent monopoly on the term and its disciplinary associations can blind scholars to its much longer and more diverse history, and for the same reason any pat definition of philology would run the risk of barring access to the rich plurality of interpretations it has acquired over the course of nearly two and a half millennia. In fact, every definition of philology remains part of its history: to be a philologist means to appropriate a term and to revive or recover a practice. This has never been more the case

---

1. The most complete survey of the history of philology remains Sandys 1964, but see also Brink 1986, Wilamowitz-Moellendorff 1982. Pfeiffer 1968 and 1976 seem to belong to this group but in fact represent a far more sophisticated undertaking; likewise Momigliano's historiographical work (see Momigliano 1994). Henderson 2006 is a fascinating opening on a new approach. On the genre of the philological introduction see Hummel 2000.

than today. Though it has been the object of a number of direct critiques,[2] philology has also been subject to a series of very high-profile revivals in the last half-century.[3] But when philology is recovered, the dynamics of its recovery often involve an element of forgetting, so that what is revived is only a fragment of the much larger assemblage of practices, epistemic orientations, and gestures of recovery associated with the term over its millennia-long history. A kind of narrowing and focusing takes place, one whose ultimate aim is often to buttress the meaning and value of the project currently called "philology," whatever that project might be. A recent example, from Sebastiano Timpanaro's justly celebrated *Genesis of Lachmann's Method*, illustrates this well. In the following passage, Timpanaro discusses Angelo Poliziano's methods of textual criticism.[4] Poliziano, he says,

> already understood that the manuscripts (at least the oldest and most valuable ones) had to be collated not occasionally but systematically, registering all the readings that diverged from the vulgate text, including those that were certainly erroneous but that might turn out to be useful for restoring the text. This is the criterion he asserted in the *subscriptiones* to the writers *De re rustica*, to Pliny, Statius, Pelagonius, and Terrence; he had a full and justified awareness of its methodological novelty, even if earlier Humanists and, probably, medieval scribes had already begun to apply it. In this regard he was a precursor of Ernesti and Wolf and was already beginning to overcome the erroneous concept of *emendatio ope codicum*, which implies that collations are made not constantly but only occasionally.[5]

One does not have to read too carefully to discern the strongly teleological movement of this narrative: Poliziano *already understood* the importance of systematic collation, a locution implying that important ground had been

---

2. The paradigm for twentieth-century critiques of philology is Ferdinand de Saussure (1986; first ed. 1916). In order to establish "linguistics" as a legitimate and autonomous field, Saussure (re)defines philology as seeking "primarily to establish [*fixer*], interpret and comment upon texts" using criticism (*critique*) as its methodology (13–14). More recent, and setting the tone for the apparent abandonment of philology in the age of "high theory," is Wellek and Warren 1956.

3. See de Man 1982 (reprinted in De Man 1986); Gaisser 2007; Gumbrecht 2003; Kallendorf 1994; Said 2004; Ziolkowsky 1990a (=1990b); and the additional examples discussed in Altschul's contribution to this volume. The appearance that philology was ever abandoned was not altogether accurate: not only has it continued to be a major term of disciplinary identification in classical studies, but it has remained a not-so-invisible force in some of the central texts associated with comparative literature, especially Auerbach 1949, 1965 and 1969 (see Lerer 1996); Curtius 1953: 1–15; Szondi 1986: 2–22 ("On Textual Understanding" [*Über philologische Erkenntnis*]; see Szondi 1962).

4. On Poliziano see Celenza's contribution to this volume.

5. Timpanaro 2005: 48.

staked and that that this was done correctly; he was a *precursor* of Ernesti and Wolf, which sets his scholarship in a line of ascent culminating in contemporary textual criticism; and he was *beginning to overcome the erroneous concept of emendatio ope codicum*—beginning, but not successful (that would have to wait for the nineteenth and twentieth centuries); and overcoming a method that was, simply, wrong. Timpanaro's story about the so-called "method of Lachmann" aims, in part, to justify and if necessary correct current practice in textual criticism, particularly in classical studies.[6] Certainly contemporary textual criticism can be described as a rigorous and sophisticated art with a history of producing valuable results in the form of generally accepted and widely used classical texts. But we might wonder about the narrative teleology that Timpanaro imposes on his material: why must Poliziano's philology be described in terms that seem to presume that today's textual methods are better? One might claim that modern text-criticism just *is* better, on the grounds that it has come closest to recovering the words and the cultural contexts of historical texts; that is, it is "just more right" than anything that has come before. If this is the case, however, a critical reader would be justified in pointing out that such a claim depends on the assumption that the past has been recovered, that modern philology has somehow achieved a relatively greater presence of the past in the present. It could be argued that Timpanaro's teleological account is no more than the narrative echo of a view of history and the relationship between historical epochs that is surprising and even paradoxical: the past is now, we have it, and historical narration merely illuminates and justifies this founding anachronism. (It changes nothing to observe that the best and the most perspicuous textual critics do not usually insist that texts have been absolutely or perfectly recovered. That would mean that the past is fragmentarily present, not fully: but the central assumption, that it is more present and less fragmentary than it once was, remains.) But hasn't this always been the case? Hasn't every era felt that its model of the past was, finally and for good, the right one, and didn't it strive to develop techniques and methodologies in which it could trust, just so it could rest confident in its recovery of the past? From a certain disquieting perspective the belief that ours is the best philology proves just the opposite, namely, that, at least in its claim to be the best, it is just like all its predecessors.

---

6. The "Method of Lachmann" is the technique of establishing an abstract genealogy of manuscripts by the differential analysis of error. Although it is usually ascribed to Lachmann, in its current form it was systematized by Maas 1963 (first German ed. 1927). See the contributions of Maynes and Altschul in this volume.

But surely no justification of the present of philological practice actually depends, in the first instance, on such a historical vision. On the contrary, someone might suggest, it relies on observations that are methodological rather than historiographical. Textual criticism today is better than its past instantiations because it is based on a rigorous logic that accurately abstracts from the maximum available evidence the correct ideal relationships between manuscripts. Here the teleological narrative is justified from the point of view of technique: today's tools are just better than before. But this explanation also fails, and for many of the same reasons. Since one of the fundamental criteria of philological technique is its ability to recover the past, a technical defense of current practice ends up falling back on historiography: the presence of the past again becomes a methodological principle. If this is avoided, however, the results are even more questionable. We are then required to ask about the temporality of technique itself, and the manner in which it constructs its own history; and here again it seems that technique has improved simply because it is in the nature of technique to have achieved perfection, simply because the history of technique is always the result of a retrojected teleology—a claim that, in the end, reintroduces circularity and begs the question of history in its own way.[7]

My point is not that there is something terminally wrong with Timpanaro's story, but rather that his way of telling it exemplifies the process by which every philology appropriates the term and its history to itself. This collection trains its regard on that dynamic of appropriation, both to document it and, by attending to a multiplicity of historical instances without privilege or prejudice, to contest it.

Studies like Timpanaro's are written from within a tradition of study that aspires to be scientific, an aspiration encouraged both by the institutional contexts in which it has flourished and by the needs of its public in other disciplines (this is true even when the part of philology that is historicized is interpretive or historiographical rather than text-critical, where claims to "scientificity" are harder, perhaps, to maintain). Outside this tradition,

---

7. To put this differently: a technical justification of the progress of textual criticism would, in the end, need the kind of questioning inaugurated by Martin Heidegger in *The Question Concerning Technology* (Heidegger 1977) and pursued today under the general heading of science studies. See the important start offered by Müller-Sievers 2006. Historians of philology will need to take account not only of philology as *technē* but also of how philological technique produces subjects and communicative apparatus: for this, the superb contribution of Daston and Galison 2007 does much more than blaze a trail (though it deals with the history of science, not philology). There has been a great deal of technical reflection on philology in classical studies, and this is growing, partly in response to pressures from other fields: see the *Hypomenata* series edited by Glen Most, a very important collection of materials, and Gibson and Kraus 2002.

however, the progressive widening of the objects of humanistic study, which has taken place in tandem with a changed awareness of the historical contingency of humanistic study itself, means that philology is no longer just a mode of scholarship, but has become one of its objects. Literary historians in particular are turning in increasing numbers to the history of philology, in its institutionalized instantiations in the German sphere of the nineteenth century, in the rise of Renaissance scholarship, or in the considerably less disciplined but for that reason more engaged and literary habits of classical scholarship in eighteenth- and nineteenth-century England.[8] As the institutions in which it has thrived—the university and the research institute, the book, the archive, even the self—have come under scholarly scrutiny, philology has begun to offer itself to analysis within new and different frames of reference. To be sure, these new histories will continue to encounter resistance among those who are only interested in its value as an instrument for the discovery of long-lost truths—there will always be, in other words, those who find such studies "as useless as they are boring," as one notable classicist once wrote.[9] But given that the negotiation and formation of the classical past is a crucial element in the cultural history of modernity, it is unlikely that philology will cease to be an object of interest to cultural historians and literary scholars across the humanities. Indeed, as the artificial epistemic divisions that prevailed in the 1980s and the 1990s between classics and the rest of the humanities increasingly crumble, it seems more and more inevitable that the cultural history of philology will cease to pause, as it often does today, at the threshold of technical detail and will begin to offer closer and deeper readings not only of the results but also of the methods of philological research.

There are good reasons to suppose that even within the enclave of instrumental philology there is little resistance to such renewed historicization. Certainly Timpanaro was not adverse to this kind of work, as his total *oeuvre* makes abundantly clear. Indeed, even where textual criticism is concerned, two streams of reflection have coexisted for over a century, and these represent in microcosm the division I have just adumbrated between histories of philology aimed at consolidating its position as an instrumental science and those whose interest is its role in the production of multiple modernities. As textual criticism developed a technique for the systematic collation of manuscripts in the service of deducing an archetype, there evolved

---

8. I couldn't begin to exhaust the bibliography here. Note especially Aarslef 1983; Barkan 1999; Celenza 2004; Clark 2006, Grafton 1983, 1988, 1991, 1997 (among many other important contributions); Levine 1987; Prins 1999; Porter 2000, 2004, 2006.

9. Lloyd-Jones 2004, in a review of Gildenhard and Ruehl 2003.

simultaneously an increasing interest in the concrete history of textual traditions, which viewed individual witnesses not merely as abstract systems of signs whose variations could be used as clues for the construction of stemmata, but also as culturally specific products tied to their place and time and linked in a tradition that has historical sense on its own. The history of twentieth-century textual criticism was largely an attempt to balance these two approaches.[10] That the attempt has been generally successful, and that the two approaches to the study of texts have been combined with fruitful results, does not change their radically divergent implications, which Timpanaro saw particularly clearly: "[T]he history of tradition became more and more the history of ancient and medieval culture; in Wilamowitz, in Traube, in Eduard Schwartz, for example, it acquired a richness and complexity unknown to the scholars of the preceding generation, but at the same time it became less and less capable of furnishing a secure criterion for constituting the text [. . .]."[11] When the study of textual traditions reaches a state of autotelic stability the result is a new field of study and a new view of the history of texts, one that is interested not merely in the recovery of a version deemed "original" but in the differing ways in which such a text has combined and recombined with changing material, graphical, and cultural contexts. The history of philology, in other words, ceases to be a justification of the current state of affairs and becomes an object of study in its own right. The fact that, despite their significant differences, these two impulses can and often do work together is an optimistic indication that new work on the history of philology will find avid readers when it begins to speak in more detail about the technical history of the field. It is on the basis of this optimism that the present collection is deliberately ambiguous as to specific disciplinary relevance—are we presenting essays in the history of philology for the benefit of "philologists" or for those interested in philology as a cultural phenomenon in its own right? My hope is that both kinds of readership will benefit, and that these essays may establish a beachhead and provoke deeper probes into the technical structures of philology that also remain mindful of its significance within the cultural history of modernity itself.

Such a crossing of scholarly viewpoints is both natural and potentially transformative. It is natural because, as several of the contributions to this volume make clear, there is no philology without the history of philology: indeed, philological inquiry, at its most rigorous and its most sustained, inevitably and always involves an equally rigorous and sustained inquiry

---

10. See especially Pasquali 1952.
11. Timpanaro 2005: 125.

into its own history, both as this is instantiated in its long string of predecessors and as it influences its contemporary forms. Whether philology is to be understood as textual criticism, as a fundamental and intimate orientation to the material details of textuality, or as a viewpoint in which textual *realia* are linked to broader cultural concerns, it always involves an engagement with texts and with texts about texts. But because every text is the result of human agency and because any human agency which leads to the production or the interpretation of a text has a good claim to being called philological, each philology is by definition engaged with other philologies, and this predicament amounts to an imperative that philology also be the history of philology. But far from simplifying matters, this observation leads to surprising and unsettling results which expose both philology and history to a radical questioning and a possible transformation of their premises. Since historiography also has a history, and this history has not been stable but has involved a series of shifting constructions of historical time, the history of philology must come to terms not only with changing practices within philology itself, but also with the changing ways in which philology has constructed its own history. In addition, just as philology is also and necessarily historiographical, historiography is always dependent on philology, which it tasks with uncovering and establishing textual evidence. A feedback loop is thus engendered, a root recursion that is not commonly theorized but should not be overlooked: which philology will historiography depend on, and which historiography, in turn, does that philology presume? These are questions that every philologist, and every historian, no doubt asks. What the history of philology has the potential to reveal is that the choices made in adjudicating the mutually informing paradigms of history and philology constitute a crucial element in the poetics of culture generally, and can influence not only how modern conversations about the past are conducted, but also the very nature of that past and the specific dynamics of its reconstruction and appropriation. This means more than that philology and history are generative of historical consciousness. It means in addition, and more worryingly, that the relationship between past and present, between the means of study and its object, are much more convoluted and interpenetrating than is often assumed.

It may be that what emerges at the intersection of philology and history is the possibility that the study and the invocation of the past is both informed by and formative of that past. To be sure, there was a world before us: that is our scholarly interest. But that world, like ours, was produced from a confrontation between the materials of the past and the poetic capacities of the present, and neither our time nor the time before can be viewed as a simple, serene, or stable and unchangeable synchronic slice. We inform it; it informs us; this is a time of times, as it was then also.

THOUGH, AS I HAVE suggested, it may be prudent to resist single definitions of philology as well as historical narratives that emphasize a single period as the time of its greatest fulfillment, we might nonetheless be able to isolate a characteristic by which it could be recognized. Such a characteristic lies, I propose, in philology's fraught relationship with itself and the need to tell its own history. At the moment when philology begins to critique its predecessors and cognate fields, it opens a perspective critical of its own aspirations: that philology can and does critique other modes of scholarship, or even other philologies, implies that it contains a moment within it capable of self-critique.

Here the example of textual criticism may again prove illuminating. The task of the modern critical edition is to produce a single text and apparatus on the basis of a comprehensive examination of all relevant witnesses. Since every critical edition is based on historical principles, and since every textual witness is itself the product of an act of philology, every critical edition is the product of a philology engaged with the history of philology. But the fact that each textual witness (including, where these exist, previous critical editions) is itself a theory of the text based on some vision of its history means that the history of philology presented by a critical edition is also a critical history of previous histories of philology. Somewhere in the structure of text-critical practice, in other words, there lies an operation that is fundamentally and unavoidably critical of the process of producing a text, that refuses to take at face value any single textual presentation, and that acknowledges that every history of a text is implicitly a history (singular) of textual histories (plural). This operation is at one and the same time fundamental and antithetical to the process of producing a critical edition: fundamental because without it the critical survey of textual witnesses would never get off the ground, and antithetical because the refusal to accept any textual instantiation uncritically must be obviated to some degree if the critical edition is to present a text of its own. If such is the structure of even the most normative philology, it can hardly be surprising that from time to time a project arises that seeks to strip away unifying, ideological tendencies and refuse historiographical closure, opening a view on the complexities of textual engagement.

It can happen that this radical element in philology expresses itself in terms of an equally radical historicism. This indeed is what transpired in the philology invoked by Walter Benjamin. Benjamin's engagement with philology, latently present in many works, became most explicit in the context of a dialogue with Adorno over the first draft of *The Paris of the Second Empire in Baudelaire*.[12] To Adorno's complaint that he had entered a "bewitched" space characterized by "the wide-eyed presentation of the facts,"[13] Benjamin's response is subtle and complex, and apparently self-canceling. He begins by insisting that the essay Adorno has read represents the properly philological part of a three-part study whose last part will present the theoretical mediation Adorno missed.[14] But this line of defense prefaces a second claim which effectively negates it: granted that the philological fact must be demystified and the "bewitched" space where magic and positivism cross abandoned, this demystification, says Benjamin, takes place in the reader and thus need not be present in the text. He uses an analogy to make this point: a painting's vanishing point does need not be visible because the true point of convergence of the perspectival lines is in the viewer. Similarly, the demystification of those facts generated by means of philology takes place by placing it in historical perspective. This means (and the draft of *Paris of the Second Empire* bears this out) submitting it to a radical and full historicization that eschews theoretical mediation. The analogy with painting in this passage plays the crucial role of establishing that the creation of a fully historicized account, that is, a radically philological one, would cause the reader to experience his own time as the viewer of a perspectival drawing experiences his own space: as a monad (or, as Benjamin would put it elsewhere, as a dialectical image).[15] This statement of method is then followed by the claim that Benjamin's philological practice is in fact directed against

---

12. Adorno and Benjamin 1999: 286 (November 10, 1938); translated also in Benjamin 2006, from which I cite. Deeper discussion is provided by the contribution of Ian Balfour to this volume.

13. "The exclusion of theory confirms the empirical. It gives it a delusively epic character on the one hand, and on the other deprives phenomena, as mere objects of subjective experience, of their true historico-philosophical weight. This could also be expressed by saying that the theological motif of calling things by their names is inherently prone to lapse into a wide-eyed presentation of mere facticity. If one wished to give the matter really drastic expression, one might say that the work has situated itself at the crossroads of magic and positivism. This site is bewitched. Only theory could break the spell . . . " (Benjamin 2006: 102).

14. "The philological approach entails examining the text detail by detail, leading the reader to fixate magically on the text. That which Faust takes home in black and white, and Grimm's veneration of the minuscule, are closely related. They have in common the magical element, which it is left to philosophy—here, the concluding part—to exorcise" (Benjamin 2006: 108).

15. "The appearance of self-contained facticity that emanates from philological study and casts its spell on the scholar is dispelled according to the degree to which the object is constructed in historical perspective. The lines of perspective in this construction, receding to the vanishing point, converge in our own historical experience. In this way, the object is constituted as a monad. In the monad, the textual detail which was frozen in a mythical rigidity comes alive . . . " (Benjamin 2006: 108).

philological practice: what Benjamin calls the application of philological technique is provoked by the innermost connection between myth and "the attitude of the philologist." The implications here are that (1) "the attitude of the philologist," as Benjamin sees it, is marked by a high degree of ideological (that is, "mythical") thinking, which we can understand in this context as being teleological; and that (2) this teleological thought must be countered from within by using the resources and the tools of philology itself, not by less but by more historico-philological rigor. Enough of Benjamin's project in both the Baudelaire book and its matrix the *Arcades Project* were finished before his death for us to be able to see that the historical perspective he was trying to draw included philology: he was, in other words, engaged in a historicization of philology meant to critique philology's engagements with history. He planned to do this, however, not by abjuring history but by intensifying it to the point where it would overwhelm philology and force it onto a new setting. This was also, inevitably—and on this point Adorno stuck—a philologization of history, and, indeed, of philology as well.

I have cited Benjamin, but signs of the critical element in philology are most easily identified in what have come to be seen as the most characteristic hallmarks of "serious" philological scholarship: the dutiful noting and cataloguing of alternative views, the compilation and responsible reporting of bibliographical references, and, in critical editions, the presentation of textual variants. The imperative to catalogue and present those alternatives from which any given philologist would distinguish his/her own project indicates the constant presence and undeniable force of radical self-criticism. That is: even when a vision of philological history is presented in a tendentious and unifying light, this ideological presentation is exceeded and undercut by the complex paratextual and argumentative apparatus it throws up about it, and which appears to the attentive reader as an open and disseminating network of alternative philologies.

Philology's constitutive critical element has two characteristic elements: (1) a commitment to extremely slow reading that results in (2) unfastening and opening the text to a vertiginous contingency. Insistence on slow reading is a first and crucial element. The "magic" of philology which Benjamin wanted to dispel comes, he says, from philology's insistence that the reader "examine the text detail by detail." The philologist's slowness has no limits. Indeed, the radical element in philology begins to be vitiated when a limit or a locus for reading is established, in the tropological structure of language, for example, or in ideologies or identities, and even in the notion of a text that truly captures "what the author really wrote." We could suggest that philology ceases to be radical when slow reading transforms into close reading because a surface or limit has been established along or against which the reading moves, as a hand moves over a hard and impenetrable surface. Resisting such reification, philology churns up debris in the form of suspected readings and emendations, commentaries, marginal annotations, insights generated by figure and rhetoric. Above all, it produces the impression that any given text could be given otherwise.

When this begins to take place, however, the second radical element of philology comes into play. To read into and beyond the text means to begin to see the places where the joins don't fit, where words and lines seem odd or out of context. At the greatest extreme texts begin to look like collocations of ill-fitting fragments or traditions of variance that could never be turned into a single "perfect" form. By what may seem to some an intolerable reversal, the result of slow reading is a perspective *before* the text, in the sense that a radical reading will force the reader to make choices, to create and formulate a text for him/herself.

These two elements can be corroborated in the characterization given to philology by Edward Said.[16] Said, like Benjamin, sees philology as a matter of reading: "reading is the indispensable act, the initial gesture without which any philology is simply impossible" (60). It is, to be more precise, "a detailed, patient scrutiny of and a lifelong attentiveness to the words and rhetorics by which language is used by human beings who exist in history" (61). This involves an imperative to make a slow and careful engagement with literary texts into the basis for developing alternatives to the forces Said saw impinging on enlightenment, freedom, and humanity. Said sees philology as an amalgam of receptivity and resistance, each linked to a different moment of reading. "Receptivity" attends to what Said joins with Leo Spitzer in calling the revealing detail that could bring the whole into focus and let a reader access the text as the author saw it (66–68).[17] By contrast, "resistance" achieves a systematic *recusatio* of jargons and sound-bites and enforced but specious disciplinizations.

This does not seem to have any connection with the formative interventions typical of textual criticism. When we read Said's text more slowly, however, the picture becomes more nuanced. The act of reading involves two times: that of the reader and that of the written, or, perhaps, the "now" of

---

16. Said 2004.
17. "To work from the surface to the 'inward life-center' of the work of art: first observing details about the superficial appearance of the particular work [. . .] then, grouping these details and seeking to integrate them into a creative principle which may have been present in the soul of the artist; and, finally, making the return trip to all the other groups of observations in order to find whether the 'inward form' one has tentatively constructed gives an account of the whole" (Spitzer 1948: 19, cited in Said 2004: 64–65).

textual encounter and the "then" of textual production. This makes philology anachronistic. But it does not exhaust the multiple temporalities involved in philological reading, for both the philologist, who reads in order to resist, and the author who writes for the same reason, are out of sorts with their times. "Art is not simply there: it exists intensely in a state of unreconciled opposition to the depredations of daily life" (63). This is a triple untimeliness at least, based on non-dialectical oppositions between (1) the reader's time and the text's time, (2) the reader and his/her own time, and (3) the author and his/her time. Perhaps the defining emblem for this constitutive philological anachrony can be found in the description of close reading that Said takes from Spitzer. For Spitzer, the only way out of the moment of blankness when a text says nothing is to read and reread. Rereading is, for Said, the clue to philology's resistance. When he insists that it is the privilege of time that allows the American academic the ability to resist the prefab languages of the marketplace, the essential characteristic of this time is the luxury to read a book unhurriedly, which means to read it more than once, to bring the experience of different days to its pages, and even to decide to read against its bound sequence, unbinding and resorting, if only in the mind, what the publisher packaged as a legible work, a cultural commodity. As a commodity made to be sold and sold to be read once and in the prescribed sequence, the book is one of the most important sites of resistance for this philological project: one reads to resist the book. And here, despite Said's silence on the theme, textual criticism returns as the specter of slow reading: for what is this resistive reading if not a principled and systematic unbinding of all the materialities of the bound and binding book and a willingness, even a commitment, to see it not for how it initially appears but as a constellation of fragments strewn across time and space?

SEVERAL COMMON themes emerge from the essays that follow. The first is philology's fraught contact with philosophy. Every philology must involve rigorous thought as well as textual practice; but thought, in taking leave of texts, leaves philology behind as well. Where and how philology should accommodate itself to thought is a constant concern in its history. A second returning theme is the role philology plays in the production and evaluation of the annotations, marginalia, and other accretions that reflect the labor of reading over time. If philology is intimately connected to reading, and if this reading cannot stop at the surface of the text, one result is that philologists also engage in an incessant writing of their texts. In textual criticism this can be seen in the role philology plays in establishing what the text is: in interpretation it leads to the addition of side- and sub-texts which seek, by means of their material presence on the page, to forge meanings for future readers. Finally, there is a recurrent concern with materialism, with texts as bodies and embodiments, and how philology construes such embodied histories. Every philology runs up against the concrete *realia* of texts, those aspects of textual communication that are more than linguistic or literary—paper, ink, *mise-en-page*, handwriting and typefaces are only some of the most evident examples. Such concerns are perhaps due to the fact that philology encounters itself most intimately in the traces of the making and transmission of texts: since every text is the result of a philological production, the history of that production will inevitably need to account for all its aspects, not just the linguistic. The matter of the text is more than just a null-point of meaning, the site where translation and interpretation fall mute and effects of presence are most intimately felt. It is also the place where every history of philology, necessarily a rigorous self-investigation, a kind of immanent critique, touches its other with infinite intimacy.

Kathleen McNamee's "Reading Outside the Library" shows classical scholarship at work on its texts in the earliest accessible phase of its history: in marginalia found in Greek papyri.[18] Many of the marginalia she discusses may have been the result of schoolchildren copying the lectures of their teachers; these teachers in turn were working from personal compilations of scholarship emanating from larger centers like Alexandria (the "library" of her title). By emphasizing that even here the annotation of literary works involved the collection of scholarly notes from other sources as well as the addition of original elements, McNamee indicates that the practice of philology and an awareness of the history of philology coincide early in the tradition. In showing how work from such centers found itself in the margins of the books of private readers, McNamee also suggests that philology was as much an aspect of the practice of reading in school or at home as it was a profession carried out in great libraries under the patronage of kings. Indeed, her breakdown of the kinds of activities that led to the addition of marginalia in Greek papyri includes scenes not only from the household and

---

18. These ancient notes offer important early examples of the kind of notes also found in many medieval manuscripts of classical literature, commonly referred to as scholia. Scholia typically preserve exegetical explanations, textual variants, and fragments of learned commentaries from earlier works of scholarship. The scholiasts who copied or compiled these collections of notes were, to be sure, philologists interested in the immediate elucidation of their texts; but they were also historians of philology who collected what they considered their predecessors' most important observations. But by the time the great medieval scholia were made, the orientation to textuality they embody was already very old. On scholia and their history, see McNamee 1995, 1998; Reynolds and Wilson 1991; Wilson 1967, 2007.

the schoolroom, but also from the scriptorium: the first layer of annotations are corrections of errors introduced when the scribe copied his exemplar. These textual practices cross the book at all the stages of its history and use—tentative confirmation, perhaps, that philology is as much about the consolidation of the literary object as it is about its study.

McNamee's study of marginalia in Greek papyri suggests that the history of philology must also be the philological study of previous philologists. In "Philologizing Philologists," Craig Maynes deepens this insight by emphasizing that every act of philology is also an act of scholarship directed at philology, since the activity of the authors who originated classical texts and of the subsequent textual agents responsible for its transmission can be characterized as philological. Insisting that textual transmission is both a diachronic process of tradition and a sequence of individual philological activities defined by their own local and synchronic contexts, Maynes elaborates the crucial internal connection between the history of philology and the establishing of a text. Since philology is not one thing but a sequence of changing things, the history of textuality (which is also always the history of philology) must come to terms with a field that is by nature variegated and multiple. That is: a critical edition is not only concerned with the *formal* plurality of literary texts, but also with a cultural and epistemic plurality, since every edition is dependent on constantly changing historical constructions of how the individual judgment of each textual agent plays a role in textual production. This produces a scholarly situation in which the study of even the least canonical of texts inevitably involves a synoptic view not only of the text through history, but also of the *culture* of the text through history. The stakes are high, here, but Maynes pushes further, observing in addition that even modern attempts to represent this complex textual, cultural, and epistemic multiplicity are themselves multiple. Maynes' analysis of the philological history of Claudius Namatianus' fourth-century C.E. Latin poem *De Reditu Suo*—which, incidentally, calls into question the correctness of the traditional author's name and poem's title—begins with a detailed analysis of the variations prevailing between the early modern textual witnesses in their titles, incipits, and explicits, thus continuing McNamee's focus on the extra- or para-textual materials which make up so much of philology's historical archive. Here again, in other words, sorting out the history of the text means sorting out the history of the philology on or, more correctly, around it. Crucially, Maynes' analysis of the historical embodiments of philological practice includes not only the history of interpretation and textual emendation but also the history of the use of the material objects themselves, as early scholars "recycled" old manuscripts to repair other ones, or erased them in order to write on the newly "cleaned" pages. Philology not only produces texts: it also recycles and on occasion destroys them.

When, in the third-century B.C.E., Eratosthenes distinguished himself from the Stoic-influenced κριτικοί (critics) and the overly-pedagogical γραμματικοί (grammarians) by arrogating the title φιλόλογος (philologist) to himself, his point, according to Suetonius, was that his research was far too multiform and variegated—too interdisciplinary—for any of the vocational names then in circulation.[19] The promiscuousness of philological interest is, perhaps, a direct result of its prevailing concern with texts, any and all of them, regardless of their "disciplinary" affiliations or "ownership," and it has been perennially controversial, since philologists who thus interest themselves in everything can easily be charged either with lacking deep knowledge of any single thing or with intruding in regions where they have no business. Under this aspect, philology seems to be Kantian philosophy's unacknowledged kin. If for Kant the role of philosophy was to adjudicate the cognitive claims of the "faculties" (what today would more appropriately be called the "disciplines") by investigating their principles and their conditions of possibility, philology undertakes a similar project in its insistence on the rigorous consideration of the documentary, textual, or linguistic bases for higher-order claims. This is bound to be upsetting, and philology does upset. Christopher Celenza's contribution discusses one such philological incursion in the early modern period: Angelo Poliziano's choice to teach the Aristotelian *Organon* in the late 1480s and early 1490s. This choice unsettled some, and Poliziano found himself needing to respond to the charge that he was teaching texts for which he had no proper training, since he was not a philosopher. His response, the *Lamia,* a *praelectio* to his course on the *Prior Analytics,* argues via a redrawing of disciplinary boundaries that to be a philosopher is impossible—the bar is just too high—and that given this situation the best one can hope for is to bring the tools of the student of language and literature to bear even on philosophical texts. Celenza insists, however, that the *Lamia* is not engaging in a "contest of the faculties" (invoking Kant). Philology's mode is different from that of philosophy: its immanent critique is based on reading. Nonetheless, philology and philosophy converge in Poliziano's account since the basis for philological analysis, that is, the analytical study of language, turns out to be the Aristotelian *Organon*, which is, therefore, not merely philosophical. Consequently, the ideal philosopher, which Poliziano insists he is not, resembles the actual humanist scholar, crossing disciplines and reading obscure and

---

19. Suetonius, *De Grammaticis et Rhetoribus* 10.4.

non-canonical sources. Such a strategy subtly and quietly disqualifies the philosophers who objected to Poliziano's incursion into their territory: they lack the textual and linguistic skills to engage Aristotle as closely as Poliziano will, and their claim to be philosophers appears to be based on a misreading of the *Organon* itself. Careful reading, Celenza shows Poliziano suggesting, represents the only true way of seeking wisdom.

Nonetheless, it can happen from time to time that philology disciplines itself and seeks to close down or escape its own radical core. In "Philology and the Emblem," Bradley J. Nelson begins with the observation that the emblem—that combination of epigram, allegorical image, and commentary which has been a constant presence in European print culture for nearly five centuries—is an inherently philological form, and then capitalizes on this fact to make the further claim that philology can become emblematic in its turn. In Nelson's analysis, emblematization designates a process in which the interminable crisis in representation definitive of modernity is blocked or assuaged by a presence which pretends to be transcendental and immediate. I write "emblematization" rather than "the emblem" here because in Nelson's analysis, the emblem itself emblematizes: that is, it is itself an example of a process which is far more widespread but to which it lends its name by metonymy. Philology plays a double-edged role in this story: it is, on the one hand, a primary example of the process of emblematization: the products of philological work on Golden-age Spanish drama are seen as producing emblematic presences. But at the same time, as a means of production, philology is also a crucial player in the deterritorialization of the sign that underwrites the crisis the emblem aims to waylay. Thus Nelson's own philological insistence on the materialities of production, which shows that the "emblem" was in fact the product of multiple agencies involved in the process of making a book and in no way the result of a unifying authorial intention, works against the apparently philological energies of the emblem itself. For the emblem would block access to these materialities. In a complex set of slippages between material analysis and effects of presencing, philology both constructs and deconstructs its objects. This double movement is embodied in the process of emblematization itself, which, in its attempt to produce what Hans-Ulrich Gumbrecht calls an "effect of presence," disconnects its objects from their original contexts and thus reproduces the very disjunctions it seeks to mitigate. Nelson concludes by suggesting, in harmony with many of the other contributors in this volume, that philology can temper and become more aware of its constant engagement with presence-effects by becoming more ludic, or, as he puts it, more carnivalesque.

Jonathan Sachs ("On the Road: Travel, Antiquarianism, Philology") focuses on the work of one scholar-traveler working in the middle of the eighteenth century. Robert Wood's *Essay on the Original Genius and Writings of Homer* proposed (among other things) that Homer was illiterate and did not write the *Iliad* and the *Odyssey*. He based this argument on two important journeys around the eastern Mediterranean, and Sachs argues that the "orality" thesis in Wood can only be understood in the context of Wood's locative hermeneutics, that is, his sense that reading in place was the most effective way to understand the Greek epics. Sachs shows Wood combating earlier commentaries on Homer with evidence drawn not from books or textual analysis but from his own experience of the lands Homer knew. In a move parallel to that of Nelson, he links this to Gumbrecht's understanding of philology as intimately concerned with a desire for presence: Wood's belief that the places in which the Homeric epics were set can make those texts more comprehensible to the modern reader amounts to an attempt to transform geography into an emblem, a luminous presencing of times long lost. Philology has always been, as McNamee underlines in this volume, a matter of annotating texts by adding words and comments in the margins, and Sachs' discussion shows this process continuing in the eighteenth century: many of the insights in the *Essay* are drawn from the extensive marginalia in his interleaved copy of the epics. Sachs shows that, although for many of Wood's contemporaries the practice of adding marginalia involved collating one text with another, Wood's own practice collates text with place. His marginalia track the similarities between what the epics contain and what Wood sees in the "primitive" life of the inhabitants of what was once the Greek east. In this process of collation, space becomes a figural stand-in for time, as the sights of eighteenth-century Turkey and Egypt provide clues for the nature of ancient Ionia. This is, then, a philology that is also historicist, but one whose historicism depends on an anachronistic misreading of the present as the past: a resorting of chronology that Sachs identifies as "ludic" and locates, following James Porter, at philology's constitutive core. This is to say, in other words, that philology is at one and the same time rigorously focused on the text and ecstatically moving away from it, committed to a historical vision and yet incapable of achieving this by anything other than the most non-historical of perspectives.

Philology has frequently been concerned not only with its history but also with its name; from time to time it displays anxiety over the fact that the very expression "philology" is, in some of its instantiations, an apparently un-philological misapplication of the word. For most of what philology practices, the correct ancient name was *grammatica,* the term used by

Poliziano in the *Lamia*. In "What is Philology?" Nadia Altschul explores some of the instabilities that surround philology at the levels of semantics and scholarly practice in medieval studies, focusing in particular on philology's sometimes difficult relationship with the close study of texts, on the one hand, and the broad consideration of culture, on the other. Altschul, observing that philology is not only textual criticism but also includes an important element of cultural analysis that is no longer cognate with nineteenth-century forms of historicism, proposes that the whole philological field can be subdivided into *ecdotics* on the one hand (a Graecism borrowed from Spanish and Italian usage to describe the scholarly study of textual editions in all its forms) and *cultural studies* on the other. By defining itself as ecdotics and cultural studies, she argues, philology might be able to integrate with other cultural studies whose orientation is not towards the past but to the present. Unstated in Altschul's proposal, but unquestionably present as a challenge, is the possibility that just as a "cultural studies of the past" might deepen other cultural studies' historical perspective, so too might it flatten medieval studies' historical view, allowing for scholarly narratives and analyses which combine multiple times in its purview. What Altschul is proposing, in other words, is a reinvigorated contact with the anachrony typical of philology and addressed in other forms throughout this volume.

James Porter ("Nietzsche, Rhetoric, Philology") takes as his subject the materialism of Nietzsche's early writing and lectures on classical rhetoric. Strikingly, Nietzsche places rhetoric *before* language, not after it: that is, he insists that language is the result of a process of genesis that is rhetorical (and not vice versa). The rhetoric that "produces" language is bodily and gestural—and that at the level not of the arms or the vocal chords, but of the physiology of perception and the physical translations that relate perception, thought, and expression. Porter shows that this position is the result of an engagement with ancient works of rhetorical theory, on the one hand, which are themselves importantly exercised by the role of the body in the production of speech, and with the modern criticism of these works in the figures of Lange and Gerber, on the other. At stake in Nietzsche's physiology of rhetoric is his "ongoing use of classical philology as a mode of critiquing contemporary ('modern') culture." But this is a critique that, rigorously and perhaps fanatically, resists all hypostatization—even of "matter," "rhetoric," or "language." The result is a writing that is neither argumentative nor probative, but rather stages positions drawn from others—from antiquity and from its modern interpreters—and draws texts and readers into a vertiginous and unsettling process of questioning. For this reason, Porter argues, readers of Nietzsche must also resist hypostatization, resist leveling reading to the uncovering of a consistent "story" or "position." This, he claims, means they must read philologically. Such a philology would be, like Nietzsche's own, attached only to its own refusal of closure. Porter's *recusatio* includes the closure imposed by Paul de Man at the level of language and tropes: this is a Nietzsche, and a reading of him, that is more ungrounded and hence more radical than (American) deconstruction.

Ian Balfour ("The Philosophy of Philology and the Crisis of Reading: Schlegel, Benjamin, de Man") also tracks the intersections of philology and deconstruction. Tracing the filiation which joins F. Schlegel to Walter Benjamin and Paul de Man, Balfour unpacks the fraught relations between philosophy and philology that are also addressed, in this volume, by Christopher Celenza. Balfour asks what happens when philology becomes the object of philosophical thought. Thinking about philology turns out to produce some uncomfortable results, the first of which lies in the fact that philology can function as a crucial legitimating factor for philosophy itself: as Schlegel puts it, philosophy without philology is nothing at all. But this means more than that there can be no properly philosophical thought without rigorous attention to texts and language. For all three of Balfour's authors, philology not only "underwrites" philosophy: it is also a crucial medium of philosophical reflection. Critique can take place only via the philological, a move that returns philology to the center of attention, for to think about literature philosophically one must philologize. Philology becomes capable of radical critique, in Balfour's account, because of its resolute and inalienable historicism: for philology a text is (and must be) fundamentally different, and therefore in a crucial relation to at least two times and places of which one is that of the philologist. The alien nature of the philological text leads to critique in different ways in Schlegel, Benjamin, and de Man—in Schlegel the otherness of the text begins as a *datum* before it is elevated to an essential content of critical thought, while in Benjamin the relationship between the present and the past occurs as a subterranean correspondence, even a kind of cryptic predestination, and in de Man the temporal spacing of the text arises out of his construction of the literary event. But in each case the result is a vision which, from viewing philology as a means of critique, leads inevitably to a vision of reading as fundamentally and forever in crisis—the more in crisis the more serious it gets. Philology, in other words, carries reading beyond the complacent belief that what it does is skim a signifying surface or even process a linguistic communication and into a space characterized above all by vertigo—a condition diagnosed as well, as we have seen, in Porter's engagement with Nietzsche.

CHAPTER 1

Reading Outside the Library

Kathleen McNamee

The subject of this essay is the primary evidence for practical applications of philology in the Greco-Roman world. For present purposes, I use "philology" in a broad sense, to embrace various sorts of practical attention applied to manuscripts in order to bring a reader as close as possible to a proper understanding of an author's words. The evidence treated here consists of the marginal and interlinear notes in some three hundred fragmentary manuscripts of Greek and Latin literature that were copied in Egypt between the second century B.C.E. and the seventh C.E. Collectively, these books are referred to conventionally as "papyri," since papyrus was the commonest writing material in that time and place, although the body of evidence includes texts written on parchment.[1] Their annotations leave traces of various steps that ancient readers took in their efforts to understand, in greater or less detail, books that were written at a time already distant even for them. I see these marginalia, most of which convey only the most elementary information, as evidence of the practice of a sort of philology according to the definition I offer for that word.

Ancient marginalia also give, therefore, a sense of *how* readers read, a central issue in this book and one that can serve as a jumping-off point. Various approaches to reading are detectable in annotations. One, which can only be called reading in the most generous definition of that term, is the kind practiced by the corrector of a handwritten book. It was this person's responsibility to discover where a newly copied text deviated from its model

---

1. The evidence is collected and analyzed in McNamee 2007.

and to set it right. To do this effectively, the corrector's manner of reading must necessarily be mechanical rather than intellectual. What he sought was deviation, not sense. Comprehension of what he read could, in fact, be a liability, if his interest in content distracted him from errors. The differences between this type of reader and the next, which are subtle, are differences of intention.

Another kind of reader—let us call him the reviser—followed the same procedure as the first. He also compared one text with another and recorded their deviations from each other, but he used a carefully edited copy of the text as the basis for his comparison rather than the original scribe's exemplar, and he worked from a different perspective. This person recognized a certain enhanced authenticity in the secondary text, and he valued it as a relatively reliable witness to the author's *ipsissima verba*. Occasionally, he recorded a name beside the variant. Such attributions may signify simply that the comparison text belonged to the person named. In most cases, however, where the names appear to belong to known scholars, we surmise that the reviser found the reading in a manuscript containing that scholar's edition of the text, or that he found it in a learned commentary in which the scholar's reasons for championing this particular reading were supplied. The specific attribution suggests, in either case, that the later reader had special interest in grasping the relative merits of different versions, and in probing the author's meaning more deeply than a corrector would ever need to.[2] Both the corrector's and the reviser's approaches to reading, rooted as they are in technical accuracy, deal exclusively with the concerns of textual criticism. Together, they represent the ancient equivalent of the "radical core" of philology that Sean Gurd has discussed in the introduction.

Another approach to reading that characterizes many papyrus notes has nothing to do with a reader's concern (or lack of it) for accuracy. It reveals, rather, his preoccupation with understanding the author's language and with assembling the background information he needed for the text to make sense. Notes reflecting this approach might metaphrase an author's words, or construe them to eliminate syntactical difficulties, or supply background information. Whether their content is humble or learned, their purpose is the same, namely, to provide the reader with an objective understanding of the author's words.

Textual accuracy and factual explanation represent only two possible concerns of a reader in approaching a text. Ancient writers on literature

---

2. By "reviser" I mean here the reader who ordered that the manuscripts be compared, or who thoughtfully compared them himself, rather than any scribe in his employ who might perform the collation. The automatic work of such a scribe is like that of a corrector.

adumbrate others (see below, e.g., for Dionysius Thrax's six-point definition of the study of literature). Still others can be discovered in scholia, whose sources are ancient.[3] Alternative ways of attacking a text might involve, for example, special attention to the study of etymologies, analogies, or allegories, or to the sound of the text when recited aloud. Such concerns were clearly immaterial to the people who wrote the notes, however, for papyrus marginalia contain virtually no trace of them. The textual and factual notes that did concern them, and the context in which those notes were added, will be the focus of the rest of this essay.

Let us begin with the general context from which annotated papyri emerge. All those under consideration (and indeed most papyri) were discovered in Egypt at the sites of cities and towns that flourished in the late Hellenistic and Roman periods. As the economic strength of the Roman empire waned in late antiquity, these cities and towns were gradually abandoned and reclaimed by the desert. Thanks to Egypt's exceptionally arid climate and a water table that is sufficiently low in many of the former settlements, many of the objects that inhabitants forgot or discarded—cast-off books and papers included—were preserved under coverings of sand and earth. In the delta and near the coast, things were different. With a climate less sere and a water table much higher, scarcely any ancient writings survived.

A significant consequence of this fact of topography is that although the capital Alexandria was one of the cultural centers in the ancient world, virtually no papyri have survived from there. This is a great misfortune, since Alexandria was the site of the fabled library established by Ptolemaic kings soon after Alexander's founding of the city and maintained by them for many generations. From the start the library's royal patrons intended it to be the most comprehensive and the most authoritative assemblage of books the world had seen, and to this end they put it under the care of eminent scholars whom they maintained in comfort in the Museum, the influential research institution located, along with the library, within the royal palace.[4] The prestige and influence achieved by the work of these Alexandrian scholars was immediate, strong, and lasting. In condensed and excerpted form it survives as medieval scholia. Their principal interests revolved around textual criticism—"philology" in the strict sense of the term—and this has shaped the interpretation of classical literature to this day. Alexandria was not the only center of learning.[5] But the ancient books that survive come almost

---

3. For example, the so-called exegetical scholia (bT) on Homer included in Erbse 1969–88 represent the genre.

4. Pfeiffer 1968; Canfora 1989.

5. The most celebrated library apart from Alexandria's was that at Pergamum, where resident

entirely from its environs. This is a small but important point: papyri survive in substantial numbers not in Alexandria itself, the cultural center, with its elevated water table. They come, rather, from towns and cities considerably removed from Alexandria.[6] To what extent did the work of the Museum scholars, strongly philological in nature, percolate into Greco-Roman cities in villages in Egypt? The answer is complex, as this essay will show.

We can be fairly sure of one or two things. Educated people, even learned people, certainly lived in Egypt outside of Alexandria. Eric Turner has shown that at least one Alexandrian scholar made a home (more likely, a second home) in Oxyrhynchus.[7] Furthermore, there are written materials from Oxyrhynchus, Hermopolis, and even from villages such as Socnopaiou Nesus that carry impeccable scholarly credentials, including named references to known Alexandrian scholars. Only a few such references are to unrecognizable authorities. Papyri also suggest that children could receive a decent education outside the capital, although those whose families had the means and the desire completed their studies in Alexandria. This was quite certainly the center of intellectual life in this part of the world. It had the indispensable library and the Museum, which both facilitated scholarly intercourse; there is no evidence for similar scholarly foundations elsewhere in Greco-Roman Egypt. Thus, the unfamiliar scholars' names that appear in a few papyrus notes are less likely to indicate the existence of rival local schools than to reveal the limitations of our knowledge.

Let us turn now to the papyrological evidence and consider how much, and in what manner, the philological work of Alexandrian scholars penetrated the reading experience of people in the rest of Egypt. Although the very fragmentary nature of the papyri makes it rare to find evidence of more than one or two kinds of note in a single text, it seems safe to say that a book belonging to a Discerning Reader of Greek literature in the time of the Roman empire is likely to have contained evidence of various philological interventions corresponding to the approaches to reading outlined above. To illustrate how, in practical terms, these interventions could have found

---

scholars influenced by Stoic philosophy favored an allegorical approach to literature. Other libraries existed at Antioch and Pella. In addition, Aristotle's Academy at Athens remained influential for centuries after his death, and there were important foundations of higher learning at Constantinople, Antioch, and Gaza, as well as law schools at Beirut and Alexandria: Pfeiffer 1968: 234–51 (Pergamum); Cribiore 2007: 42–82 (higher education in Athens and the Roman East) and passim (Antioch); Collinet 1925.

6. With some notable exceptions, for example, the papyri found at Derveni, Herculaneum, and Dura-Europus: Kouremenos, Parássoglou, and Tsantsanoglou 2006; Sider 2005; Fink, Gilliam, and Welles 1959.

7. Obbink 2007: 271–82; Turner 1952 and 1956.

their way into the margins and between the lines of ancient books, I have devised a scenario involving imaginary readers who are not learned scholars. Scholars, after all, were only a tiny minority of the ancient literate population.

Imagine the year is 200 C.E., the place Oxyrhynchus, an Egyptian city several hundred miles south of the Alexandrian library and Museum, a seat of Greek scholarship for nearly five centuries. A scribe copies a manuscript of Aristophanes' *Birds* for our Discerning Reader. Someone—perhaps the scribe, perhaps a slave or apprentice—compares the copy with its exemplar and enters corrections. In this model, he has accomplished Step One, which corresponds to the first type of reading: the correction of out-and-out errors. The second person's theoretical object is to purge the copy of any deviations from the exemplar. These are undesirable, of course, because they corrupt the poetic text and therefore alter its meaning. The corrector's objective is only theoretical, however. Chances are good that his practical application of theory is imperfect.

The Discerning Reader, therefore, aware of human frailty and realizing that the exemplar itself cannot be a perfect replica of the author's original text, takes the trouble to compare his new copy with another one. The friend who lends him the second copy assures him it is quite reliable. He copies its variant readings into his new book, sometimes between the lines, sometimes in the margin. Some discrepancies are between one main text and the other. Others show up as later additions in the margins or between the lines of the second manuscript. The Discerning Reader may prefer to do this job himself to ensure good results. Alternatively, he may give it to a secretary he trusts. Either way, we will have completed Step Two, the addition of variants, corresponding to the second sort of reading considered above.

The Discerning Reader now nervously lends his fairly reliable copy of the *Birds* to his oldest son, a boy in his teens. The boy is reading the play with his teacher, the grammarian (γραμματικός, *grammaticus*), and needs help understanding the text. Because much of Aristophanes' vocabulary and idiom elude him and his classmates, the teacher habitually has to offer explanations in class. He assists them in reading, that is, according to the third method. Presumably, the grammarian reads the explanations aloud from an informal copy that he made for himself, some time earlier, of a glossary on just this play. The boy writes *exactly what he hears* into the margins and between the lines of his father's book. I do not know whether he tells his father about this. Whatever he faces at home, we can be certain that the innocent vandalism gives him a better understanding of what Aristophanes has to say, since now he has a rendition of the difficult words in his own vernacular. When the boy writes synonyms in the margins or, as often, between the lines, he completes Step Three, the addition of notes providing elementary exegesis.

Contrary to the belief of many twenty-first-century students of ancient Greek, however, vocabulary alone is not sufficient for comprehension. The grammarian therefore also provides his students with the factual information they need to get the jokes. He identifies the foibles of the politicians Aristophanes pillories, fills in historical background, fixes the location of any topographical features mentioned in the play, explains the democratic process in Athens, supplies the context for a poem alluded to by the playwright (if the reference is to a poem the class previously studied, he will probably have students recite it in full). The teacher gets most of this secondary information from a *hypomnema,* a line-by-line commentary on the play. At least a line-by-line commentary was the intention of the commentator who first composed it. The version belonging to our grammarian probably has gaps in coverage. Like the glossary he made for himself, he probably also copied this *hypomnema* from a loaner. He left out the parts that did not serve his purposes, and probably also those he did not understand. The resulting string of excerpts probably contains, in addition to factual material, some useful glosses and metaphrases that are missing in his glossary, and passages of scholarly argumentation for or against a variant reading or two. All this he passes along to the class. As the teacher reads new information aloud, the Son of the Discerning Reader again tries to capture the recitation verbatim and write it down in the margins of his father's book.[8] If his haste makes him careless, his spelling is likely to reflect the itacistic pronunciation of contemporary Greek. On some days, the grammarian may allow him and his classmates to copy directly from his book into theirs. Through varied activities like these, explanatory notes will have found their way into the margins of the book: Step Four in the philological cycle. Like the preceding phase, this is also connected with the third sort of approach to reading, since the reader's concerns are rooted neither in textual accuracy nor in interpretation, but (still) in factual information.

The class finishes the *Birds,* and the boy returns the book to his father, who may receive it with some dismay. Pause now to imagine what the book of the Discerning but Oblivious Reader looks like once his son is finished with it. The margins contain corrections written by a corrector, variants copied by someone else from a second edition of the text, glosses from a

---

8. This is one way of explaining how it happens that so many annotations correspond verbatim, or nearly so, with other ancient commentary.

glossary and glosses from a commentary, and explanations from the same commentary. Some of this information came via the teacher's lectures, some was copied from the teacher's manual, some from other copies of the play, and still the story is not finished.

Five years later, the man's second son is reading the *Birds* with a different teacher. With fatalistic resignation, the Discerning Reader hands over his marked-up copy of the play. Son Number Two annotates it too, adding information his brother had not included (as well as some that he failed to notice in the crowded margins). In fact, the second child's teacher has a library superior to that of the grammarian who taught the first. It includes not one but two commentaries on the play, and the second grammarian reads aloud to the class from both. The margins of the Discerning Reader's book now contain a sort of anthology of textual and explanatory information deriving from a large number of sources. No other kinds of notes appear. It would be hard, at this point, to detect which source produced which glosses, explanations, and variants. We might try to sort things out if we could distinguish the handwriting of the two children from each other and from the writing of the two revisers. Even if this were possible, however, there would be no sure way to distinguish which of the notes by Son Number Two originated in which of the two commentaries his teacher consulted. We have reached, admittedly in an informal sense, Step Five, the compilation of exegetic material.

The book is a mess. A certain thoughtful friend of the Discerning Reader sees it, covered as it is with different people's scrawls, and he decides he must have a copy of the entire compilation. He sees how useful the secondary information will be when it is time for his daughter to study Aristophanes.[9] He borrows the book, therefore, and brings it to a scribe to have it transcribed, complete with annotations, in the fair handwriting of a single professional amanuensis. Of course, this latest scribe may alter the main text—he may even believe he ought to do so—by incorporating the corrections he finds in the exemplar. He may also adopt the variants, or transcribe them as marginalia, depending on the orders of his customer. One thing he certainly will not do is use his own judgment to pick and choose the variants he thinks are right. Most of the time, the work done by professional scribes was quite mindless.

Up to a point, then, the new manuscript contains a text that very nearly integrates the two unannotated models that the Discerning Reader used at the beginning of our story. Variants present in the new book already existed

---

9. On the education of girls at the grammatical level, see Cribiore 2001: 74–101.

in those manuscripts and also, very likely, in the wider textual tradition of Aristophanes. The scribe may also have introduced additional variants unwittingly. Perhaps he misread a marginal gloss, thinking it a correction, incorporated it into the text, and thus invented a new variant. If the new lection fits the meter and makes some sort of sense, the fact that it was a mistake might even escape detection for a long time. The latest scribe will also, inevitably, introduce his own new errors, and perhaps his corrector will miss *them*. That corrector, in turn, may also make false corrections of his own. In any of these ways, another, slightly variant version of the *Birds* would come into circulation. By the time the thoughtful friend of the Discerning Reader hands the new manuscript to his daughter, Step Six will be finished, the alteration of a text on the basis of previous interventions. A second cycle of philological intrusions will already be halfway done.

At every stage in this fiction, the fundamental objective of the players—the Discerning Reader, thoughtful friend, the two grammarians, and perhaps even their students—is philological. Everyone in the chain gives careful attention to the form of the literary text in an effort to understand Aristophanes correctly. Does any of them reach a perfect understanding of the author's meaning? Of course not: no one has access to the exact words of the poet, much less to any layered meanings he intended. This is a situation modern classicists understand well. It was also the prevailing situation in antiquity.

Now let us turn to the ancient books themselves for illustrations of the various steps of the model. The surviving material is voluminous but spotty in every imaginable way. As we have seen, it comes from secondary cities and from towns and villages of Egypt, not from Alexandria. Archeological find spots are poorly documented, or not at all. The contents of ancient manuscripts are an indiscriminately mixed lot of authors—some widely read but with scarcely any annotation, some less popular and with rather a lot, some with abundant notes in texts from earlier centuries but hardly any from late antiquity, some the reverse. The evidence is very fragmentary: even though a text lacks notes altogether, the lost portion may have once been thickly annotated. Even the oldest annotated texts are several recopyings away from the authors' originals. Marginalia themselves, furthermore, vary greatly in subject and learning, and the motives of annotators are never really as clear as the story suggests. The model intimates that most marginalia come from a school context, and in fact I think this is usually the case. But there is not even any objective way to know who actually wrote the notes. Even if professional scribes made the annotations, this tells us little. Some marginalia on typical school subjects have the air of a schoolmaster's lecture whereas others are learned. Many annotated papyri, finally, are subliterary texts—commentaries, recipe collections and the like—that were assuredly not schoolbooks. With these caveats in mind, and with the model as guide, let us look at the texts.

Correction

Corrections in papyri, first, are often made by the original scribe, sometimes in the course of writing. Methods vary. Mistakes are sometimes erased and rewritten, sometimes dotted (expunged, literally), with the right text added above the error. For long alterations, scribes sometimes wrote a siglum beside the faulty lines and wrote the correct text in the upper or lower margin, with a matching symbol. The words ἄνω or κάτω, "above" or "below," as appropriate, sometimes accompany the siglum. Some corrections are cases of indisputable error made good, for example:[10]

a. The restitution of essential letters, without which the text is not Greek:
MP³ 561, v–vi, Homer, *Iliad* (ostracon).
1.15 **cκή]πρω[ι**
altered to cκή]πτρω[ι

1.110 **ἐκήβολο̣ [ἄλγεα τεύχει**
altered to ἐκήβολος [ἄλγεα τεύχει

b. The correction of a scribe's visual errors, for example, the misreading of ε as c:
MP³ 48, ii, Fragment of Aeschylus.
]κ̣οιcινc̣ν̣[
altered to]κοιcινεν[

---

10. Papyri are identified here by Mertens-Pack³ catalogue number (MP³): P. Mertens and M.-H. Marganne, *Mertens-Pack³ on Line* (available at http://promethee.philo.ulg.ac.be/cedopal/get PackCombi.asp) (May 2009). Following the MP³ number are the date (by century, Roman numerals indicating centuries c.e. and Arabic numerals those b.c.e.), the author, and the text. Abbreviations: *CGFP*: Austin 1973; Page: Page 1951; Pf.: Pfeiffer 1949–1953; *PLF*: Lobel & Page 1963; *PMG*: Page 1962; Rutherford: Rutherford 2001; *SH*: Lloyd-Jones & Parsons 1983. *TrGF*: Snell, Kannicht & Radt 1971–2004; Voigt: Voigt 1971. I use standard conventions of editing in transcribing papyrological texts: square brackets—[]—indicate letters lost in a lacuna and restored by the editor; round brackets—()—indicate letters added to complete abbreviations; ⌊ ⌋ surround letters absent in the papyrus due to a lacuna but attested in another source; ⟦ ⟧ surround words or letters erased in the ms. Dots under individual letters indicate letters of doubtful but likely reading; dots with no letters above them indicate illegible letters. Bold-faced text indicates the wording of the scribal text; unbold indicates the annotation.

c. Erroneous repetitions that entered the text when a scribe's eye jumped from the line he was copying to a similar one nearby—the "saute du même au même:"[11]
MP³ 26, ii, Fragment of Aeschylus.
νύμφ[ι]ον ἤδη (wrongly repeated from 7 lines above)
altered to νύμφ[ι]ον οἷον

Corrections like these are fairly straightforward. In some alterations, however, it is less obvious what the scribe is up to, for example:

d. MP³ 7, iii, Aeschines, *De Falsa Legatione*.
Κίμωνος εἴποντος ὅτι φοβεῖται μὴ δικαιολογούμενος περιγένοιτο ἡμῶν ὁ Φίλιππος
φοβεῖται altered to φοβοῖτο

e. MP³ 177, ii, Bacchylides 17.
ὄρνυco ἐc
altered to ὄρνυc' ἐc

φοβοῖτο in (d) is the reading of later manuscripts. But was the scribe's initial φοβεῖται part of a gloss that wrongly found its way into his exemplar, or his faulty substitution of the indicative form for the optative, a mood rarely employed in his day, or is it a hitherto unknown (and implausible) variant? Technically, either form works. In (e), it is unclear whether the corrector meant to bring the text into line with an exemplar or was recording advice from a teacher about oral delivery—a warning, that is, not to let the *scriptio plena* fool the reader into pronouncing the omicron. If so, this is not a textual emendation but an instruction for recitation.

Variants

Variant readings, the second kind of modification made in the Discerning Reader's manuscript, must have had great importance for readers for whom an accurate text was paramount. Variants are sometimes distinguished, in papyri, by being written with a dot on each side. The ones most worth trusting as genuine readings are accompanied by a scholar's name. About a dozen names are preserved in such a context. Some are known. Many can only tentatively be identified because of the inclination of scribes to abbreviate:

---

11. Dain 1964.

a. MP³ 616, ii, Homer, *Iliad*.
2.707 **ὁ δ' ἄρα πρότερος**: Ἀρίσταρχ(ος) ὁ δ' ἅμα πρότ(ερος)
"Aristarchus read ὁ δ' ἅμα πρότ(ερος)"
Munro and Allen (1920) report one ms. with Aristarchus' ἅμα, which they print, and the rest with ἄρα.

b. MP³ 1473, ii, Sophocles, *Ichneutae*.
TrGF 4.314.146 **ἐκμεμαγμένοι**:–μενα Ἀρ(ιστο)νί(κος)(?)
"?Aristonicus read -μενα"

c. MP³1361, ii, Pindar, *Paean* 2.61.
ἐνκατέθηκαν: · γ· Ἀρ( )
"Ar . . . read ἐγκατέθηκαν"

As we saw, a variant, attributed or not, may have come from collation of manuscripts, or it may have been copied from a commentary. If the former, it would be nice to know more about the source. How exactly did the variant come to be associated with a single scholar who, for the most part, is now unknown to us? How many recopyings separated this copy from his original? How carefully written and corrected was the comparison manuscript from which the variant came? Where did that manuscript normally reside—in a private collection? In the Alexandrian Library? Who had access to it? Why those people?

Corrections and variants—Steps One and Two of the model presented earlier—represent the kind of activity traditionally associated with philology. Other kinds of intervention in ancient manuscripts deal more with meaning and less with text. At Step Three in the model, glosses and metaphrases were the notes the Son of the Discerning Reader first scribbled in his father's copy of *Birds*. Synonyms and metaphrasings helped him at the most fundamental level. In papyri, notes like this outnumber notes on factual background two to one. Their ratio to textual notes is even greater, about three to one.

The Table (see pp. 45–46) lists authors whose texts contain elementary exegesis (column A), textual comments other than variants (column B), or notes providing factual background (column C). The authors listed first are those whose manuscripts contain the largest number of elementary notes. The three outliers at the top of the list, however—Callimachus, Theocritus, and Pindar—need to be set aside, since for each author a single, long, and exceptionally heavily annotated manuscript skews the results. Among the remaining names—Isocrates, Aristophanes, Homer, various lyric poets—are the principal authors perennially read at the secondary level and the advanced primary level by schoolchildren, as ancient writers on education tell us. (Two of the three poets we excluded were also, in fact, read routinely in schools, and their work survives in many papyri.) According to Quintilian, the best authors for children at the secondary level are Pindar, Alcaeus, Stesichorus, and Simonides (*Inst.* 2.5.1–5). Statius' father, a grammarian at Naples, taught Pindar, Ibycus, Alcman, Stesichorus, Sappho, Callimachus, Lycophron, and Corinna (also Sophron, who does not appear here) (*Silvae* 5.3.146–58). These curricula consist only of poetry, but Quintilian holds that certain prose authors are also appropriate for schoolchildren, especially at the later stages of grammatical education or the early stages of a rhetor's instruction. We know, in fact, that Libanius taught Thucydides' *Peloponnesian Wars* to his rhetorical students (*Or.* 1.148–50), and the heavily annotated Kellis Isocrates (MP³ 1240.03) is patently a schoolbook, although the class that used it was probably no farther along than the advanced elementary level. Virtually all the marginalia that proliferate in late Aristophanes codices, finally, come from pedagogical sources, as Günther Zuntz (1975) demonstrated.

The point is this: that any list of the authors principally taught at the intermediate level in antiquity coincides fairly well with a list of papyri that contain unsophisticated notes on word meanings. If there had been something like a student bookstore for the pupils of grammarians in Roman Oxyrhynchus, most of the authors listed at the top of the Table would be on the shelf. Certainly all of them would show up, in different groupings, on the combined reading lists of local teachers. If the shopowner also sold second-hand books, several would contain simple glosses and metaphrases added by schoolchildren.

Elementary Glosses and Rephrasings

The source of the elementary notes surviving in papyri was typically a glossary specific to the work being studied, with words and their meanings listed in the order in which they appeared in the literary text. This was the usual form of glossaries, as we know from the multitude that survive, particularly for Homer.[12] Such a collection was certainly the source of the Kellis notes, which are packed into the margins of the codex without any of the concern that annotators regularly show for aligning notes with the text they explain.

---

12. Naoumides 1969 demonstrates that short, text-specific glossaries predominate over comprehensive lexica in papyri.

The simplicity, not to say banality, of the glosses in this text is a clear sign that it was used at a fairly elementary level:

MP³ 1240.03, iv, Isocrates, *Ad Demonicum*.
«πρέπει»: χρή   "'It is fitting:' it is right"
«ὁρῶ»: βλέπω   "'Observe:' see"
«οὐ μικρά»: πάνυ   "'Not a little:' very much"

Notes like these hardly look like philology in the narrow sense of the word. They do, however, bring a schoolchild closer to a correct understanding of a text, or they ought to. I offer them as examples of practical philology, according to my broader definition.

Background Information 1: Scholarly Notes

We reach now the final category of evidence, represented in Step Four: notes that offer background information that a reader needs to understand a text thoroughly. Comments like these we may loosely divide into two uneven groups. The smaller set are those found in scholars' texts, the larger consists of all the rest. The vagueness of this description indicates the difficulty, not to say the impossibility, of deciding whether a given manuscript is a scholar's text or not.

One obstacle is the broad connotation of the word "scholar" itself. At one extreme, it describes an Alexandrian scholar of lasting influence like Aristophanes of Byzantium or Aristarchus. At the other, it refers to the intelligent protégé of an intelligent and conscientious grammarian, whether in Alexandria, Oxyrhynchus or elsewhere, who has access to a good library. Scattered between these extremes are hundreds of Museum scholars, students, and grammarians living in the cities of Greco-Roman Egypt during the millennium for which we have papyrus evidence. A second difficulty is that the clearest criteria for identifying scholars' texts to date are formulated in a way that casts the net even wider. For Eric Turner, these are books that show clear signs of informed revision, have critical signs that indicate the text was used in conjunction with a scholarly commentary, and contain marginal notes.[13] Informed revision like that represented by the annotated variants considered earlier is certainly a mark of such a manuscript. Critical

---

13. Turner 1956 and 1980, especially 93–96.

sigla are not.[14] Although they probably indicate that a reader has compared the manuscript with a commentary, not all surviving papyrus commentaries are learned. Nor are marginal notes. We have already seen that notes supplying elementary exegesis are vastly more common than any other kind of comment. For present purposes, then, I consider a scholar's text to be one in which any of several kinds of additions have been made, including variants, detailed textual notes like that in (a) below, informational notes attributed to named authorities as in example (b), or—in general—marginalia providing detailed background information. Here another problem arises, however. Detailed notes are not, simply for that reason, scholarly. Note (c), below, for example, comes from a papyrus with multiple indications that it belonged to a learned reader. At the end of the following list, I include also a 'faux-scholarly' note (example d). Despite its accurate and specific detail, the information it supplies is irrelevant to the context. The manuscript in which it appears, moreover, although remarkable for its dense and lengthy annotation, contains no evidence of truly scholarly intervention:[15]

a. MP³ 79, 1 B.C.E.–1 C.E., Alcman.
π]αρεγγρά(φεται) ἐν [το]ῖς ἀντιγρά(φοις) αὕτη
?ἡ ᾠδὴ ἐν τῷ] πέμπτῳ καὶ ἐν ἐκείνῳ
ἐν μὲν τῷ] Ἀρ(ιστο)νί(κου) περιεγέγρα(πτο), ἐν δὲ τῷ Πτολ-
(εμαίου)
ἀπερ[ί]γρα(πτος) ἦν
"This ... is wrongly inserted in ... copies in the fifth (book) ... and in that (book) it was bracketed in Aristonicus' copy but was not bracketed in Ptolemy's."

b. MP³ 998, i, Homer *Iliad*, 23.842 or 845.[16]
ἔρριψε
τὸ ῥῖψαι ἐν τῷ ι γράφεται·
εἴρηται γ(ὰρ), φ[η]cὶν ὁ Τρύφω[ν],
παρὰ τὸ ῥῖμμα κ(αὶ) ῥίπτειν
"ῥῖψαι is written with an iota (i.e., iota only: not epsilon iota, ῥεῖψαι). For it is said to come, Tryphon says, from ῥῖμμα and ῥίπτειν"

---

14. McNamee 1992.
15. McNamee 1994.
16. This text was also used by someone who was certainly not a scholar and who added the charmingly simple gloss «κ]ρυερά»: ψυχρά ("'icy cold': freezing cold"). This says nothing, however, about whether the person who wrote the comment on morphology was a scholar or a scholar's student, since the simple gloss may come from a much later pen.

c. MP³ 1360, iii, Pindar, *Paean* 20.19 (Group S1 Rutherford).
ἀ]μφίπολ[οι] Κεφ[αλ]λαν[
ἡ Κεφαλλή(νη) πρότερ[ον τοῦ Ἀ]μφι-
τρύω(νος) Δουλίχιο(ν) ἐκαλεῖτο· ἦν δ' ὑ-
πὸ τὸν Πτερέλαον· ἀ(πὸ) δ(ὲ) Κεφάλ(ου)
τὴν προσηγορίαν ἔσχ[ε]ν
"Cephallene before the time of Amphitryon was called Dulichium, and it was under the control of Pterelaus. It got its name from Cephalus"

d. (A 'faux scholarly' annotation) MP³ 1356, vi, Pindar, *Pythian* 1.52–53.
φαντὶ Λαμνόθεν ἕλκει
τειρόμενον μεταβάσοντας ἐλθεῖν
ἥροας ἀντιθέους Ποίαντος υἱὸν τοξόταν
[«φαντὶ Λαμνόθεν»: οἱ γὰρ Ἕλληνες ἐκ Λήμνου μετεστείλαντο
τὸν ἥρωα. ὁ δὲ Φιλοκτ]ήτης πόαν ἐπέθε-
[το ἐπὶ τὸ τραῦμα καὶ οὕτως ὑγιάσθη]
"('They say from Lemnos . . .': for the Greeks summoned the hero from Lemnos. And Philoctetes put an herb (on his wound and in this way was cured.)"

Background Information 2: Informational Notes That Are Not Scholarly

By contrast with examples (a) through (c) above, the intellectual content of explanatory marginalia in most papyri is neither scholarly nor even particularly high. As in the case of elementary notes, background comments in this second group are thickest in papyri of the same three poets for whom disproportionately large fragments survive. Again, though, if we set these three authors aside, we find that most factual notes in this set appear in copies of authors read in schools: Aristophanes, Aratus, Alcaeus, Homer, Aeschylus, Sophocles, Menander, Alcman, Plato, Hipponax. Within this larger group we may distinguish three general types of informational notes. The first supplies factual information about the organization or performance of the text:

a. Identifying speakers or persons addressed:
MP³ 1487, v-vi, Theocritus 15.59.
πρὸς γραῦν τινά
"To an old woman"

b. Explaining the circumstances of production or the setting of a play (the note having been excerpted, in this case, from a "hypothesis," i.e., a plot summary):
MP³ 46, ii–iii, Aeschylus, *TrGF* 3.451v.
ἡ μὲν] cκηνὴ τοῦ δρᾴ-
ματο]c ὑπόκειται ἐν
   ]· ὁ δὲ χο(ρὸc) cυνέcτη-
κεν ἐ]κ πολιτῶν γε-
ρόντω]ν· ὁ προλογίζ[ω](ν) [
"The scene of the play is in. . . . The chorus consists of ?old citizens. . . . The person speaking the prologue (is) . . . "

c. Drawing attention to the tone of a speech:
MP³ 145, v, Aristophanes, *Clouds* 3.
οὐδέποθ' ἡμέρα γενήcεται
«οὐδέποθ' ἡμέρα γενήcεται»: τοῦτο καὶ
ὀργιζόμενοc καὶ ὑποκρινόμενοc
δύναται λέγειν
"This he can say in both an angry and a dramatic manner"

The second deals with language and expression, for example issues of morphology, dialect or syntax. Here are the subjects dear to the hearts of grammarians from the Alexandrians onward.

a. Metaplasm (an unconventional alteration in a word's form):
MP³ 1338, iv–v?, Parthenius, *SH* 611.11–20.
πίcυρον, ὡc ἀπὸ
εὐθείαc τοῦ πί-
cυροc......
...... πίcυρεc,
ὡc ἀπὸ εὐθείαc
τοῦ πίcυρ ἀλ-
λὰ μεταπλα-
cμόc (ἐcτιν), ὡc
χρυcάρματοι,
ἐρυcάρματεc
"πίcυρον (lemma): as if from a nominative πίcυροc. [?He does not write] πίcυρεc, as if from a nominative πίcυρ. Rather, it is a metaplasm (a form created from a stem different from that of the nominative singular—*KM*), like χρυcάρματοι, ἐρυcάρματεc"

b. Dialect (Aeolic, Boeotian):
MP³ 59, ii, Alcaeus, Voigt 77 i.16.
οἱ Αἰολεῖc ci[?]υτ( ) ... [?
πολλ[.]ν λέγοι ἂν τῃ [
[C]απφὼ κατ[...]γλ[
"The Aeolians (say). . . . Sappho would say . . . ?"

MP³ 251, Corinna, *PMG* 654 i.22.
ἐν χρουcοφαῖc
ἐc
"To"
I.e., the equivalent of the Boeotian form ἐν (ἐc in the vernacular), which means "to." The annotator does not supply the corresponding fact, that Boeotian χρουcοφαῖc is equivalent to Attic χρουcοφάc.

c. Morphology and dialect:
MP³ 55, i, Alcaeus, *PLF* 30.
«ἀ]γόντον»: πρ(οcτατικὸν) [ἀ]ν(τὶ τοῦ) ἀγέ[τωcαν
"ἀ]γόντον: imperative, instead of (the Attic form) ἀγέ[τωcαν, 'let them go'"

d. Meter:
MP³ 201, iv, Callimachus, *Ectheosis Arsinoes* Pf. 228.1.
¡Ἀγέτω θεόc, οὐ γὰρ ἐγὼ δίχ₁α τῶνδ' ἀείδειν
τὸ μ(έν) μέτρ(ον) Ἀρχεβούλ(ειον) λογαοιδ(ικὸν) καλ(εῖται)·
πεντάμετρον· ἡ α' ἐπιδέχετ(αι) ἀνάπαιcτ(ον)
cπονδεῖ(ον) ἴαμβ(ον), αἱ ἑξῆc ἀναπαίcτ(ουc),
ἡ ἐcχάτ(η) βακχεῖον καὶ ἀμφίβραχυν,
ἐπεὶ ἀδιάφορ(οc) ἡ τελευτ(αία) cυλλαβή
"The meter is called the Archeboulian logaoedic, a pentameter: the first position (θέcιc?) allows anapaest, spondee, or iamb; the following positions anapaests; the last a bacchius and amphibrachys, since the final syllable is indifferently (short or long)"

Figures of speech attract a great deal of attention.

a. Irony:
MP³ 61, ii, Alcaeus, Voigt 120.5 (ed. A. Porro).
ταῦτα c[ὺν εἰ]ρωνείᾳ εἴc τινα

γήμαντα [πρὶν γε]νειάcαι
"These things (are said) with irony toward a man marrying before he has a beard"

b. Ellipse, expressions *para prosdokian*:
MP³ 361, ii, Epicharmus, *Odysseus Automolos*, CGFP 83.8–18.
ἐ]νθὼν τεῖδε θωκηcῶ τε καὶ λεξοῦ[μ᾽ ὅπ]ωc
ι ῥάιδιν᾽ ε ι ἴμειν ταῦτα καὶ τοῖc δεξιωτέροιc ι ἐμεῦ[c
εἴλη]πτ(αι) πα(ρὰ) προcδοκ(ίαν), ὡc εἰ ἔλεγε καὶ τοῖc ἀμαθεcτάτοιc τὸ καθ[. . .
" . . . has been left out as contrary to expectation, as if he meant to say, 'even to the stupidest people' [instead, that is, of the author's 'even to the people smarter than I'] . . . "

c. Pleonasm:
MP³ 87.01, ii, annotation in a commentary on Anacreon.
τα]υτολ | ο]γίαc
" . . . repetition"

These were the fundamental subjects of grammatical education since at least the second century B.C.E., when Dionysius Thrax formulated his influential definition of γραμματική—the subject, after all, of secondary instruction in antiquity.

Background Information 3: Notes Supplying Context

There is one more category of information that ancient grammarians were expected to pack into the intellectual kit they provided their students: background facts. Although the specific subject of particular notes of this kind varies widely according to the nature of a text, the topic that dominates is mythology. Myth is a fundamental substratum of ancient commentary on works by the dramatic poets and by Homer, all of whom children read early in their schooling. Recondite myths are also the delight of the Hellenistic poets, who were read by advanced students. A paramount task for a grammarian, therefore, was to make sure that students knew the facts of the case as they read. Marginalia on myth range from terse simplicity to concise recitations of key facts to long-winded, fully documented recitations of stories:

a. MP³ 917.3, I, Homer, *Iliad* 14.325.
ἣ δὲ Διώνυcον Cεμέλη τέκε χάρμα βροτοῖcιν
οἴνου εὑρετή[c, -ν
"Inventor of wine"

b. MP³ 1338, IV-V?, Parthenius, *Arete*.
τὸν Ζέφ(υρον)· ἐκεί-
νῳ γ(ὰρ) ἐγα-
μήθη ἡ Ἶρις
"Zephyrus, for Iris was married to him"

c. MP³ 1360, iii, Pindar, *Paean* 8.143ff (Group B2 Rutherford).
]. []. ἐκπεcόντοc χρηcμοῦ Ἐργίνῳ cτρατευομ(έν)ῳ ἐπὶ Θήβαc
   ἑτέρου[
λέγει] γ(άρ)· "ἀλλ' οὕτωc τῷ Ἐργίνῳ ἔπεμψαc χρηcμοὺc τῷ
   ἐπὶ τὰc Θήβαc[
ἑλκ]υ̣cαμένῳ τὸ ξίφοc," ἀν(τὶ τοῦ) cτρατεύcαντι· τὸ γ(ὰρ)
   ἑλκόμ(εν)ον ἀν(τὶ τοῦ) ἑλκ̣[υc]άμ(εν)ον [εἴρηται.
Κλύμ](εν)ον ἀναιρεθῆ(ναί) [Εὐφορί]ων μ(ὲν) ὑπὸ Περιήρουc,
   Ἑλλάνι(κοc) δ[ὲ
ὑπ]ό τινοc Καδ[μείων?] κ̣[(ατ') Ὀ]γ̣χηc̣τὸν(?) μαχόμ(εν)ον, Ἐπι
   μενίδη̣[c
δ' ἐν̣ ξ' Γε̣[νεαλογ]ιῶν ὑπὸ Γλαύκου ἐρίcαντα τῷ ζεύγει τ [
δύο δὲ πόλ]εμοι ἐγέν̣ο(ντο), ὁ μ(ὲν) Κλυμένου ἀναιρεθέντο(c),
ὁ δὲ τοὺc ἐπὶ] δαcμὸ(ν) π̣[(αρ)]ὀ̣ντ(αc) Ἡρακλέο(υc)
   ἀκρωτηριά[cαντοc
". . . another oracle for Erginus was delivered while he was campaigning against Thebes. . . For he (Pindar) says (about Apollo,) 'But thus you sent oracles to Erginus who had drawn his sword against Thebes.' ('Had drawn his sword') instead of 'who had campaigned.' For 'drawing the sword' was said (by the poet) instead of 'having drawn.' Euphorion(?) (says) that Clymenus was killed by Perieres. Hellanicus, though, (cf. Paus. 9.37.1) . . . by one of the Cadmeians . . . as he was fighting at Onchestus, and Epimenides (*FGrH* 457) . . . in the 60th book of Genealogies (says he was killed) by Glaucus as he competed with the chariot. . . . There were two wars, the first when Clymenus was killed, . . . the second when Heracles mutilated the men who were there to collect tribute" (after Rutherford).

In fact, ancient authors make clear that an occupational hazard of grammarians was giving in too readily to wretched excess in the teaching of myth.[17] The example from Pindar's *Pythian* 1 (above, Background Information 1, note d) illustrates just this fault. In the first *Pythian,* Pindar likens Hiero to Philoctetes: both of them triumph over physical pain. The commentator in the papyrus supplies a complete but boiled-down account of Sophocles' version of the Philoctetes myth, including the story of the herb that eventually healed his sore, although there is nothing about the cure in Pindar. Why include an irrelevancy in a note on the *Pythian?* Because, as I suspect, the annotation is meant for students. Not only does it betray the same obsession with myth as the other notes in this papyrus. It also would give the teacher the opportunity to remind his students of the details of Sophocles' play, which they had very likely read before they got to Pindar.

Of course notes on myth appear in scholars' texts also, where the information supplied tends to be very precise, as in the note on Pindar *Paean* 8 (above, note c). Here the highly specific citations of authoritative sources compensate in some degree for a mythographic excess that Quintilian might have deplored. In fact, though, difficulties may lurk even in citations like these, since some mythographical compilers added the luster of learning to their work by incorporating bogus references.[18] The very precision of these phony citations seems, superficially, to testify to their *bona fides.* The enhanced credentials of mythographical collections doctored like this— precision masquerading as accuracy—must have added to their appeal in some circles, and both grammarians and scholars probably played a part, knowingly or not, in transmitting falsified testimonials in commentaries and notes. The point is not that the citations of Epimenides and Hellanicus in the *Paeans* manuscript are phony, for the scholarly credentials of this text are otherwise strong. The point is that even in scholarly texts like this, the information in mythographic notes cannot be accepted without question: even the scholarly annotator of a book like this may have been fooled.

Following mythographic notes in frequency, in distant second place, are notes on geography and history, the latter not always distinguishable from myth. Historical notes appear in predictable contexts, for example, in copies of Alcaeus' political poems for which the reader needs to know the circumstances and the principal actors; in Pindar's *Paeans,* where the achievements of the cities being honored needs to be explained for readers of later generations; or in Callimachean passages that honor members of the house of Ptolemy.

---

17. Quintilian warns against it (*Inst.* 1.8.18–21). Juvenal lampoons parents who expect their sons' teachers to know every possible mythological detail (7.229–36).

18. Cameron 2004: esp. 173–74, which concerns this note.

a. MP³ 60, i–ii, Alcaeus, Voigt 114.1.
κατὰ τὴν
φυγὴν τὴν
πρώτην, ὅ-
[τ'] ἐ(πὶ) Μυρcίλον
καταcκ[ευ]αcάμ[(εν)]οι
ἐπιβουλὴν οἱ π(ερὶ)
τὸν Ἀλκαῖον κ(ατα-)
φανέντες δ(ὲ) π(αρα-)
φθάcα[ντ]ες πρὶν
ἢ δίκη[ν] ὑπο-
[c]χεῖν ἐφ[υ]γον
[εἰ]c Πύρρ[α]ν

"At the time of the first exile, when those who sided with Alcaeus, having prepared a plot against Myrsilus but having been exposed, got away before being brought to justice and fled to Pyrrha."

b. MP³ 1361, ii, Pindar, *Paeans* 2.3–4.
cέθ]εν Ἰάονι τόνδε λαῷ [παι]ᾶνα [δι]ώξω
ἄποικοι γάρ εἰcιν οἱ Ἀβδηρῖται [Τηΐων·Τέωc]
δ' ἐcτὶ τῆc Ἰωνίαc πόλιc η[

"For the Abderites are colonists (of the Teians. Teos) is a city of Ionia . . . "

c. MP³ 186, vi–vii, Callimachus, *Aetia 4* (*Coma Berenices*) Pf. fr. 110.45.
βουπόροc Ἀρcινόηιc μητρόc, καὶ διὰ μέ[ccου /Μηδείων ὀλοαὶ
νῆεc ἔβηcαν/ Ἄθω
«Ἀρcινόηc μητρ(όc)»
κατὰ τιμὴν εἶ-
πεν ἐπεὶ θυγά-
τηρ Ἀπάμαc κ(αὶ)
Μάγα

"Of your mother Arsinoe:" he (i.e. Callimachus) said this out of respect, since she (i.e. Berenice) is the daughter of Apamas and Maga"

Notes on geography are about as numerous as those on history.[19] In general, they simply identify as river, mountain, or strait a physical feature mentioned in the text. Sometimes they also identify its location.

---

19. Assuming, that is, that we discount the proliferation of geographical notes in one particular copy of Callimachus, a poem about Sicilian cities.

a. MP³ 373.2, ii, *fragmenta* (Euphorion?).
   Ληλάντοιο
   "Λήλαντον· | (ἔcτι) δ(ὲ) ὄροc κ(αὶ) πόλ(ιc)"
   "Lelantum: it is a mountain and a city." (An error: in fact, it is a plain between Eretria and Chalcis.)

   ]Ἀονίο[ι]ο
   Βοι[ωτίου]
   "Boeotian"

   Κ̣άλ(ηc) ποταμ(ὸc) Μυγδονί | αc περὶ Βιθυνίαν
   "Cales is a river of Mygdonia in Bithynia"

b. MP³ 371, ii, Euphorion, *Hippomedon Maior*, SH 416.
   Πόλ]τυοc ὡc Αἴν[ο]υ τε ερ̣ ι̣άδαο π̣[
   ] πρότερον μ(ὲν) Πολτυμβρίαν κ[α]λουμ(ένην) [ ] αι αὖθι[c
   ἐ]καλεῖτο δ(ὲ) Πολτυμβρία ἀπὸ Πόλ̣τυοc τ[οῦ] β[α]c̣[ι]λ(έωc)
   [αὐτῆc
   ὡc] Ἑλλάνικος̣
   " . . . formerly called Poltymbria. . . . but thereafter it was called Poltymbria from Poltyos its king, as Hellanicus (says)"

Since factual error like that in (a) above is rather rare, there is a sort of pleasant irony in the fact that one of these infrequent mistakes appears in a note on geography in a copy of a poem by the geographer Eratosthenes:

c. MP³ 364.2, 1 B.C.E.—i C.E., Eratosthenes, *Hermes*, SH 397
   ἡ νῆcοc ⟦Πάφοc⟧
   Κύπροc, ἡ μη-
   τρόπολιc Πάφοc
   "The island is ~~Paphos~~ Cyprus, the chief town Paphos"

Subjects other than myth, history, and geography get much less attention. They deal with proverbs, local ritual, local custom, botany, astronomy—whatever a newcomer to a text needed to know to acquire a full appreciation of the author's meaning.

a. Proverbs:
   MP³ 59, ii, Alcaeus, Voigt 71.1–2 .
   φίλοc μὲν ἦcθα κἀπ᾽ ἔριφον κάλην

καὶ χοῖρον. οὕτω τοῦτο νομίσδεται
φί[λο]ς δέ, φη(σιν), ἦ[σθα......]ον ὥστε σὲ καὶ ἐπὶ χοῖ-
ρ[ο]ν καὶ ἔριφον [καλεῖν, τοῦτ'] (ἔστιν) εἰς τὰ παρασκευάς-
ματα τυχ[<10> τ]οῖς γ(ὰρ) ξένοις μετὰ
σπουδῆς πο[ιοῦσιν ?τ(ὴν) εὐ]ωχίαν· παροιμία δ' (ἐστὶν)
ἐπ' ἔριφ[ο]ν καὶ χο[ῖρον καλεῖν, ὅθε]ν λέγει «οὕτω τοῦτο νομ-
(ίζεται)»

"'You were a friend (of such a kind,)' he says, 'that I would invite you for pig and for kid,' that is, for any(?) events happening (at my home). For they especially enjoy preparing feasts for guests. 'To invite for kid and pig' is a proverb. Whence he says 'this is the custom.'"

b. Botany, animal husbandry
MP³ 1487, v-vi, Theocritus 2.48–49
ἱππομανὲς φυτόν ἐστι
ἐὰν γεννήσῃ ἡ ἵππος· [??]
φ[υτὸ]ν προλάβῃ ὁ ἱπποβουκόλ(ος) [κ(αὶ)?]
καθαρίζει τὴν ἀκαθαρσίαν [?]
ι[ ]. [.] πώλους [<12]

"If the mare gives birth, the herdsman gets a plant(?) in advance (and) cleans the filth (in order that?) . . . foals . . ."

The presumed source, indirectly, of nearly all the marginalia in papyri is the work of Alexandrian scholars. Whether in textual studies, in grammar, or in non-linguistic subjects like history, geography, and ethnography, their approach was much the same: they assembled evidence methodically from disparate sources, and they classified it logically. In the third century B.C.E., Zenodotus inaugurated textual criticism by collecting and systematically collating manuscripts of Homer, and Callimachus classified the contents of the Ptolemaic Library by genre and author, among his other undertakings. A century later, Dionysius Thrax analyzed the study of language and of literature and on this basis formulated a definition of grammar, broadly understood, whose influence still endures. Other scholars, with the contents of the Alexandrian Library at their disposal, wrote works of secondary scholarship—on laws, place names, rituals, tribes, rivers, myths, and the like. Their research found its way back into commentaries by Alexandrian and other scholars on literature, and most factual annotations in papyri, as well as many textual notes, are vestiges of their work. Indeed, ancient marginal and interlinear notes in general illustrate, quite nicely, key elements in Dionysius' terse definition of γραμματική:

Grammatike is familiarity with the expressions typically used by the poets and the writers of prose. It has six parts. First, well practiced reading with attention to pitch and pronunciation; second, *explanation of the poetic tropes* embodied in the text; third, the *interpretation in common speech of glosses* and *questions arising from the text;* fourth, the development of etymologies; fifth, the demonstration of analogy; sixth, the assessment of the poems, which is the finest of all the parts of the craft.[20]

As we have seen, most ancient notes are concerned with the same set of subjects: explaining poetic tropes, interpreting unfamiliar language, and answering questions arising from the text. Like γραμματική, their object is to help a reader come closer to comprehending an author's meaning. Usually, it seems, that reader was the student of a grammarian, who drilled the student in forms, meanings, and facts. If the proficiency of such a student ever reached the point at which he was ready to engage in the sixth and "finest" part of literary education, the assessment of poems (κρίcιc ποιημάτων), this is not reflected in papyrus marginalia.

This, then, was the general state of philology several hundred miles south of the Alexandrian Library, in Oxyrhynchus, not only in the second century when the Discerning Reader and his children were reading Aristophanes there, but also for several centuries before and after, at least until the evidence gives out about the time of the Arab conquest. Of course, my survey of the evidence has handled many questions inadequately or not at all, for example, the identity of the annotators in ancient papyri (not all were Sons of Discerning Readers); the mechanical process entailed in writing or copying notes into books, especially when the books are in roll form; the tone of discourse in marginalia and commentaries (it is not really as invidious as tales of life at the Museum make out); the preservation of commentaries (one wonders how long they survived uncontaminated and in a form their authors would recognize, whether there were dominant versions, whether there were competing versions); finally, the disputed links between ancient marginalia and medieval scholia. I hope I have succeeded, however, in my initial purpose, namely, to illustrate the practical applications of philology in antiquity on the basis of the annotations of ancient manuscripts, and to give

---

20. γραμματική ἐcτιν ἐμπειρία τῶν παρὰ ποιηταῖc τε καὶ cυγγραφεῦcιν ὡc ἐπὶ τὸ πολὺ λεγομένων. μέρη δὲ αὐτῆc ἐcτιν ἕξ· πρῶτον ἀνάγνωcιc ἐντριβὴc κατὰ προcῳδίαν, δεύτερον ἐξήγηcιc κατὰ τοὺc ἐνυπάρχονταc ποιητικοὺc τρόπουc, τρίτον γλωccῶν τε καὶ ἰcτοριῶν πρόχειροc ἀπόδοcιc, τέταρτον ἐτυμολογίαc εὕρεcιc, πέμπτον ἀναλογίαc ἐκλογιcμόc, ἕκτον κρίcιc ποιημάτων, ὃ δὴ κάλλιcτόν ἐcτι πάντων τῶν ἐν τῇ τέχνῃ (Uhlig 1883).

a sense of what was entailed in reading the classics in Greco-Egyptian cities some distance from the Library at Alexandria. Readers there leave traces of their concerns with textual accuracy and basic comprehension. If we wish to investigate the reading habits of people keen on other matters—authorial intention or interpretation of texts, for example—we must seek other sources than these marginalia.

Table

Annotated Authors, with Tallies of Three Kinds of Note

	No. of texts	A *elementary exegesis*	B *textual criticism*	C *factual background*
Theocritus	6	197	3	52
Callimachus	11	86	1	50
Pindar	11	80	26	51
Isocrates	2	49	0	0
Aristophanes	16	46	0	30
Homer	21	40	42	17
Alcaeus	13	37	14	10
Thucydides	7	17	2	0
Ap. Rhodius	4	13	1	2
Euripides	12	13	1	1
Corinna	1	11	0	1
Menander	13	11	1	7
Plato	9	11	4	4
Cercidas	1	10	0	2
Parthenius	2	8	0	6
Alcman	3	8	10	5
Sophocles	8	7	31	2
Lycophron	2	6	0	5
Demosthenes	5	6	0	0
Simonides	3	6	13	0
Hipponax	2	4	0	5
Eratosthenes	1	4	0	2
Herodas	1	4	1	0
Bacchylides	4	3	1	3
Sappho	3	3	1	0
Aratus	5	2	0	10
Aeschylus	8	2	0	11
Epicharmus	3	2	9	1
Herodotus	2	2	1	0
Ibycus	2	1	0	1

Table, continued

	No. of texts	A *elementary exegesis*	B *textual criticism*	C *factual background*
Archilochus	3	1	0	1
Hesiod	4	1	0	0
Stesichorus	4	1	12	0
Euphorion	3	0	2	5
Anacreon	2	0	1	2
Theognis	1	0	0	1
Hippocrates	2	0	0	1
Hierocles Stoicus	1	0	0	0
Didymus	1	0	0	0
Xenophon	3	0	13	0
Aristoxenus	1	0	1	0
Cratinus?	1	0	1	0
Critias?	1	0	1	0

CHAPTER 2

Philologizing Philologists: A Case Study

Philological History and the
Text of Rutilius Namatianus' *De Reditu Suo*

Craig Maynes

Modern conceptions of the term "philology," no matter how divergent, all proceed from the basic notion that philology is a field which is concerned with the use of words.[1] For those who are concerned with the use of ancient words, the meaning of the term "philology" is, largely by necessity, attenuated to the *study* of *written* words. But the study of written words has never been and will never be (indeed simply cannot be) conducted uniformly. This essay will focus on the historical fluidity of the purpose, nature and returns of studying written words. It will be concerned not with a theory of what philology is, but rather with the consideration of the potentially multiplicitous effects on our philological pursuits of what philology *has been* in its own historical incarnations.

By nature, authors are lovers of words, and many (the best ones) are also students of the written words that went before; they are themselves philologists. As such, any writer worth the title "author" (the philologist-author)

---

1. Etymologically, the term means "the love of words" (φιλο -, "loving," and λόγος, "word"). λόγος also came to imply the rational use of words, "reasoning," so by extension the term "philology" might also mean "love of reasoning." Despite these etymological definitions, the term philology was only occasionally used even by the classical Greeks in the sense of "love of words" or even "love of reasoning." Rather, they usually employed the term as signifying "love of learning" or "love of literature," and often in direct contrast to "philosophy" ("the love of wisdom"). Nonetheless, the term "philology" itself has always been polysemous and all of the above were potential meanings in classical Greek (Liddel, Scott, and Jones 1996, s.v. φιλολογέω). Modern use of the term "philology" is no less diverse, varying widely between disciplines and continents, and signifying everything from the study of literature to linguistics.

actively participates in the textual exposition of his own philological prerogatives. That is, depending on his literary program the philologist-author must recover, uncover or indeed cover over his own literary precedents in his word-loving activity of writing. The activity with which scholars of classical literature occupy themselves, whether knowingly or not, is essentially the same, but instead of being driven by a self-defined literary program, they find themselves applying the (also largely self-defined) precepts of their definition of philology to the text of the classical philologist-author. The philologist philologizes the philologist. Philology then is itself largely concerned with its own recovery.

"The philologist philologizes the philologist" means that a philologist-scholar applies self-defined and sometimes arbitrary precepts of studying written words to the written words of a philologist-author. Even the relatively narrow definition of philology as "the study of written words" can imply more than one type of activity, so in the historical application of this process, there is nothing to prevent the philologist-scholar, the agent of philology, from conceiving of himself differently and of his activity (philology) as one of literary or metaliterary (or even extraliterary) creation rather than forensic examination of literary creation. That is, the philologist-author-scholar self-consciously expresses his own love of words by engaging with the literary precedents set by previous lovers of words. In short, there are multiple modes of philology even if the meaning of the word is purposefully constrained to that familiar to classical scholarship. Thus, in any scholarly effort to "recover" philology, consideration must be given to the fact that this endeavor is, in fact, attempting to delineate the margins of a historically protean field (if not discipline) and, furthermore, that it is being conducted from within, for scholars often define their own pursuits as philological.

By its nature, classical philology has a twofold historical dimension which affects its own definition and self-interrogation. First, it relies upon the diachronic transmission of written text from ancient archetype (itself often far removed from the author) to modern edition. Here the "concrete" philological subdisciplines of paleography, codicology, and textual criticism are seen as instruments toward the end recovery of an author's original written words. But these "subdisciplines" are really disciplines in themselves, themselves conceived differently by different practitioners, themselves "concrete" only in so far as they proceed from the physical remains of the text, its documentary components.² Alongside the diachronic dimension of philology is the aforementioned synchronic variation in the mode of philology. Any manuscript must be viewed first as a cultural document, subject to contemporary and regional conceptions of philology, and only then as a witness to a text whose author rarely shared those conceptions.³ Thus, the philological history of a text, that is, the historical process of its production, transmission and reception, is an obstacle to our attempts to recover the purity of the archetype, since it has been tainted by diachronic and synchronic variation. But for this very same reason, the philological history of a text enables an examination into the variable nature of philology itself.

Such an examination will be approached here by way of a case study of a relatively obscure Latin poet: Rutilius Claudius Namatianus. That this particular author is not particularly canonical has served to attenuate the reception of his text—that is, any attention afforded his poem, either past or present, is narrowly defined. This extreme attenuation, itself a product of philological history—for who, if not philologists, defines the canon from which Rutilius is excluded?—provides insight into the very nature of the transmission and reception of a text, on which philological study relies.

Rutilius Claudius Namatianus, if that is his real name—an issue addressed below—was born into a noble family of Narbonese Gaul, perhaps of Tolosa (Toulouse), in the last half (if not the last quarter) of the fourth century

---

2. The process of editing a classical text, even through a careful, methodologically structured study of surviving documentary witnesses, always involves a high degree of qualitative evaluation, and is thus far less science than it is art. Attempts to represent textual criticism as a mechanical (and therefore purely scientific) process have been made, but always fail to account for the inherent untidiness of textual transmission (especially of ancient texts), for which there is really no remedy but common sense and critical judgment. See below. For the history of classical textual criticism, see Kenney 1974 and Timpanaro 1981 (now available in English translation as Timparano 2005).

3. As I hope to demonstrate, this is a feature of textual criticism which is too often overlooked by editors of ancient texts, whose efforts to "recover" the author's original text by comparing witnesses and arranging them into a stemma frequently fail to consider the importance of the culture surrounding the production of the witnesses themselves. G. Thomas Tanselle, in a paper on "older" textual criticism directed at editors of modern texts, briefly discusses the tendency of classical scholars to overlook the documents themselves in favor of their text: "there is a real sense in which one may still claim that a text does date from the time it is inscribed or set in type. The changes introduced by a scribe or compositor, whether out of habitual practice or out of inadvertence, produce a new text; and understanding as much as possible about the production of that text—the habits of the individual scribe, the characteristics of the period, and so on—helps one to know how certain readings occurred" (Tanselle 1990: 287).

C.E.[4] Following in the footsteps of his father, who had achieved some political success in Italy, Rutilius pursued a political career at Rome, as was the fashion for the thoroughly Romanized Gallic aristocracy of the time. In this political endeavor, Rutilius met with success during the reign of the emperor Honorius. He served as *magister officiorum* in the year 412 and as *praefectus urbi* in the year 414.[5] Rutilius lived through and witnessed the first death throes of the Roman empire in the West. The federate nation of the Visigoths, erstwhile subjects of the Eastern empire, rebelled late in the fourth century and, under the leadership of their general Alaric, eventually invaded Italy and sacked Rome in the year 410. Alaric died shortly thereafter, and his successor, Ataulf, led the Visigoths north into Narbonese Gaul, Rutilius' homeland, which they plundered for five years before being driven into Spain. Throughout the Visigothic occupation of his homeland, Rutilius was at Rome, presumably helping it recover from the sack of 410. He held his offices in 412 and 414, only returning to his devastated lands in 416,[6] after the Visigoths had vacated Gaul. His elegiac poem, most frequently entitled *De Reditu Suo,* "On his Return Journey," describes, in two books, his return journey from the recently plundered city of Rome to his even more recently plundered Gallic homeland.

Rutilius presumably wrote his poem during or shortly after the journey described in the text, but of course knowledge of the text relies on its subsequent transmission through an unknown number of intermediaries. There is no record of the text's existence until its rediscovery in the year 1493, which leaves modern editors at the mercy of an unknown number of unidentified modes of philology. However, subsequent to the poem's discovery in 1493, the application of different modes of philology can be observed in the surviving witnesses and in humanist documentation. The poem's survival is a product of humanist scholarship of the late fifteenth and early sixteenth centuries. The humanists' enthusiasm for record keeping permits the construction of a history of the process of the text's reception and transmission.

---

4. For much more detailed biography of Rutilius Namatianus and excellent summary of his historical context, see Doblhofer 1972: 17–27 and Lana 1961.

5. The *magister officiorum* oversaw the bureaucracy of Rome, and the *praefectus urbi* was the emperor's personal representative in the city (see the relevant entries in Hornblower and Spawforth 2003). By this time, the city of Rome was no longer the sole center of imperial administration, but as the traditional seat of Roman authority, it remained important both as a symbol and as the home to many influential families.

6. Or perhaps 415 or 417. Much debate has taken place over the precise date of Rutilius' journey home. See Cameron 1967; Carcopino 1963; Corsaro 1981: 11–30; Doblhofer 1972: 35–39; Lana 1961.

Primary Witnesses to the Text

Stemma

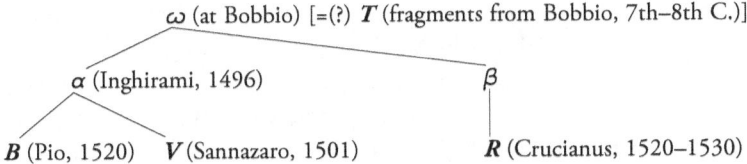

- **B** *editio princeps* (first printed edition), ed. Giambattista Pio, Bologne, C.E. 1520.
- **R** Rome, Biblioteca dell' Accademia Nazionale dei Lincei e Corsiniana, ms. Or. 202 (*olim* Caetani 158), ff. 2^r–27^v, C.E. 1520–1530.
- **T** Turin, Biblioteca Nazionale, F IV 25, f. 21/22 (frammento), seventh–eighth century C.E.
- **V** Vienna, Osterreichische Nationalbibliothek, Codex Vindobonesis Palatinus 277 (*olim* 387), ff. 84^r–93^v, C.E. 1501.

Until 1891, the text depended only upon one manuscript, *V*, produced in 1501, and the closely related but independent *editio princeps*, *B*, printed in Bologne in 1520. These two witnesses are direct descendants of the same now lost manuscript (*α*), which was produced in 1496 by Fedro Inghirami, who copied from a manuscript at the monastery of Bobbio. In the three and a half centuries before 1891, many editions of Rutilius' poem were published in continental Europe, largely in a conscious effort to disseminate obscure ancient authors, either alone or in collections of "minor" poets.[7] The variant readings of the *editio princeps*, *B*, were generally overlooked in favor of the Vienna manuscript, even though *B* was known to be an independent witness to the text. This exposes a common practice of Renaissance philology which persisted for centuries, the preferential selection of one manuscript as the "best," the *codex optimus*. The *codex optimus* might be considered the "best" because it is the oldest one and thus temporally closer to the source, or because it is the one with the least apparent textual errors, or simply

---

7. Editions published between 1520 and 1891: Almeloveen (1687), Baehrens (1883), Barth (1623), Burman (1731), Castalio (1582), Damm (1760), Kapp (1786), Maittaire (1713), Mueller (1870), Panvinius (1558), Pithoeus (1590), Simler (1575), Sitzman (1616), Wernsdorf (1788), Zumpt (1840). For a full bibliography and brief description of each of these editions, with notes on their interrelationships, see Doblhofer 1972: 71–77.

because it was physically more accessible, or because of any other number of entirely subjective factors. This subjective, *prima facie* approach to a text is generally rejected by modern methodologies of the criticism of classical texts, especially when the text has only a few primary witnesses and when a stemma is easily and convincingly constructed.[8] But for several centuries, printed editions of Rutilius which privileged *V*'s readings circulated.

In 1891, a new manuscript, *R*, was discovered in Rome—it was produced between 1520 and 1530, close in time to *V* and *B*, but it represents a completely different branch of the text's tradition, and is distanced from the α witnesses by the intervention of at least one unknown intermediary, β.[9] During the centuries between the discovery of *V* and the discovery of *R*, editors of Rutilius were afforded wide latitude in the activity of emendation and transposition of lines. The textual tradition, even if one considered *B* alongside the "better" *V*, was rather meager, and Rutilius left behind no other work by which to evaluate his style. In addition, the culture of early editing was one which valued clever emendations, often regardless of their necessity or even likelihood. Early editions are, therefore, filled with speculative emendations and supplements. The discovery of *R*, and its subsequent collation with the texts of *V* and *B*, essentially doubled knowledge of the text by providing evidence from an entirely new branch of the tradition. Stemmatically, this propels the evidence much further back in time than the exemplar of the *BV* branch (α) by facilitating the textual reconstruction of the further removed archetype (ω). The evidence of the newly broadened stemma failed to support virtually all of the speculative emendations and supplements made before the discovery of *R*.

This invites consideration of the eminent fallibility of textual editing. The methods of textual editing, although somewhat formalized by modern methodology and now usually much better documented in a critical apparatus, are essentially the same now as they were in the sixteenth century—the editor emends as seems appropriate given his own understanding of the author's style and the demands of the language in question. The process is, in other words, subjective and not always concrete. The stemmatic approach to textual criticism, the so-called Lachmann method, even in its earliest and most mechanical incarnation (that presented by Paul Maas), requires the editor to apply his critical judgement to the text in order to

---

8. This is not the place for a lengthy discussion on the methods of classical textual criticism, but those who are interested in an introduction might find West 1973 to be a good starting point.

9. The presence of β is felt mostly in *R*'s indication that its direct exemplar was lacking line 1.213 of the poem—a line which ω was able to transmit to the other witnesses.

emend the corrupt archetype that results from the process of recension.[10] Subsequent modifications to the stemmatic method have focused on the failure of the mechanical aspects of recension to account for the complexities of transmission, and have resulted in a much less mechanical approach in which editorial judgment must be exercised throughout the process.[11] While stemmatic recension is a valuable tool for most editors of classical texts, it shifts very little of the editor's task from his own judgmental capacity. The necessity in textual editing of applying the non-systematizable, unteachable and largely indefinable quality of judgment, a quality which varies from person to person, makes textual criticism a field which has always resisted any overarching methodology.[12] But in classical textual criticism this semi-artistic, anti-methodological quality of critical judgement is usually applied, according to some variation of the Lachmann method, to the emendation of an archetype which has been recovered somewhat mechanically through stemmatic recension. This produces a textual criticism which is by necessity a self-contradictory mongrel; Gurd describes it as a "cyborg discipline," generated in part by mechanical method and in part by organic invention.[13]

For an editor attempting to recover the "original" text of an ancient author, the mechanical component of textual criticism can only provide indistinct guidelines as to where to apply judgment. This of course problematizes the process since no two editors are likely to agree entirely on the proper application of judgment. Over time, then, the variable aspect of textual criticism actually produces an array of various editions, none of which may convincingly claim to approach the text of the lost original with

---

10. Maas first published his step-by-step guide to Lachmann's method in 1927. His attribution of the invention of the entire process to nineteenth-century scholar Karl Lachmann was somewhat simplistic, as it seems to have been generated gradually in the work of Lachmann and others, all of it interpreted by Maas himself. The concept of studying the genealogy of manuscripts actually dates back to the sixteenth century. See Timpanaro 1981.

11. Most influential was Giorgio Pasquali's response to Maas, which was particularly critical of the usefulness of Maas' technique when the text's transmission is contaminated by indirect relationships such as a scribe's correction of one manuscript from another, thereby allowing it to resist accurate stemmatic recension, at least of a purely mechanical variety (Pasquali 1934). Also very influential was Joseph Bédier's observation that a suspicious majority of stemmata produced by Maas' technique are bipartite. This gave rise to another influential approach, often called "best-text editing," which places even more emphasis on the editor's judgment by denying any final authority to the mechanically produced genealogical aspect of the method (Bédier 1928). Subsequent methodological developments, particularly in the field of the editing of modern texts (visited briefly below), have tended to arise from one or the other of these criticisms of Maas. See Altschul's contribution in this volume.

12. Thus in 1921, A. E. Housman expressed his now famous maxim, "criticus nascitur, non fit" ("The critic is born, not made"), in an attempt to combat any growing impressions that textual criticism might be entirely systematized or even wholly teachable (Housman 1961: 133).

13. Gurd 2005: 36–44.

complete accuracy. Gurd calls this "a field of radical textual plurality," further observing that a new critical edition will not only continue to expand the field, but will also reflect (in its apparatus) the very plurality of the field.[14] This observation is correct as long as that edition is properly critical by modern standards, i.e., it actually provides a useful apparatus with which to evaluate the plurality of the field, and also as long as the observation of the constitutive elements of the plurality is itself carried out critically. For if a text is to be viewed as the "singular plural" product of many individual acts of philology, the viewer must take care to observe also the philological plurality represented in the commission of those acts. If a critical text is viewed as a plurality constituted by its various iterations, then the text also becomes temporally displaced and corrupt, since its constituent iterations represent editions produced one after another, many of them feeding upon previous iterations, but each of them produced in its own temporally distinct philological climate. An editor (and a reader) must cope not only with textual variation and emendation, but also with the effects of previous editorial variation.

In the production of a new edition to add to the array of texts, an editor must observe textual corruptions and attempt to remedy them by applying his judgment. Added to this judgmental burden is the evaluation of the emendations proposed by all the previous editors, who were not only applying their own individual judgments to the text, but also doing so according to a variety of different philological methods. The decision as to whether or not a previous emendation warrants consideration, and thus inclusion in the text or apparatus, therefore, relies on the editor's estimation not only of the previous emendation, but also of the process by which that emendation was generated. Here method and history collide, seemingly without recognition by many modern editors. Consider the text and apparatus of the first eight lines from Ernst Doblhofer's 1972 edition of Rutilius:[15]

> Velocem potius reditum mirabere, lector,
>   tam cito Romuleis posse carere bonis.
> quid longum toto Romam venerantibus aevo!
>   nil umquam longum est, quod sine fine placet.
> o quantum et quotiens possum numerare beatos,
>   nasci felici qui meruere solo,

---

14. Gurd 2005: 44–55.

15. All translations are my own. Discussing textual issues in translation is difficult, and possible only with the most literal of translations. Thus, in order to facilitate discussion of the textual issues at hand, this translation is overly literal and does somewhat of a disservice to the poet.

qui Romanorum procerum generosa propago
    ingenitum cumulant urbis honore decus!

1 potius *VRB:* prorsus *Ke (in not.)* reditu *Baehr (in not.)*
2 tam *VRB:* quam *Pith* tam cito *VRB:* quam me ita *Barth (in not.) totum hunc versum om. V1, suppl. V2*
5 quantum *VRB:* quater *Heins* possum *VR:* possem *B Panv* non est *Heins*

Rather, you will be amazed, reader, that my swift return journey
    can abandon the benefits of Rome so quickly.
How tedious for those who revere Rome their whole lives!
    But nothing is ever tedious that pleases without end.
Oh, how greatly and how often can I count up the blessed men
    who have warranted birth in that fruitful soil,
the noble offspring of Roman princes
    who crown their innate glory with their city's dignity!

1 rather *VRB:* absolutely *Keene (in a note)* by my return journey *Baehrens (in a note)*
2 so *VRB:* how *Pithoeus* so quickly *VRB:* how I [can abandon . . .] thus *Barthes (in a note)* In *V,* the first copyist omitted this entire line, and the second copyist supplied it.
5 how greatly and how often *VRB:* repeatedly *Heinsius* I can *VR:* I might *B Panvinius* I cannot *Heinsius*

While Doblhofer's edition is excellent, and he rightly follows the readings suggested by the textual evidence and what is known of Rutilius' style, he feels compelled to report in his apparatus all of the emendations ever suggested. Note the appearance of speculative emendations of Baehrens (1883), Pithoeus (1590), Barth (1623) and Heinsius (1731), all of them made before the 1891 discovery of *R* (1891). Doblhofer has produced a critical apparatus that preserves emendations which arise from a period of wild speculation. Each of these emendations was unnecessary and unlikely, and Doblhofer tacitly acknowledges this by relegating them to his apparatus rather than printing them as his text. Doblhofer's editorial decisions here are supported in large part by *R*'s evidence bolstering that available to these philological speculators, and also by an understanding that the philological climate of the editors in question was one which put much more stock in speculation than his. In fact, a modern editor might be tempted to exclude these emendations from the apparatus altogether on the grounds that they are essentially useless to modern (as opposed to sixteenth-, seventeenth-, eighteenth-, or nineteenth-century) philological engagement with the text. However, this temptation is not Doblhofer's—there are no firm philological "rules" which dictate the essentially subjective evaluation of variants, or the reporting of previous speculation. By including these emendations in his apparatus, Doblhofer permits his reader to evaluate the treatment of the text by previous modes of philology. However, this presumes that the reader is able to distinguish such "antiquated" editorial emendations from the more modern ones (such as that of Keene in line 1, above). It takes a detailed understanding of the history of editing a particular text to evaluate the apparatus that includes previous editors' emendations, since the apparatus itself usually cannot represent fully the historical dimensions of each emendation.

Lacking a single, universal mode of editorial practice, many of an editor's choices will be guided instead by his conception of the purpose of his edition, his editorial intention. Doblhofer's *Rutilius,* for example, is clearly intended in part to provide the reader with an apparatus that indicates even the most unlikely textual speculations produced by previous editors, therefore presupposing a reader who is both interested in access to the history of editing the text and well enough versed in philological history to evaluate such emendations. A modern editor will usually establish his intentions in the preface to his edition, thereby exposing his approach to the textual evidence and his expectations of his readers. For his part, Doblhofer establishes in his foreword that his intention is to summarize previous textual scholarship, with a view to examining the Romantic nationalism that colors the (largely French and Italian) mid-twentieth-century scholarship on Rutilius.[16] He therefore has produced an edition that is particularly attuned to the historical treatment of the text.

This concept of editorial intention has always been present in the production of critical editions, which vary in editorial technique and in presentation according to the foreseen application of that particular edition. Thus, for example, while the weighty apparatus produced by Doblhofer's historical approach to the text might appeal to experienced textual critics, it would be of less use to a reader whose interests lay elsewhere, and who is thus not the edition's intended user. Such a reader might prefer Duff's much simpler apparatus (1934), intended only to report particularly difficult textual cruces

---

16. " . . . die vorliegende versucht, die Ergebnisse der in den vergangenen Dezennien geleisteten Arbeit zusammenzufassen. An dieser haben sich vor allem französische und italienische Gelehrte beteiligt; das Bewusstsein der Landsmannschaft und der gemeinsamen Zugehörigkeit zur Romania ist als Triebfeder etlicher Studien über den 'Gallier mit dem römischen Herzen' unverkennbar" (Doblhofer 1972: 7). Although his preface suggests that his text-historical examination will focus only on the recent decades (since the last German edition), Doblhofer's extremely thorough examination actually encompasses the text's entire history, not just the most recent. His point about the Romance bias towards the Gallo-Roman poet is very interesting, and will be discussed further below.

and suggested emendations which are judged deserving of consideration, or perhaps Fo's edition (1992), which provides no apparatus at all and thus presupposes a reader who is unconcerned with matters textual. Variation in editorial intention is an unavoidable function of simple practicality. Different readers have different needs, and thus require different editions. Since it is a matter of common practice, editorial intention itself has received no scholarly attention as a significant feature of the actual process of editing classical texts. However, it ought to be viewed as another problematizing factor in editorial philology, for a previous editor's self-defined intentions in supplying (or not supplying) particular types of emendations and apparatus notations, while contextually significant, are obscured in the extratemporal plurality of a later iteration of the text. The plurality of the critical text is again corrupted, this time by the various intentions of its multiple editors.

Since the nature of a particular edition and the textual instance it embodies relies on factors dictated by its editor's methodological approach and intention, the overall editorial plurality of the text is a function not only of judgmental variation, but also of editorial variation. The meticulous editor such as Doblhofer thus naturally engages with the previous products of his own profession, stretching his editorial judgment over the manifold field produced by all the text's previous iterations. In this activity, editors usually make a deliberate, but sometimes almost self-contradictory, choice to segregate from that field those very textual instances upon which everything else ultimately relies: the text's witnesses. As the foundation of textual knowledge, the surviving witnesses of an ancient text receive careful scrutiny from textual critics, but they are almost without exception treated as raw information, waiting for critical treatment to arrange and evaluate them as being more or less "correct" according to the demands of the editor's methods and intentions. The witnesses themselves, even those which might contain evidence of ancient scholarly treatment (such as corrections or marginal notations), are perceived as the grist for philological criticism, the passive subjects of philologizing.[17] But they can also be much more, as

---

17. In fact, in some ways, the more "scholarly" the witness, the more passive it becomes in the modern edition because even the "best" (i.e., that closest to a modern mode) Renaissance scholarship is seen as a philological hindrance to modern philologists' attempts "to recover" the lost ancient purity of the text. For example, in *Scribes and Scholars*, a guide still much used to introduce students to the transmission of classical literature, Reynolds and Wilson (1991: 122–63) heap praise upon many Renaissance humanists' modes of philology because they approximated modern modes, but also present humanist philological production as entirely problematic for the modern textual critic (216–18), who is forced to cleanse it from the text. This is somewhat counterproductive. As Reynolds and Wilson themselves establish for their readers, and as shall be seen below, Renaissance philology was no more uniform than modern philology. Thus the modern textual value of each instance of Renaissance tex-

they are themselves the products of philological treatment, even if the nature of that treatment varies substantially from that to which they are subjected by a modern editor.

Philological intentions quite naturally influence the returns of the self-referential practice of philology. In philologizing a philologist, the philological agent's intentions have a direct impact upon the philological product. As mentioned above, editorial intention ultimately affects the returns of editorial philology by corrupting the plurality of the ancient text. *Authorial* intention is central to the criticism of modern authors, for whom the evidence is much more abundant and much less temporally distant than that of ancient authors. Much of the recent debate in the editing of modern texts has focused on the issue of authorial intention—to what extent an editor can or should attempt to define the author's ultimate textual intentions in the face of an abundance of contemporary or near contemporary witnesses, and even of the author's own drafts or proofs.[18] This is a debate which has had little place in the editing of classical texts, where the textual evidence is much more tenuous and often so far removed from the original author that the best case scenario is the establishment of a text which more or less approximates the *substantial* elements of the author's original, leaving the rest almost entirely to editorial discretion. However, given the useful contributions to the field of textual criticism generated by the intentionalist debate, and given the classical editor's usual reliance on many centuries of unknown intermediaries which the surviving witnesses represent, perhaps more scrutiny should be given to the issue of "intermediate intentions"—the philological intentions active in the transmission and reception of the text by those witnesses. How might the historically distinct modes of philology being practiced by the witnesses influence the text? And, more importantly, how might they be of use to the text's modern editor, whose own philological goal is the production of an edition which, in accordance with modern classical philology, approximates the long-lost author's philological intentions?

Perhaps the most telling indications in Rutilius of modern philology's dependence on historical modes of philology are the facts that the author is usually still called by the name Rutilius Claudius Namatianus and that his poem is still regularly entitled *De Reditu Suo*. In fact, none of the three primary witnesses to the text agree on the name of its author or the title of

---

tual production must be evaluated individually, and many of them must be considered to be active witnesses, full-fledged members of the text's plurality, infected by intentions of their own, akin to any edition.

18. Most useful for exposing the issues and debate surrounding authorial intention are McGann 1983 and Shillingsburg 1997.

the poem. In the Vienna manuscript (V), the poem is introduced by the following *titulus* (f. 84ʳ):

> Ex fragmentis RuTilii cLaudii Namatiani
> de reditu suo e Roma In Galliam Narbonen[sem]
>
> From the fragments of RuTilius cLaudius Namatianus
> on his return journey from Rome into Narbonese Gaul

The same information is given again in the *incipit* of the second book of the poem (f. 92ᵛ):

> Rutilii claudii namatiani de
> reditu suo explicit liber iˢ. In[-
> cipit liber iiˢ.
>
> End of the first book of Rutilius Claudius Namatianus
> on his return journey. Beginning of the second book.

Thus *V* is clear in calling the poem *De Reditu Suo,* and the author Rutilius Claudius Namatianus. The first printed edition (*B*), gives slightly different information. The edition begins with the following frontispiece:

> CLAUDIUS RUTILIUS POE-
> TA PRISCUS DE LAUDI-
> BUS URBIS, ETRURIAE,
> ET ITALIAE
>
> CLAUDIUS RUTILIUS, AN
> ANCIENT POET, ON PRAISE FOR
> ROME, ETRURIA,
> AND ITALY

The first seven pages of the edition contain a dedicatory poem of the editor's own composition (on which, see below). At the top of the eighth page, Rutilius' poem is introduced with the following *titulus:*

> AD VENERIUM RUFIUM RUTILII CLAU-
> DII NUMATIANI GALLI VIRI CON-
> SULARIS, PRAEFECTORII URBIS,

> TRIBUNI MILITUM, PRAEFE-
> CTI PRAETORIO. LIBER
> PRIMUS
> CUI TITULUS ITINERARIUM.
>
> THE FIRST BOOK, DEDICATED TO VENERIUS RUFIUS,
> OF RUTILIUS CLAUDIUS NUMATIANUS,
> A GALLIC MAN OF CONSULAR RANK,
> PREFECT OF THE CITY, MILITARY
> TRIBUNE, PRAETORIAN
> PREFECT.
> THE WORK IS ENTITLED "THE ITINERARY."

The author and title are further introduced in the *incipit* of the second book of the poem:

> RUTILII CLAUDII NUMATIANI DE RE-
> DITU SUO, ITINERARII LIBER
> SECUNDUS.
>
> THE SECOND BOOK OF "THE ITINERARY" OF
> RUTILIUS CLAUDIUS NUMATIANUS
> ON HIS RETURN JOURNEY.

Thus the first edition (*B*) calls the poet Rutilius Claudius Numatianus and seems to prefer the title *Itinerarium*—a rather prosaic and non-classical word which seldom occurs even in late antique Latin. But *B* also refers once to the title *De Reditu Suo*, which suggests that α, the ancestor of both *B* and *V,* at least contained the label *De Reditu Suo*, either as a title proper or an exordium. The Roman manuscript (*R*) is far from helpful in these matters. The *titulus*, which has been truncated by the margin, gives the work no title and reads simply: (f. 2^r)

> CLAUDII RUTI[-
> LII POETAE DI[GNISSIMI
>
> OF CLAUDIUS RUTILIUS,
> A MOST DISTINGUISHED POET

The *incipit* to the second book of the poem is no more helpful regarding the poem's title, and only serves to further complicate the issue regarding the poet's name: (f. 24ᵛ)

> EXPLICIT LIBER PRIMUS
> CLAUDII RUTILII POET[A]E
> INCIPIT LIBER II
> CLAUDII RUTI[LII
> NUMANTI[-
> ANI POET[A]E
> DIGNIS[-
> SIMI

> END OF THE FIRST BOOK
> OF CLAUDIUS RUTILIUS THE POET.
> BEGINNING OF THE SECOND BOOK
> OF CLAUDIUS RUTILIUS
> NUMANTIANUS,
> A MOST
> DISTINGUISHED
> POET.

Thus *R* does not provide a title at all. It is highly likely that the archetype (ω) was missing its first page.[19] The first transmitted lines of the poem seem to represent the resolution of a thought ("rather, you will be amazed, reader, that my swift return journey (*reditum*) . . . "). While beginning a poem mid-thought might be considered a rhetorical gesture, it seems more likely that the poem has lost its first lines, in which Rutilius delivered a formal and traditional *recusatio:* excusing himself from undertaking grander poetic subjects in praise of Rome. The general confusion over the title, and the Rome manuscript's utter lack of one, support this theory—the original *titulus* was lost along with the first lines, leaving later copyists to invent a descriptive title of their own or infer one from the header over the second book of the poem. *De Reditu Suo* is then a provisional title, an unlikely "best guess," imposed upon the work by α's need to give the work some kind of descriptive title, likely taking *reditum* in the first surviving line as its inspiration. Modern editors also feel the same need, and many entitle the poem *De Reditu Suo* without comment—the modern tradition has been tainted by historical practice.[20]

---

19. This sensible suggestion was first proposed by Keene 1907: 16–17.
20. Doblhofer's excellent 1972 edition is the greatest exception. Not only does he engage with this problem very thoroughly, but he also refuses to commit to a single title given the conflicting

According to stemmatic theory, this author ought to be called Claudius Rutilius Numatianus or Numantianus, and not Rutilius Claudius Namatianus. The transposition of Claudius and Rutilius is actually relatively inconsequential, as both are properly family names, and late antique use of such double *gens* nomenclature was liable to accept either order.[21] The *cognomen*, however, is a different matter—The *VB* branch is split between Namatianus and Numatianus. *R* presents a name which starts out Num- rather than Nam-, which should break the *VB* split in favor of Num-. Since history provides no significant help regarding the names, it is left to modern editors to determine whether they prefer the name ending–atianus (*VB*'s reading) or–antianus (*R*'s reading). At the very least, according to modern methodology, NAM-atianus should *not* be their reading.

Because the historical treatment of *V* as the best witness resulted in the widespread circulation of its variant of the name, the reading of *V* still prevails, despite modern philological practice. And this erroneous practice is continued in this essay, for the same reason that other modern editors continue it: because it would border on being counterproductive to publish a modern edition of a relatively obscure text under a now non-standard form of his obscure name. One common purpose of textual criticism—to provide texts which are easily accessible to other philologists—compels modern editors to contravene the precepts of modern stemmatic theory because of the precepts of historical philology. There may also be another reason to acquiesce to this apparent contravention—the issue of names and titles will be revisited below.

Our text of Rutilius' poem is not complete. As mentioned above, it is extremely likely that the first few lines of the first book were lost along with the title. But this is not the only text missing from the poem, for the manuscript tradition has lost most of the second book, preserving only the first sixty-eight lines. All three of the primary witnesses thus must ultimately descend from a mutilated archetype (ω). However, in 1973 codicologist Mirella Ferrari published the discovery of a scrap of parchment, labelled *T* in this essay, containing thirty-nine partial lines from the lost portion of the poem's second book.[22] At some time late in the fifteenth century at the monastic library of Bobbio, a piece of a 7th- or 8th-century manuscript of Rutilius was used to repair another codex, now at Turin.

The thirty-nine partial lines presented by the fragments at Turin provide

---

evidence. His edition is cleverly titled "De reditu suo sive Iter Gallicum"—note however that this still propagates the unlikely title made familiar by historical practice.

21. Keene 1907: 15.
22. Ferrari 1973.

the earliest witness to the philological reception of Rutilius Namatianus' text. The cursive minuscule script of the text and the interlinear corrections are typical of seventh- and eighth-century Northern Italy, and especially the early manuscript production of the monastery of Bobbio, itself founded early in the seventh century.[23] As will become clear below, Bobbio was an important locale for the text of Rutilius Namatianus, as it is where α was copied in 1496. Bobbio was renowned as a center of learning and knowledge, and a place where manuscripts were purposefully collected, copied and maintained.[24] And yet, the seemingly careless treatment in the fifteenth century of Rutilius' mangled text seems to imply differently. It is very likely that T and ω are the same text—that the text copied at Bobbio in 1496, α, was copied from the source of these fragments. If, in the late fifteenth century, Bobbio possessed the exemplar for α, which was obviously mutilated, why then were pages of the missing and mutilated text being used, at the same time, as repair material? While the need to recycle dismembered papyrus pages is understandable, why did Rutilius' text not warrant repairs itself? Rather than attempting to preserve the text on this page, someone at Bobbio instead used it to repair the inside margin of a 10th-century manuscript of the Life of Saint Severinus. At some level, whether conscious or not, the philological value of the Life of Saint Severinus was seen to be greater than that of Rutilius' poem.

It is, of course, impossible to reconstruct the circumstances surrounding the damaging of the Bobbio manuscript or the recycling of a scrap of it into a patch for another manuscript. Given the cost of parchment, such reuse of materials from damaged manuscripts was common.[25] However, it is clear that at least this one fragment lingered in the scriptorium, and was afforded philological value only as recyclable, not as a witness to an otherwise lost piece of text. Evidence suggests that the philology of textual recycling was very active at Bobbio, which was a major center of another type of textual recycling, the production of palimpsests, in which the parchment's original text was effaced and then written over with another text.[26] These practices were intended to further the philological survival of the repaired/upper text at the expense of the recycled damaged/lower text. E. A. Lowe, in a study of Latin palimpsests, showed that the medieval philologists responsible for this textual recycling did not practice it with any intentional malice. Texts were

---

23. Ibid.
24. Sandys 1964: 1.452–55.
25. "Come era usuale per gli artigliani che aggiustavano e rilegavano libri, i religiosi lavorarono impiegando al massimo, per pezze e fogli di guardia, materiale vecchio, sciupato o frammentario, che avevano a disposizione in loco . . ." (Ferrari 1973: 3).
26. On the practice and distribution of palimpsest production, see Lowe 1972.

chosen for erasure largely because they were considered too obsolete or too damaged to be of use.[27] Far from being destructive, this medieval approach has actually resulted in the survival of many fragments, such as those from Rutilius' second book, and indeed of entire texts, such as Cicero's *De re publica*, which otherwise would not exist today. Realization of this irony is made possible only by the modern philologists who seek out such lost texts amidst the recycled products of medieval philology.

The modern treatment of the Turin fragments has focused on the paleographical interpretation and text-critical analysis of the text they preserve. The original text printed by Ferrari in 1973 sparked a period of intense (for Rutilius) interest, best exemplified in the published discussion among Bartolucci, Castorina, Cecchini, Lana and Tandoi,[28] each of whom provides an often fundamentally different interpretation of the text itself as well as speculation on supplements and emendations. Often, these paleographers and textual critics cannot even agree on what the letters are, let alone how to edit them. Take as an example the first preserved line of the fragments. Ferrari was very conservative in her original publication of the fragments, indicating the partial illegibility of many of the letters and declining to indulge in speculative supplement. Her first line reads:

]multus satiat . . . pan
]much ?satisfies? . . . {pan[

Fo (1992) interprets the partially illegible letters almost completely differently and supplies a minor supplement:

]multus solatia pan[is
]much bread . . . consolations

Tandoi, whose purpose was to present a sensible text of the fragments by means of liberal application of conjectural supplements, could not make much use of this first most fragmentary and illegible portion, and so not only left it without supplement, but did not even print the clearly legible letters "pa" near the end of the line:

]multus satiari . . .
]much . . . to be satisfied

---

27. Lowe 1972.
28. Bartalucci et al. 1975. See also Frassinetti 1980.

This may serve as a reminder that the so-called "concrete" philological disciplines, upon which all philological activity is founded, are often far from concrete and are liable to the demands placed upon them by different modes of philological pursuit.

Aside from the Turin fragments, the text relies on humanist copies and humanist scholarship of the late fourteenth and early fifteenth centuries. The humanist activity around this text reveals much about the protean nature of philological activity, as each humanist who approached Rutilius' poem did so in a different manner and for a different reason. As mentioned above, the monastic library at Bobbio was responsible for the text's survival. In 1493, Giorgio Merula, a respected Milanese scholar, discovered the contents of the monastic collection at Bobbio.[29] He dispatched his assistant, Giorgio Galbiato, to survey Bobbio's library and inform him of its contents. The catalogue was recorded in Merula's papers, and includes Rutilius. At this time, Merula was in the midst of a philological competition with his intellectual nemesis, Poliziano. The agonistic rivalry between Milanese Merula and Florentine Poliziano is well documented in their correspondence—it focused on the discovery and editing of Greek and Latin texts, including those discovered by Merula at Bobbio.[30] Each of these men was afforded a degree of public esteem proportionate to his perceived literary and scholarly achievements. Philological activity, scholarly value aside, was thus a means of gaining social prestige. Though it may seem callous to acknowledge, one of the returns of humanist philology is personal gain. This had an effect on the treatment of the text of Rutilius, for Merula and Galbiato apparently dismissed it entirely as a text of value, as it was not among the texts they selected for publication. That Merula made no attempt to acquire or study this otherwise unknown text seems strange for a man whose reputation was as a seeker of new knowledge. Perhaps this short, late, and obscure text simply did not offer Merula what he was looking for: substantial philological ammunition in his rivalry with Poliziano. Modern philology may be suspected of the same sort of unscholarly motivation and returns, since many philologists are driven by academic culture to produce scholarly contributions of substance, often agonistic in nature, at least partly (it must be recognized) in order to increase their own scholarly profiles. But then, perhaps this is too cynical, and Merula simply ran out of time, as he died in 1494, leaving the philological treasure-trove at Bobbio for others to explore.

---

29. See Ferrari 1970.
30. On the conflict between Merula and Politian, see Santoro 1952. The historians of classical scholarship curiously avoid dwelling on this unpleasant dispute. Sandys twice mentions it in passing (1964: 35, 85n1) and Pfeiffer 1976: 42–46 makes no mention of it at all.

Tommaso Inghirami, also known as Fedro, soon to be the chief Vatican librarian, visited Bobbio while he was in the region in 1496. He returned to Rome with some Bobbio manuscripts and with his own copies of others. Rutilius Namatianus is one of the latter. Fedro's purpose was to acquire for the Vatican library as many texts as he could—an indication of a prime philological concern of the period: the purposeful discovery and movement of texts from monastic libraries into private, controlled collections. And this philological purpose was apparently successful, as Inghirami's copy became the direct exemplar for the Vienna manuscript (*V*) and probably also for the first printed edition (*B*). The Bobbio copy, however, disappeared from the monastery in 1706, removed by a French officer and never seen again.

Much can, and has, been said about the production of the Vienna manuscript.[31] In 1501, Neapolitan poet-scholar Jacopo Sannazaro, who was about to embark on an exilic journey into France along with his patron, King Federico of Aragon, visited Rome and produced the copy of Rutilius which is now *V*. He copied Inghirami's text, or rather he, his companion Filippino Bononi, and a third scribe divided the text amongst themselves, each copying a portion.[32] This is a scholar's copy. Sannazaro carefully corrected the sections copied by his two colleagues (but not his own section)—his corrections usually bring the text into agreement with the readings of *B*, which suggests that he is merely correcting errors in his colleagues' transcription. There is also evidence that Sannazaro undertook some careful emendation, but where his readings differ from *B*'s, his variants are usually quite astute and often come at locations where modern editors also feel the need to emend the text.

Sannazaro was himself a celebrated composer of Latin pastoral and elegiac verse, and he took much of his inspiration from classical verse of the same genres. During the four years of exile which followed his visit to Rome in 1501, Sannazaro sought out in France new manuscripts of classical verse, some of which, most notably the only surviving witnesses for Grattius' *Cynegetica* and the pseudo-Ovidian *Halieutica,* are bound up with his copy of Rutilius. He has suggested emendations in the margins of these other works. It seems that Sannazaro's purpose was the collection of little-known classical poetry. His choice of texts and his scholarly treatment of them speak to his dual philological identity: poet and scholar. It is in the capacity of a poet-scholar-philologist that he produced the Vienna manuscript.

---

31. The nature and production of *V* is thoroughly examined by Doblhofer 1972: 62–66 and Ferrari 1970: 170–78.

32. The identification Sannazaro and Bononi as two of the three scribes of *V* was made by analysis of their handwriting. See Ferrari 1970.

The circumstances surrounding the production of the first printed edition, *B,* are less clear, but the edition expresses enough about itself to situate it within the philological culture of its time. It was printed in Bologne in 1520 by Giambattista Pio, a teacher and scholar who produced and published several commentaries and editions of classical authors. In this slim volume, Rutilius' poem is placed between a lengthy dedicatory poem of Pio's own composition and a small collection of miscellaneous epigrams. The volume begins with this dedication:

LEONI DECIMO PONTIFICI MAXIMO
MEDICAE FLORENTINO IOAN-
   NES BAPTISTA PIUS
      CLIENS.

TO LEO THE TENTH, POPE,
FLORENTINE MEDICI, FROM
   IOANNES BAPTISTA PIUS,
      CLIENT.

The book was printed as an act of *clientela,* and is dedicated to the learned Medici Pope Leo X, famed for extravagance, in part because of his literary patronage. Perhaps in an effort to elevate the status of Rutilius to a level more befitting a gift to the indulgent papal patron, Pio invented a more distinguished career and pedigree for Rutilius. Reconsideration of the information found in Pio's *titulus* to Rutilius' poem (above) reveals that Pio attributes to Rutilius consular status (VIRI CONSULARIS) and the office of praetorian prefect (PRAEFECTI PRAETORIO)—two honors he did not in fact achieve. Note also that Pio wishes the poem to have had the personal touch of an addressee, Venerius Rufius (AD VENERIUM RUFIUM). It is indeed conceivable that the original poem was dedicated or addressed to Rufius, a friend who succeeded Rutilius in the office of prefect of the city, and whom Rutilius addresses several times within the poem. However, the evidence of *V* and *R* seems to suggest that Pio has transformed the conceivable into fact without proof. In addition, the name Venerius arises from a textual corruption at line 1.421, where Rutilius laments his inability to fit Rufius' proper name into elegiac meter.[33] Since this poem lacked a

---

33. At line 1.421, *B* and *V* preserve nonsense: *cognomen versu veneris, carissime Rufi* ("your surname by Venus' line, dearest Rufius). Pio must have interpreted this line to mean that Rufius' family name was Venerius. *R* preserves different, unmetrical nonsense: *cognomen venens, carissime Rufi* ("selling your surname, dearest Rufius"). Given the sense required here and the tendencies of scribal errors,

proper *titulus* due to the mutilation of the Bobbio archetype, Pio invented (along with the title *Itinerarium*) a back-story which suited his needs. As a humanist's gift to a pope, it was now more meaningful, since, by way of Pio's additions, this work was in antiquity a very distinguished poet's gift to his fellow distinguished aristocrat. Although Pio was a scholar himself, his purpose in publishing this particular book was not strictly scholarly. There is little evidence that Pio attempted to correct the text of his exemplar as had Sannazaro (who had the same exemplar), and in fact it appears that Pio introduced a number of minor textual errors. The philological intention of this edition, is then, not scholarly, but rather sociopolitical: it is the product of a client-philologist, not a scholar-philologist.

The Rome manuscript, discovered in 1891, is a curious example of philological pursuit. Proudly copied by one Ioannes Andreas Crucianus, about whom we know little more than the fact that he was governor of Foligno in 1531, the text can be dated between 1520 and 1530. Examination of common errors and omissions reveals that R, like V and B, is ultimately descended from the mutilated Bobbio archetype, but that, unlike V and B, it is not descended from Inghirami's copy. Loving care went into the physical production of the script, and the manuscript includes several amateurish, but enthusiastic illustrations. Crucianus also proudly presented his coat of arms and his name numerous times during his transcription. All of this enthusiasm for the production of a text might speak to a level of excitement about philological pursuits which is seldom seen today. But Crucianus' scholarly ability clearly did not match his enthusiasm, for alongside this apparently proud achievement is an obvious and profound ignorance of the Latin language, let alone the demands of elegiac meter. In places, the text of R is so corrupt that Crucianus could not possibly have understood what he was writing down.[34] In theory, this manuscript has equal stemmatic weight as V and B combined, but in practice, its only constructive contribution to the text is to broaden the stemma and thus add weight to the readings of V and B when in agreement. But what is a modern editor to do? According to stemmatic theory and modern text-critical practice, one must consider and should report all variant readings of R as representative of an entire branch of the tradition. As an example of the returns of this philology on the text and apparatus of a few lines of the poem, consider a relatively typical passage

---

the most likely emendation, first proposed by Kalinka, is *cognomen versu veheris, carissime Rufi* ("you will be borne by my line as a surname, dearest Rufius").

34. For the purposes of criticizing Crucianus' lack of ability, it hardly matters whether he was the author of the errors or was merely copying mindlessly from a poor exemplar, since he never even indicates potential errors—a practice that was common for sixteenth-century humanists.

which is selected simply because it will be discussed further below (Rutilius Namatianus 1.349–60):[35]

> Lux aderat: tonsis progressi stare videmur,
>   sed cursum prorae terra relicta probat. 350
> Occurrit Chalybum memorabilis Ilva metallis,
>   qua nihil uberius Norica gleba tulit,
> non Biturix largo potior strictura camino,
>   nec quae Sardonico cespite massa fluit.
> Plus confert populis ferri fecunda creatrix 355
>   quam Tartesiaci glarea fulva Tagi.
> Materies vitiis aurum letale parandis:
>   auri caecus amor ducit in omne nefas;
> aurea legitimas expugnant munera taedas
>   virgineosque sinus aureus imber emit. 360

349 tonsis progressi stare videmur *BV*: tensis progressu stare videmus *R* **350** prorae *BV*: pronae *R* **351** ilva *BV*: silva *R* **352** nihil ... gleba *BV*: mihi ... terra *R* **355** fecunda *BV*: secunda *R* **356** tartesiaci *BV*: tartasiaci *R* **359** expugnant *BV*: expunat *R* **360** aureus *BV*: aure *R*

> Daylight arrived. Driving on with oars, we seem to stand still,
>   but the land left behind demonstrates the ship's motion. 350
> We pass by Ilva, famed for the mines of the Chalybes,
>   than which Norican soil has produced nothing more valuable,
> nor is Biturigean ore stronger, despite being smelted in a copious forge,
>   nor the molten mass which flows from Sardinian sod.
> The fertile mother of iron bestows more upon the people 355
>   than the gold-hued gravel of the Tartessian Tagus.
> Deadly gold is a substance that produces vices:
>   blind love of gold leads to every crime;
> golden gifts overcome the torches of lawful marriage
>   and a golden shower buys maidenly embraces. 360

349 Driving on with oars, we seem to stand still *BV*: With taut things by progress we see standing *R* **350** ship's *BV*: prostrate's *R* **351** Ilva *BV*: forest *R* **352** soil ... noth-

---

35. The text, apparatus, and translation are my own. For clarity, the variants are reported positively, and translated with an amount of carefully considered inanity. Crucianus likely did not understand what he was writing down, but must have had some passing familiarity with Latin, since most of his errors produce nonsense by means of actual (but erroneous) Latin words.

ing *BV:* land ... for me *R* **355** fertile *BV:* favorable *R* **356** Tartessian *BV:* Tartassian *R* **359** overcome *BV:* ovircums *R* **360** golden *BV:* with an ear *R*

Here, in only twelve lines of the poem, *R* offers erroneous variants eight times, ranging from minor orthographic errors (e.g. *pronae, secunda*) which nonetheless confuse the sense, to truly bewildering nonsense (e.g. *tensis progressu stare videmus*). This is representative of *R*'s textual contribution throughout the poem, and it means that the editor's apparatus is largely consumed with recording *R*'s errors. Yet *R*'s contribution is considered important because it represents an independent branch of the stemma. By virtue of modern philological methods, *R* enjoys a privilege which is not afforded *B* or *V,* despite the obvious deficiencies (in modern eyes) of its own philological method.

This then is the philological history of the reception and transmission of the physical text. Modern editions are dependent upon three witnesses produced by very different modes of study. For modern, scholarly purposes, it is hard to deny the obvious superiority of Sannazaro's careful and scholarly copy, the product of his brand of philology, which happens to coincide most closely with the modern brand. Sannazaro's scholarly transcription and astute emendation tends to highlight the shortcomings both of Pio's relatively careless transcription of the same exemplar and of Crucianus' obviously poor grasp of Latin. True, Pio's edition permits the reconstruction of Inghirami's copy and the identification of places where Sannazaro emended Inghirami's text; and Crucianus' manuscript broadens the stemma, and thus our quantitative (if not qualitative) knowledge of the text. But even a conservative modern edition, based in stemmatic recension, produces a text approximating a copyediting of the Vienna manuscript alone, but with an apparatus laden with inferior variants, especially from *R.* In many ways, for the modern mode of philology, *V* really is the *codex optimus* because of Sannazaro's mode of philology.

With this in mind, the subject of Rutilius' name might be revisited. The historical treatment of Sannazaro's text as the *codex optimus* produced the version of Rutilius' name which is now in current usage. Consideration of the modes of philology in effect in the other witnesses, and their general textual ineffectiveness even in modern terms, tempts modern editors, whether consciously or not, to trust and approve Sannazaro's variant despite the demands of stemmatic analysis and criticism, not because his text *per se* is "best," but because his scholarly and literary mode of philology coincides most closely with the modern and because he sought similar returns in the production of his text.

The philological returns sought by Pio's eager but uncritical printed edition and Crucianus' eager but almost illiterate manuscript were obviously different. Each took pride in his work, one as an offering to a powerful patron, the other as a private pleasure. A clue as to Pio's reasoning for offering this particular poem as a gift, perhaps also the reason that Crucianus was so proud of his text, can be seen in the frontispiece to *B:*

> CLAUDIUS RUTILIUS POE-
> TA PRISCUS DE LAUDI-
> BUS URBIS, ETRURIAE,
>   ET ITALIAE

> CLAUDIUS RUTILIUS, AN
> ANCIENT POET, ON PRAISE FOR
> ROME, ETRURIA,
>   AND ITALY

Rutilius' poem, although technically a travel poem, does indeed present *laudes Urbis, Etruriae et Italiae.* This inspires one final consideration. Philology is not evident only in the processes of textual reception and transmission, it is evident also in the process of literary creation. Rutilius himself took part in a philological process, not just by writing the poem, but by writing a poem which made use of the precedents provided by literary tradition in the expression of his own agenda. He was, in other words, a philologist-author.

In the aftermath of the Visigothic sack of Rome and destruction of the Italian and Gallic countryside, Rutilius directed his literary efforts toward depicting Roman tradition surviving and thriving, even amidst the ruins. Even before the journey begins, before he leaves Rome itself, Rutilius delivers, in an elegant and learned rhetorical style, a 164-line encomium of Rome. He begins with regrets that he must travel along the Italian coast by sea because the roads north are no longer safe. Then he reflects on Rome's greatness and its cosmopolitan nature, which leads him to exhort Rome to rise up again, to become stronger by her defeat, just as she had done several times in the days of the Republic: (Rutilius Namatianus 1.139–46)[36]

> illud te reparat quod cetera regna resolvit;
>   ordo renascendi est crescere posse malis.
> ergo age, sacrilegae tandem cadat hostia gentis;

---

36. Text and translation are my own.

submittant trepidi perfida colla Getae.
ditia pacatae dent vectigalia terrae;
   impleant augustos barbara praeda sinus.
aeternum tibi Rhenus aret, tibi Nilus inundet,
   altricemque suam fertilis orbis alat.

The very thing which dissolves other nations renews you;
   your ability to grow by misfortune is your usual manner of rebirth.
Come then, let the impious race finally fall as a sacrifice;
   let the panic-stricken Goths stretch forth their treacherous necks.
Let the pacified lands give tributary riches;
   let barbarian loot fill your august lap.
Let the Rhine plow for you forever, let the Nile overflow for you,
   and let the fruitful world nourish its nurse.

This travel poem is actually less about travel than it is about the continuance of "Romanness," *Romanitas,* in the face of recent disaster. Rather than focus on the journey itself, Rutilius has structured his poem around a series of Roman vignettes which take place at the many purposeful pauses in his journey. Perhaps most notable is his stopover in Triturrita at the end of Book One, where he takes part in a boar hunt which might have been lifted from the pages of Virgil.[37] In fact, Virgil was clearly at the front of Rutilius' mind, for in his efforts to present an image of Roman rebirth, the poetry of the Augustan age of rebirth provided excellent literary precedents. Rutilius' poem self-consciously displays thorough familiarity with his classical predecessors. At this relatively late date in Latin literature, Rutilius writes in a refined and elegant style which is modeled largely on that of the early empire, itself much influenced by Hellenistic conventions.[38] While some echoes of other late authors such as Ausonius can be detected in Rutilius, the presence of golden age poets Virgil and Ovid is so pronounced as to require little detection at all. Garth Tissol has outlined Rutilius' use of melancholy travel imagery inspired by and alluding to Ovid's exilic poetry—making use of literary (that is philological) precedents to express his own message.[39] Rutilius' use of Virgil is also extremely evident. For example, consider now the content of a passage which was quoted above for purely textual reasons: (Rutilius Namatianus 1.349–60)

---

37. See Capponi 1986 for the literary allusiveness of this hunting vignette.
38. Cf. Bertotti 1969; Lana 1961; and especially Merone 1959.
39. Tissol 2002.

Lux aderat: tonsis progressi stare videmur,
    sed cursum prorae terra relicta probat.
Occurrit Chalybum memorabilis Ilva metallis,
    qua nihil uberius Norica gleba tulit,
non Biturix largo potior strictura camino,
    nec quae Sardonico cespite massa fluit.
Plus confert populis ferri fecunda creatrix
    quam Tartesiaci glarea fulva Tagi.
Materies vitiis aurum letale parandis:
    auri caecus amor ducit in omne nefas;
aurea legitimas expugnant munera taedas
    virgineosque sinus aureus imber emit.

Daylight arrived. Driving on with oars, we seem to stand still,
    but the land left behind demonstrates the ship's motion.
We pass by Ilva, famed for the mines of the Chalybes,
    than which Norican soil has produced nothing more valuable,
nor is Biturigean ore stronger, despite being smelted in a copious forge,
    nor the molten mass which flows from Sardinian sod.
The fertile mother of iron bestows more upon the people
    than the gold-hued gravel of the Tartessian Tagus.
Deadly gold is a substance that produces vices:
    blind love of gold leads to every crime;
golden gifts overcome the torches of lawful marriage
    and a golden shower buys maidenly embraces.

Rutilius describes his journey past the island of Elbe (Ilva), which is famed for the quality of its iron. This is in fact an elaboration of a passage of Virgil. In Book Ten of the *Aeneid,* Aeneas' supporters gather to fight for his cause: (Virgil, *Aeneid* 10.172–74)

> sescentos illi dederat Populonia mater
> expertos belli iuvenes, at Ilva trecentos
> insula, inexhaustis Chalybum generosa metallis.

> To him Populonia had given six hundred of
> of her sons, skilled in war, but Ilva three hundred,
> an island rich with the inexhaustible mines of the Chalybes.

Ilva, "rich with the inexhaustible mines of the Chalybes," is just one of the supporting city-states listed in this catalogue of Aeneas' troops. Here Rutilius philologizes Virgil, and in doing so maintains the very same philological impetus which Virgil had begun four centuries earlier, for Virgil himself was of course alluding to (and so philologizing) Homer's famous catalogue of ships. This is no mere passing allusion (in either Rutilius or Virgil), but a small part of a much more portentous series of allusions. For, in Virgil's passage, 10.166–84, Aeneas' supporters come not just from Elbe, but from Cosa, Populonia, Pisa, Caere, Minio, Pyrgi, and Graviscae as well. And Rutilius, in his poem, is careful to elaborate upon every one of these places as he passes or visits them.[40] The Roman places of Italy which were original supporters of the first Roman, the ancestor of the Roman race, are thus held up by Rutilius as continuing the Roman tradition. Rutilius not only knows his Virgil but uses him to his own philological end. Rutilius' *laudes Italiae* are themselves founded upon the unified vision of Roman nationalism so central to the worldview of his Augustan exemplars. Because Rutilius' poem foregrounds an agenda of Italian rebirth, it was naturally attractive to the Italian humanists, who also lived in a time of Italian national pride and renaissance. A quick glance at any bibliography on Rutilius will reveal the continuance of this philological trend: the study of Rutilius continues to be dominated by Italian scholars.

In the production of any modern edition, the editor finds himself contending with the accumulated effects of multiple variant forms of philology, let alone with variant forms of text. Starting with the original author, philology is constantly but not consistently applied to the production, reception and transmission of the text. Thus, in addition to being at the mercy of the chance survival of texts, modern philologists are essentially at the mercy of historical modes of their own discipline. In part then, any fully aware modern philologist must proceed from the understanding that he or she is taking part in this same process, engaging with and manipulating the returns of philology itself.

---

40. For this, see Maaz 1988.

CHAPTER 3

Angelo Poliziano's *Lamia*
"Philology" and "Philosophy" at the University of Florence

Christopher S. Celenza

> Let's tell stories for a while, if you please, but let's make them relevant, as Horace says. For stories, even those that are considered the kinds of things that foolish old women discuss, are not only the first beginnings of philosophy. Stories are also—and just as often—philosophy's instrument.[1]

These lines open Angelo Poliziano's *Lamia,* a *praelectio* or preliminary oration, which he delivered in the fall of 1492 to open the course he was teaching on Aristotle's *Prior Analytics* at the Florentine university. In the work, Poliziano is responding to objections from contemporaries, who suggested that he did not have the training necessary to carry out this task, since he was not a "philosopher." The text seems, in hindsight, to be an alternate version of the mission of philosophy, even as it is a response to debates that were taking place in the intellectual world of Italian humanism in the late 1480s and early 1490s. More than this, the text represents a signal moment in the history of philology. Poliziano explicitly and implicitly asks his readers and listeners whether the self-proclaimed "philosophers" in the context of the Florentine university were engaging in the mission of philosophy, according to its ancient Greek etymology, the "love of wisdom." Suggesting that

---

1. "Fabulari paulisper lubet, sed ex re, ut Flaccus ait; nam fabellae, etiam quae aniles putantur, non rudimentum modo sed et instrumentum quandoque philosophiae sunt," Poliziano, *Lamia* 1. Section numbers for the text and translation of the *Lamia* refer to those established in Celenza 2010; all translations are my own, drawn from that volume. An expanded version of this essay appears in that volume as "Poliziano's *Lamia* in Context." In addition to the literature cited on the *Lamia* in Wesseling 1986, see Blanchard 1995: 52–60; Zini 1996: 185–91 and 1999. Recent literature on Poliziano can also be found in Fera and Martelli 1998. Still essential is Vasoli 1968, especially 116–31.

75

they are not doing so, he proposes something different, a transdisciplinary discipline, or as he calls it early on, "this particular profession of ours" (7), which turns out to be something remarkably like philology.

I

To understand the *Lamia*, it is necessary to set it in the context of Poliziano's evolving intellectual interests and teaching career, before moving on to an analysis of the text.

Poliziano had an early and abiding interest in philosophy of all sorts, including Aristotle. Jonathan Hunt's work has shown that in 1480, when Poliziano was in his middle twenties, he engaged in an intense set of philosophical conversations with Francesco di Tommaso (c.1445–1514), a Dominican based at Santa Maria Novella in Florence.[2] Early on, too, Poliziano studied with the Byzantine émigré Andronicus Callistus. Poliziano celebrated Callistus in his *Elegy* to his respected humanist friend Bartolomeo Fonzio, saying that Callistus "loosed the knots of high-flown Aristotle."[3] Poliziano was also a student of Johannes Argyropoulos (1415–87), well recognized by contemporaries as a teacher of Aristotle, and someone whom Poliziano himself called in his *Miscellanea* "by far the most famous Peripatetic of his day."[4] Finally, Poliziano's relationship with Giovanni Pico della Mirandola also pushed him toward the posture of excluding no philosophical text, whatever its disciplinary provenance.

Poliziano testifies in numerous places to these interests, and the course of his career, as well as various interactions with his contemporaries, shows the directions in which he was willing to travel. His early years saw him break onto the cultural scene in Florence after translating books two through five of Homer's *Iliad*, which he worked on from 1469 until 1475.[5] The early 1470s also saw Poliziano compose two poetic works, an elegy for Bartolomeo Fonzio and an *epicedion*, or funeral poem, for Albiera degli Albizzi, the intended wife of Sigismondo della Stufa, a Medicean, who died before her sixteenth birthday.[6] In those two works Poliziano gives hints of his philosophical background at the time, when he was still in his late teens.

---

2. Hunt 1995.
3. "Rursus in Andronici doctum me confero ludum / Qui tumidi nodos laxat Aristotelis." *Ad Bartholomeum Fontium* vv. 193–94 (Poliziano 2003: 34). For the meaning here of "tumidi" see Bausi's note on these lines.
4. For the Poliziano quotation see below, n10; for Argyropoulos and Aristotle see Field 1988: 107–26; Hankins 1990: 1.350.
5. See Bausi 2003: xii–xiii.
6. Both edited by Bausi in Poliziano 2003.

The elegy for Fonzio is especially interesting. Poliziano structures it as a recounting of his day, and in going through his day he mentions those with whom he studied. Marsilio Ficino figures prominently, with over thirty verses dedicated to him.[7] To the young Poliziano, Ficino appears as a natural philosopher who teaches "how much the stars fly, as, wandering, they run along," who refutes the "impious words of insane Lucretius," makes war on Epicurus's folly, and who is a new "Orpheus, measuring out Apollonian poetry."[8] There is a brief allusion to Ficino's metaphysical hierarchy (verses 179–80), but to Poliziano at this early stage it was Ficino the anti-Lucretian, anti-Epicurean natural philosopher who stood out. Later, toward the end of his *Miscellanea*, Poliziano downplayed his early studies with Ficino and Argyropoulos, claiming with almost two decades hindsight that because of his "nature and age" he was "more inclined to the allures of the poet Homer."[9] Yet his enthusiasm for philosophy is more marked in these earlier works.

As his early work progressed, so too did Poliziano's relationship with the Medici family. He played the familiar humanist game of networking well and wound up in Lorenzo's inner circle before long.[10] From 1480 on, Poliziano taught poetics and rhetoric at the Florentine *studium generale* with Medici sponsorship. It is from this final period, 1480 until his death in 1494, that some of his most lasting works emerged. His four *Silvae* (the *Manto*, on Virgil; the *Ambra*, on Homer; the *Rusticus*, on Virgil's *Georgics* and Hesiod's *Works and Days;* and the *Nutricia*, a survey of the history of poetry from ancient through modern times) date from this final period, as do the first "century" and the never published second *centuria* of the *Miscellanea*.[11]

Hindsight allows us to see Poliziano's teaching sharpening his critical faculties: his *Silvae* were poetic introductions to the authors he was teaching,

---

7. *Ad Bartholomeum Fontium* vv. 155–88.

8. "quanto currunt vaga sidera lapsu" (v.157): "Impia non sani turbat modo dicta Lucreti, / Imminet erratis nunc, Epicure, tuis . . . " (vv.173–74); " . . . Qualis Apollinei modulator carminis Orpheus . . . " (v.183).

9. "Etenim ego, tenera adhuc aetate, sub duobus excellentissimis hominibus Marsilio Ficino Florentino, cuius longe felicior quam Thracensis Orphei cithara veram (ni fallor) Eurydicen, hoc est amplissimi iudicii Platonicam sapientiam revocavit ab inferis, et Argyropylo Byzantio Peripateticorum sui temporis longe clarissimo, dabam quidem philosophiae utrique operam, sed non admodum assiduam, videlicet ad Homeri poetae blandimenta natura et aetate proclivior, quem tum latine quoque miro ut adolescens ardore, miro studio versibus interpretabar. Postea vero rebus aliis negotiisque prementibus, sic ego nonnunquam de philosophia, quasi de Nilo canes, bibi fugique, donec reversus est in hanc urbem maxime Laurenti Medicis cum benivolentia, tum virtutis et ingenii similitudine allectus princeps hic nobilissimus Ioannes Picus Mirandula. . . . " (*Miscellanea* in Poliziano 1498 [speaking about his early studies]: K ii[v]–K iii[r]). Also cited in Garin 1979: 344, n1.

10. See Bausi 2003: xi–xxxiii.

11. For the *Silvae*, see Poliziano 2004 and the critical edition of the texts in Poliziano 1996.

highly different in form from more standard university *praelectiones*. Texts of this genre were usually in prose and customarily followed a pattern describing what was useful about the proposed subject and the problems that the course would treat.[12] Poliziano's omnivorous attitude to literature also led to his immersing himself ever more deeply in Greek as well as Latin, archaic as well as late authors, and texts from every possible disciplinary tradition, including medicine, natural philosophy, law, and logic.

During the first four to five years of his teaching career at the *Studium,* as Lucia Cesarini Martinelli has argued, Poliziano sought to distinguish himself from certain Florentine teaching traditions.[13] To give one example, in a Florence that had always valued the *Aeneid,* Poliziano chose instead to lecture on Vergil's bucolic poetry.[14] In the second period, from roughly 1485–90, Poliziano seemed secure enough in his professional status to begin to treat more traditional themes, but always in his own distinctive ways. This period saw courses on Vergil's *Aeneid* and on Homer; Poliziano also lectured on his own poetic *praelectiones,* actually teaching and explicating for students his *Manto* and his *Ambra.* The final period, from 1490 until his death, was marked by Poliziano's focus on Aristotelian texts, and it signals both an evolution of his existing interests as well as a form of resistance against institutional intellectual segregation.

Poliziano's bottom-line prestige and competitiveness rose as well. His salary rose during the 1480s and the language of his contracts shows that he was accorded an increasing level of freedom of teaching. Gradually, he came to want to teach Aristotle.[15] Poliziano lectured on Aristotle's *Ethics* in 1490–91, and he made it clear that he believed many of his colleagues in the university knew so little Greek and Latin that they missed Aristotle's meaning in many cases.[16] The *praelectio* to the *Ethics* course was entitled *Panepistemon,* and in a certain respect the later *Lamia* can be seen as a companion piece to it.[17] As the Hellenic etymology of its title implied, the *Panepistemon* represented an attempt to offer a representation of all knowl-

---

12. Some more standard *praelectiones* can be seen in Müllner 1899: 3–197; cf. also Cardini 1973: 287–382, who publishes different preliminary orations of Cristoforo Landino. There is a fine overview of the genre of the *praelectio* in Campanelli 1994.

13. Martinelli 1996.

14. Martinelli 1996: 480.

15. Verde 1973–94: 1.263–392 and 2.26–29. There is further discussion in my "Poliziano's *Lamia* in Context" (Celenza 2010).

16. Wesseling 1986: xiii–xiv. For Poliziano's philologically oriented method of teaching the *Ethics* (he lectured only on books 3 and 4), see Lines 2002: 101–05, with App. A, #113 and App. C, #48; Lines (App. A, #113) also suggests Poliziano lectured on the *Ethics* in 1491–92. For a useful overview see also Lines 2001.

17. See "Panepistemon," in Poliziano 1498: ff. Y viii(v)–Z vi(v); Mandosio 1996 and 1997.

edge, which Poliziano proffers in a schematic fashion, almost like a diagram in words; he is intent on including those fields that traditionally lay outside the purview of the liberal arts:

> But now I intend to interpret Aristotle's *Ethics*. In so far as it is possible to do, I will approach this kind of analysis in such a way that not only the fields of learning that are termed liberal or the arts or that have to do with machines are gathered together within the boundaries of this classification, but also those commonly considered low and sedentary which, despite their reputation, are just as necessary for life.[18]

For Poliziano, "there are three genres of teachings among human beings: inspired, invented, and mixed. In the first genre there is situated our theology; in the second, philosophy, the mother of the arts; and in the third, divination."[19] By "inspired," then, Poliziano means Christian theology (the religions of the ancient pagans fall under the "invented" category); "invented" (*inventum*) signifies branches of learning that are or have been "found" or "discovered" by human beings; and "mixed" refers to divination, the faculty of foreseeing, or prophecy. It is the "invented" category that occupies most of the *Panepistemon*.[20]

The variety of fields that Poliziano includes demonstrates that he sees "philosophy" as having a broad scope and as including all fields of human wisdom, however humble. For Poliziano, philosophy is threefold: theoretical, practical, and rational, which, Latinate that Poliziano is, he terms "spectativa" (as opposed to the Hellenizing but more usual "theoretica"), "actualis" (instead of "pragmatica") and "rationalis" (permitted, since it derives from the authentic Latin word "ratio"). Yet within those rubrics one finds references not only to metaphysics, physics, and ethics, but also to grammar, history, cooking, carpentry, and tumbling, the latter art belonging to what Poliziano calls the "jesting craftsmen" ("illos nugatorios artifices").[21]

---

18. "Mihi vero nunc Aristotelis eiusdem libros *De moribus* interpretari consilium est, ita divisionem istiusmodi aggredi ut, quoad eius fieri possit, non disciplinae modo et artes vel liberales quae dicuntur vel machinales, sed etiam sordidae illae ac sellulariae, quibus tamen vita indiget intra huius ambitum distributionis colligantur" ("Panepistemon," in Poliziano 1498: f. Y viii[v]).

19. "Tria sunt igitur inter homines genera doctrinarum: inspiratum, inventum, mixtum. In primo genere theologia nostra, in secundo mater artium philosophia, in tertio divination sita est" ("Panepistemon," in Poliziano 1498: f. Y viii[v]).

20. "Theology" (the "genus inspiratum") occipies one short paragraph in ibid., f. Y ix(r); "Philosophy" occupies ff. Y ix(r)–Z vi(r); "Divination" ("which is also called prophecy by our people"—"quae prophetia quoque dicitur a nostris") occupies one folio, in ibid., f.Z vi(v).

21. Poliziano 1498: f.Z iv(r)–Z v(r).

The list of fields included within the "genus inventum" is astonishingly large. As sixteenth-century efforts to refine and offer better reference books grew (a phenomenon coincident with the standardization of printing with movable type), Poliziano's *Panepistemon* had a noteworthy fortune.[22] If Poliziano's *Panepistemon* offered a schematic representation of the world's human wisdom, the *Lamia* can be seen as an attempt to provide a narrative for his schematization: not overtly so, but as a representation of just how widely one needed to think if the "love of wisdom" was to be approached in its integrity.

After his *Ethics* course, Poliziano taught Aristotle's logical works. He brought to bear some of the then newly available late ancient commentators on Aristotle; and he was conscious of his own teaching style. As he wrote, closing the *Praelectio* to his logic course of 1491 (*Praelectio de dialectica*) and addressing his students:

> I am going to take care that nothing be brought away from this enterprise that I cannot defend either with reason or by an appeal to trusted authorities, and I won't blunt the sharp edges of your mind with exceeding loquacity, confusing language, or mountains of 'questions.' Indeed, a clear brevity and a swift run-through will be characteristic of my speaking style. Moreover, though I won't be interposing doubts at every turn, I also won't omit them all either, so that your mental muscles will be exercised (rather than simply fatigued) as advantageously as possible.[23]

If Poliziano was careful to conclude his *Praelectio* by telling students what to expect style-wise, he was scrupulous about telling them how he had prepared to teach Aristotle. Earlier in the text, Poliziano had presented a list of authors into whose work he had delved. The list is indicative of Poliziano's tastes and aims, and the manner in which he frames it bears more than passing similarity to the *Lamia*, evoking similar anxieties and resentments already pressing upon him. He is well aware that people will ask who his teachers were in this branch of erudition (dialectic), since he has not spent much time with it

---

22. See Mandosio 1996: 160–63, who cites Champier 1537 (160, n163) and Gesner 1548 (162, n168).

23. "Curae autem nobis erit ne quid huc afferatur quod non vel ratione tueri vel auctoritate possimus. Nec vero aut verbositate nimia, aut perplexitate orationis, aut quaestionum molibus vestrae mentis acies retundetur. Etenim perspicua brevitas atque expeditus erit nostrae orationis cursus. Dubitationes autem nec omnes nec ubique aut interponemus, aut omittemus, sic ut vestra quam commodissime exerceantur ingenia, non fatigentur" (*Praelectio de dialectica,* in Poliziano 1498: bb ii[r]). The passage is also partially cited by Wesseling in Poliziano 1986: 113.

previously.²⁴ First, he answers, there were those who came from the "family of Aristotle," the *Aristotelis familia*, whom he names, interestingly, all in the plural form, as if to indicate that he knows them so well it would be otiose to be more specific. This very same move serves to highlight the fact that he was reading these recondite authors in Greek and thereby superseding what many contemporary teachers of philosophy could accomplish: "If you were to ask me, then, who my teachers were in Aristotelian learning, I could show you heaps of books, in which you will count the Theophrastuses, the Alexanders [Alexander of Aphrodisias], the Themistiuses, the Ammoniuses [Ammonius of Alexandria, 435/45–517–26], the Simpliciuses, the Philoponuses and others, moreover, from the family of Aristotle."²⁵

Poliziano continues his list by saying that there are now those who follow in place of the late ancient commentators mentioned above. They are: Walter Burley (1275–1344; Poliziano is probably referring to Burley's commentary on the *Six Principles* attributed to Gilbert of Poitiers);²⁶ Erveus, or Hervaeus Natalis (c.1260–c.1323), a French Dominican; William of Ockham (1280/5–c1349); Antisberus, or William Heytesbury, (c.1313–72); and Strodus, or Ralph Strode, a fellow of Merton College in Oxford who flourished from 1350–1400 and was the "philosophical Strode" who was one of the two dedicatees of Chaucer's *Troilus and Criseyde*.²⁷ All these thinkers had actively engaged in the great flourishing of attention to problems of language and logic that occurred during the late thirteenth and fourteenth centuries.

The desire to exclude no text and to read widely irrespective of disciplinary parameters, as manifested in these lists, leads one to think of Pico della Mirandola and more broadly of the generational moment these humanists

---

24. "Prius tamen quam longius progrediar, respondendum mihi tacitis quorundam cogitationibus video, qui quoniam ante hoc tempus partem hanc philosophiae nunquam attigerim, quaerent ex me fortassis quo tandem magistro usus dialecticae me doctorem profiteri audeam" (Poliziano 1498: bb i[r])

25. "Et ego igitur, si ex me quaeratis qui mihi praeceptores in Peripateticorum fuerint scholis, strues vobis monstrare librarias potero, ubi Theophrastos, Alexandros, Themistius, Hammonios, Simplicios, Philoponos, aliosque praeterea ex Aristotelis familia numerabitis, quorum nunc in locum (si diis placet) Burleus, Evreus, Occam [*cod.* Occan], Antisberus, Strodusque succedunt. Et quidem ego adulescens doctoribus quibusdam, nec his quidem obscuris, philosophiae dialecticaeque operam dabam, quorum alii graecarum nostrarumque iuxta ignari literarum, ita omnem Aristotelis librorum puritatem dira quadam morositatis illuvie foedabant, ut risum mihi aliquando, interdum etiam stomachum moverent. Pauci rursus, qui Graeca tenebant, quamquam nova quaedam nonnullis inaudita admirabiliaque proferre videbantur, nihil tamen omnino afferebant quod non ego aliquando antea deprehendissem in iis ipsis commentariis, quorum mihi iam tum copia fuit, huius beneficio Laurentii Medicis, cuius totum muneris hoc est, quod scio, quod profiteor" (Poliziano 1498: bb i[v]). This passage is also partially cited by Garin 1979: 344, n1.

26. See below on (ps.-)Gilbert.

27. Chaucer 1926: 5.1856–60.

inhabited. Poliziano and Pico had evolved such a close friendship and intellectual alliance in the 1480s that Poliziano closed his own *Miscellanea* with a fulsome statement praising Pico. Pico, in Poliziano's view, was "most expert in philosophy as a whole, even as he was an expert in the literatures of different languages, and both furnished and trained in all the best disciplines, almost to an extent that it could not be believed."[28] Poliziano's close friendship with Pico also helps contextualize the *Lamia* in an important way.

Poliziano and Pico carried out their work in a social community whose members were linked by bonds of commonly held assumptions. While each member had his own particular contributions to make, to understand their works fully one must conceive a theory of collective authorship. Even if the achievements of each member remained his own, the agendas for research and discussion were set within the context of the community's ongoing conversations.

One key member of this community was the Venetian Ermolao Barbaro (1454–93). As Pico wrote to Barbaro, highlighting this community: "I, and our own Poliziano, have often read whatever letters we had from you, whether they were directed to us or to others. What arrives always contends to such an extent with what there was previously, and new pleasures pop up so abundantly as we read, that because of our constant shouts of approbation we barely have time to breathe."[29] Fundamentally, the approach to knowledge-making was collaborative. A new letter would arrive, and it would serve as a stimulus for debate and conversation to the group as a whole, whoever the destined recipient might have been. A response would be written, but the response was informed by the conversations that attended the letter.

The most famous letter exchange between Pico and Barbaro concerned the relationship between eloquence and philosophy.[30] Barbaro wrote to Pico complaining of scholastic philosophical language and condemning scholastic philosophy in general, urging Pico not to dedicate so much time to these thinkers. Pico, in the first short section of the letter just quoted, admitted he had been spending perhaps too much time in the pursuit of this type of philosophy.[31] Then, in the letter's principal part, he argued through the persona of a scholastic philosopher that the truth of the doctrines was more

---

28. "Iam idem totius philosophiae consultissimus etiamque varia linguarum literatura et omnibus honestis artibus supra veri fidem munitus atque instructus" (Poliziano 1498: K iii [r]). Also cited in Garin 1979: 338, n1.

29. "Legimus saepe ego et noster Politianus quascumque habemus tuas aut ad alios, aut ad nos epistolas; ita semper prioribus certant sequentia et novae fertiliter inter legendum efflorescunt veneres, ut perpetua quadam acclamatione interspirandi locum non habeamus" (Garin 1952: 806).

30. The best recent treatment, with ample bibliography, is in Bausi 1996.

31. The letter can be found in Garin 1952: 804–23.

important than the style in which a philosopher wrote: content over form. Still, Pico made these arguments not in the Latin of scholastic philosophy, but by employing an elegant Ciceronian Latinity in keeping with the best practices of his generation. He ended the letter by saying in a short coda that these were not his own real opinions, but that, in a dialogical fashion, he had maintained them only to stimulate Barbaro to go even further in his defense of eloquence.

Barbaro's return letter to Pico (a letter which we can easily imagine Poliziano avidly read as well) included an anecdote; in it Barbaro recounted what a scholastic philosophical colleague, "audaculus et insolens," at his own university, Padua, said about Pico: "This Pico, whoever he is, seems to me to be a grammarian," or a *grammaticus*, "who has stepped into shoes too big for himself."[32] Amid these excited conversations about the direction the search for wisdom should take, we can see the origins of Poliziano's *Lamia*. Seven years later, Poliziano intends to define what a *grammaticus* really is, and in so doing to flesh out what sort of training, competence, and purview the *grammaticus* possesses.

As to why Poliziano opted to teach the *Prior Analytics* when he did, his teaching sequence, as well as his overall philosophical aims, help to explain his choices. The year before, that is, in the academic year 1491–92, he had taught Aristotle's *Categories, On Interpretation,* and *Sophistical Refutations.* Near the end of the *Sophistical Refutations,* Aristotle claims that he was original in his treatment of syllogisms and syllogistic logic, the subjects of the *Prior Analytics,* and that although there had been predecessors to study in the case of rhetoric, there were none such in the case of logic.[33] Poliziano was patently attracted to this notion that the study of language and logic represented a frontier for Aristotle, even as Poliziano's own *ad fontes* mentality allowed him first to read, and then symbolically to leap over, the many thinkers who had gone before him. Who else but Poliziano would have thought of writing, as an opening university oration on the subject of logic, a multilayered prose treatise outlining an independent view of what true philosophy represented?

---

32. "Quorum e numero unus aliquis in gymnasio patavino (nihil confingo, Pice; ridiculum omnino sed veram historiam denarro) audaculus et insolens, cuiusmodi fere sunt qui litteras humaniores et odio et ludibrio habent: 'Picus,' inquit, 'iste quisquis est, grammaticus opinor, parvo pedi calceos magnos circumdedit. Quid enim opus est tam multis rhetoriis? Aut quid ranis propinat? (addidimus ipsi, et quidem Seriphiis). Ecquis est, inquit, tam stolidus atque sensu carens, qui patronum hunc egregium cum altero, quisquis est, nefario grammatista colludere non intelligat? Mihi quidem videtur flere ad tumulum novercae, nullam homini fidem habeo . . .'" (Garin 1952: 846).

33. Aristotle, *Soph. Elench.,* sec. 34.

II

As often happened in humanist philosophical literature, the spur for the work was a polemic. This time, self-identified philosophers in the Florentine University had been suggesting that Poliziano was not philosopher enough to interpret these Aristotelian texts. In his *Lamia*, Poliziano strikes back publicly against his detractors.[34] The Latin word "Lamia" (which appears in Horace's *Ars poetica*, Apuleius' *Metamorphoses*, and Tertullian, among other places) refers to a sorceress who sucks the blood of children; it is also associated with childishness.[35] For Poliziano, the *Lamiae* in Florence represent purveyors of a kind of vampiric, backbiting, reputation-mongering rapacity. His choice to inveigh against them seems part of the close-knit yet competitive cultural world of Florence, especially in the late 1480s and early 1490s.[36] Poliziano's critique of the culture he saw around him goes deeper, however, than the local environment. Its importance lies rather in the fact that it is a noteworthy part of the humanist movement from Petrarch on, whereby intense attention to language fueled a reevaluation of the nature of wisdom and of philosophy, the love of wisdom. Poliziano is not engaging in a mere contest of the faculties: this is not a question of "rhetoric" or "philology" versus "philosophy." Instead, the *Lamia* shows Poliziano demonstrating that alternate ways of doing philosophy (or pursuing wisdom) were possible. It is a culmination and recapitulation of the work done within an identifiable stream of the humanist tradition that stretches from Petrarch through Lorenzo Valla and beyond.

Poliziano begins the *Lamia* by emphasizing the utility of the "fable," which he designates with the words *fabella* and *fabula*. The first word of the *Lamia* has "fabula" at its root, even as the treatise's first sentence sets the tone (1): "Fabulari paulisper lubet, sed ex re, ut Flaccus ait; nam fabellae etiam quae aniles putantur, non rudimentum modo sed et instrumentum quandoque philosophiae sunt."[37] Poliziano's Latin here is relevant, echoing as it does one of his favorite authors, Apuleius (c. 123–c. 170 C.E.), specifically the *Florida*, 15.24, where Apuleius describes the island of Samos and its most famous inhabitant, Pythagoras: "Prorsus, inquam, hoc erat primum *sapientiae rudimentum:* meditari condiscere, loquitari dediscere." ("This, I say, was

---

34. Poliziano also deviates from the normal *praelectio* pattern of providing an *adhortatio*, or "exhortation" to his prospective students; see Wesseling 1986: xx.

35. See Horace, *Ars poetica*, 340; Apuleius, *Metamorphoses*, 1.110.3 and 5.164.6; for childishness, Tertullian, *Adversus Valerianum*, 3.

36. For the differing intellectual perspectives present in the Florence of the 1480s and 90s, see Celenza 2004: 103–6, with literature.

37. Tr. above, in the epigraph to this chapter.

wisdom's first *implement:* to learn how to meditate, and to unlearn how to speak.") Apuleius had been describing Pythagoras's penchant to enjoin his students to silence (15.23): " . . . nihil prius discipulos suos docuit quam tacere" ("the first thing he taught his students was to be silent"). Poliziano has an ancient source in mind, yet he goes in a different direction, since one obviously cannot tell "stories" by remaining silent. From the beginning of the *praelectio,* then, Poliziano's practice is clear: he will imitate his ancient sources, but he will not follow them blindly; he will copy but not copy; he will comment but not compile.

Poliziano then commences with one of a number of "fables," just as he will conclude the treatise with one. The initial fable compels us to look beyond Latinate sources to the vernacular tradition in which he, like all other Renaissance intellectuals, was embedded. It was his grandmother, Poliziano avers, who first exposed him to the Lamia (2): "Even from when I was a little boy, my grandmother used to tell me that there were these Lamias in the wilderness, which devoured crying boys. Back then, the Lamia was the thing I dreaded the most, my greatest fear."[38] Now, too, in his rustic hideaway near Fiesole, Fonte Lucente, the women who come into town to procure water speak of an abode of Lamias, concealed in the shadows (ibid.). Grandmothers, women: for a Latin reader of the fifteenth century this gender distinction served to highlight a certain category of people: those without formal training in Latin.

There is indeed a vernacular tradition to the word and concept "lamia." Medieval uses of the word in Italian vernaculars prior to Poliziano indicate different meanings, all of them negative. The *Pungilingua* of fra Domenico Cavalca (c. 1270–1342), for example, offers a caution against flatterers, likening the flatterer to the lamia, "a cruel beast who after nourishing its pups tears them apart and devours them."[39] Boccaccio's *Decameron* offers another meaning: the lamia as a woman whose beauty is fatally attractive.[40] Closer to

---

38. "Mihi quidem etiam puerulo avia narrabat esse aliquas in solitudinibus Lamias, quae plorantes gluttirent pueros. Maxima tunc mihi formido Lamia erat, maximum terriculum" (Celenza 2010: 2).

39. "E Geremia profeta si lamenta di questi adulatori sotto simiglianza di lamie, e dice 'Lamiae nudaverunt mammas, lactaverunt catulos suos.' Lamia è una bestia crudele, la quale, poichè ha allattato i suoi categli, sì gli straccia e divoragli. E significa gli adulatori, li quali lattando uccidono gli amici loro, almeno quanto all'anima . . . " (Cavalca 1837: 126). Cavalca refers to *Lamentations,* 4.3. "Lamiae" in the Vulgate represents a translation of the Septuagint's Greek version of the Hebrew bible, where the Septuagint had "drakontes," which can mean "serpents" or "sea-serpents," though the Septuagint's version was itself a mistranslation of the Hebrew word for "jackals." See Albrektson 1963: 174–75.

40. Giovanni Boccaccio, *Decamerone,* 9.5: "A cui Calandrin disse: 'E' non si vuol dire a persona: egli è una giovane qua giú, che è piú bella che una lammia, la quale è sí forte innamorata di me, che ti

Poliziano's time, the word was used by Luca Pulci (1431–70) in a prefatory letter to his *Driadeo d'Amore,* directed to Lorenzo de' Medici.[41] Pulci relates that Lorenzo is missed by the countryfolk, especially the aged, "those who claim not only to have seen nymphs and demigods of this sort but even to have spoken with lamias, and to have seen flying through the air serpents and other animals so wondrous that they wouldn't even be found in Lybia."[42] For Pulci, lamias are mythical creatures, parallel to nymphs and "demigods," who properly inhabit rustic locales and with whom long-time inhabitants of those locales discourse. Poliziano's *fabella,* then, would remind his readers and listeners of something they had heard over a fire or perhaps encountered in the (vernacular) reading they did for amusement. Yet, for Poliziano, these creatures are found not only in the mythical world of rusticity. They also inhabit the contemporary city and, as Poliziano is about to argue, form part of the social economy of the intellectual marketplace.

As to the Lamia's nature, Poliziano tells his listeners that, according to Plutarch, this creature possesses "removeable eyes"—"oculos exemptiles" (3). When the Lamia leaves her own home, she attaches her eyes, so as to see everything that happens in all the traditional public places; returning home, the Lamia puts her eyes back on the shelf. The Lamia is "always blind at home, always sighted in public."[43] Poliziano assumes that backbiting gossips will be immediately familiar to his audience (5), and he adds an anecdote:

> When I was walking around, by chance one day a number of these Lamias saw me. They surrounded me, and, as if they were evaluating me, they looked me over, just like buyers are accustomed to do. Soon, with their heads bowed crookedly, they hissed together, "It's Poliziano, the very one, that trifler who was so quick to call himself a philosopher." Having said that, they flew away like wasps who left behind a stinger.

What was their central concern? Poliziano suggests an answer:

---

parrebbe un gran fatto: io me ne avvidi testé quando io andai per l'acqua." Boccaccio's usage implies that this meaning of the Lamia was obvious enough not to require explanation.

41. Pulci 1916. A work less famous to posterity than the *Morgante* of his better known brother Luigi Pulci (1432–84) and first drafted in the middle 1460s, Luca's *Driadeo* had a considerable circulation in late fifteenth-century Florence. See Tavernati 1985. See also Baldassarri 1998; in general on the Pulci family, Carrai 1985; and Jordan 1986.

42. "... coloro che non solamente dicono aver veduto ninfe e questi semidei, ma eziandio parlato con le lamie e veduto per l'aria volare serpenti ed altri animali mostruosi che in Libia non se ne vide mai tali" (Pulci 1916: 19).

43. "Ita semper domi caeca, semper foris oculata" (Celenza 2010: 4).

Now as to the fact that they said I was "so quick to call myself a philosopher," I really don't know what it was about the whole thing that bothered them: whether I was a philosopher—which I most certainly am not—or that I wanted to *seem* to be a philosopher, notwithstanding the fact that I am far from being one.[44]

There were people, in the small social economy of Florentine intellectual life, who began to object to the fact that Poliziano taught matters Aristotelian: the *Ethics,* the various logical works. Poliziano's objection is that they subjected him to negative scrutiny because of their sense that they belonged to a closed, professional community: self-identified philosophers.

To overcome this opposition, Poliziano proposes an originary investigation that has to do with "philosophy" itself: "So why don't we see, first of all, just what this animal is that men call a 'philosopher.'"[45] And then Poliziano follows this initial premise with a startling assertion (ibid.): "Then, I hope, you will easily understand that I am not a philosopher. . . . Not that I'm ashamed of the name 'philosopher' (if only I could live up to it in reality!); it's more that it keeps me happy if I stay away from titles that belong to other people."[46] Poliziano evinces respect for the mission of philosophy, describes it as something he feels unable to achieve, and, given the way the appellation "philosopher" has become corrupted by unreflective use, finally suggests he is happy to forego the title "philosopher." He then lays out the structure of his *praelectio:* "First, then, we'll deal with the question, 'what is a philosopher' and whether being a philosopher is a vile or bad thing. After we have shown that it isn't, then we'll go on to say a little something about ourselves and about this particular profession of ours."[47]

To discover what a philosopher (and by extension what "philosophy") is, Poliziano engages in a complex internal dialogue of praise and blame,

---

44. "Harum igitur aliquot praetereuntem forte conspicatae me substiterunt et, quasi noscitarent, inspexere curiosius, veluti emptores solent. Mox ita inter se detortis nutibus consusurrarunt: 'Politianus est, ipsissimus est, nugator ille scilicet qui sic repente philosophus prodiit.' Et cum dicto avolarunt, quasi vespae dimisso aculeo. Sed quod repente me dixerunt prodiisse philosophum, nescio equidem utrumne illis hoc totum displiceat philosophum esse, quod ego profecto non sum, an quod ego videri velim philosophus, cum longe absim tamen a philosopho" (Celenza 2010: 6).

45. "Videamus ergo primum quodnam hoc sit animal quod homines philosophum vocant" (Celenza 2010: 7).

46. "Tum, spero, facile intellegetis non esse me philosophum. Neque hoc dico tamen quo id vos credam credere, sed ne quis fortasse aliquando credat; non quia me nominis istius pudeat (si modo ei possim re ipsa satisfacere), sed quod alienis titulis libenter abstineo . . . " (Celenza 2010: 7).

47. "De hoc igitur primum, mox etiam de eo agemus, utrumne esse philosophum turpe ac malum sit. Quod ubi docuerimus non esse, tum de nobis ipsis nonnihil deque nostra hac professione loquemur" (Celenza 2010: 7).

of naming and of withholding names, that marks the treatise's structure. He begins with the origin of the word "philosopher," reputedly coined by Pythagoras.[48] Poliziano's method of arriving there, however, is unique. He does not name Pythagoras, and he clearly intends in this part of the treatise to treat the matter in a satirical vein:

> I've certainly heard that there once was a certain man from Samos, a teacher of the youth. He was always clothed in white and had a fine head of hair; born often enough, even reborn, he was noticeable for his golden thigh. His name was 'He Himself'—at least that's what his students used to call him. But as soon as he took one of those students under his wing, in a flash he took away his power of speech![49]

Poliziano alludes here to the Pythagorean custom reported in some ancient sources of compelling newly arrived students to be "listeners" (*akousmatikoi*), allowing them to speak in the school context only after five years of training, after they had become sufficiently learned (*mathematikoi*).[50]

Poliziano goes on to list a number of the *symbola* of Pythagoras. Well after their use as ritual markers and precepts to be obeyed in ancient Pythagorean communities, these short gnomic sayings acquired a body of interpretive literature in late antiquity and the middle ages.[51] They enjoyed a minor revival in the fifteenth and sixteenth centuries, as the vogue for proverbial literature increased.[52] Yet it is clear from Poliziano's tone that his intent is mildly subversive as he introduces the *symbola* almost with the rhythm of a stand-up comedian (8): "Now if you hear the precepts of 'He Himself' you are going to dissolve with laughter, I just know it. But I'm going to tell you anyway."[53] He goes on to present a number of precepts: "'Do not . . . punc-

---

48. If Pythagoras, who wrote nothing, knew or used the words "philosophy" or "philosopher," it is likely that the meanings behind them were different even from those of Plato. The original anecdote (that Pythagoras coined the word "philosophy" when conversing with the tyrant Leon of Sicyon) is from Heraclides Ponticus and, as W. Burkert pointed out, "made its way, via the doxographers, into all the ancient handbooks;" Burkert 1972: 65. See Burkert 1960; Hadot 2002: 15 and 285, n1 with the literature cited there.

49. "Audivi equidem Samium fuisse olim quendam iuventutis magistrum, candidatum semper et capillatum, femore etiam aureo conspicuum, natum saepius ac renatum. Nomen illi erat "Ipse:" sic discipuli certe vocabant sui. Sed eos discipulos, ut ad se quenque receperat, statim prorsus elinguabat!" (Celenza 2010: 8).

50. On this tradition, see Burkert 1972: 192–208.

51. For the functions that the *symbola* (or *akousmata*) served in ancient Pythagorean communities, see Burkert 1972: 166–92.

52. Leon Battista Alberti, Marsilio Ficino, and others commented on them. See Wesseling 1986: xxv–xxviii; Celenza 2001: 4–52 and Vuilleumier 2000: 21–80.

53. "Praecepta vero si Ipsius audieritis, risu, scio, diffluetis. Dicam tamen nihilo secius" (Celenza 2010: 8).

ture fire with a sword.' 'Don't jump over the scale.' 'Don't eat your brain.' 'Don't eat your heart'" (and so on), closing his list with an allusion to the Pythagorean prohibition on eating beans and some mockery of Pythagorean reincarnation and vegetarianism.[54]

The comedy continues, with a rhythm that can be sensed as much in the Latin as in translation (11): "If I weren't afraid of the jeering that I think is already starting to bubble forth, I'd have something else to relate. Well, I'll relate it anyway. You can laugh if you feel like it."[55] The two stories that Poliziano then relates concern legends about Pythagoras's taming of wild animals, which are worth quoting extensively (11–12):

> He used to teach animals, wild ones as well as tame. Of course, one remembers that there was a certain Daunian bear. Awesome in its size, the bear was terrifying in its savagery and was a bitter plague on bulls and men. This man (if indeed he was only a man) called to it soothingly. He petted it with his hand, had it in his home for a while, and fed it bread and apples. Soon thereafter he sent the bear away, making it swear that it wouldn't touch any other animal after that moment. And the bear went tamely into its mountains and forests. Thereafter, it didn't injure a single other animal.
>
> Don't you want to hear about the bull? He saw the bull of Taranto once by chance in a pasture as it was munching away, stripping off the greens from a bean field. He called the herdsman over to tell him to inform the bull not to eat that stuff. The herdsman said, "But I don't speak bull. If you do, you'll do a better job of it." Without delay, He Himself went right up to the bull and talked to him for a minute, right in his ear. He ordered the bull not to eat any bean-like food, not only now but forever. And so that bull of Taranto grew old in the temple of Juno. He was thought to be holy, and he customarily fed on human food that the happy crowd gave him.[56]

---

54. "'Ignem,' aiebat, 'gladio ne fodicato.' 'Stateram ne transilito.' 'Cerebrum ne comedito.' 'Cor etiam ne comedito'" (Celenza 2010: 9).

55. "Ni cachinnos metuam qui iam clanculum, puto, ebulliunt, habeo aliud quoque quod narrem. Sed narrabo tamen. Vos, ut lubet, ridetote" (Celenza 2010: 11).

56. "Bestias docebat, tam feras quam cicures. Et sane ursa Daunia quaedam fuisse memoratur, magnitudine horribili, feritate formidabili, pestis acerba bovum atque hominum. Hanc ad se hic vir (si modo Ipse erat vir) blande vocavit, manu permulsit, domi habuit aliquandiu, pane aluit et pomis. Mox dimisit, adiurans ne quod animal post id attingeret. Illa vero in montes suos et silvas abiit mitis, nec animantium deinde obfuit cuiquam.Vultisne etiam de bove audire? Bovem Tarenti in agro quodam pascuo forte conspicatus, viridem adhuc fabaciam segetem morsu truncantem, rogavit bubulcum moneret bovem suum ne illam depasceretur. Huic bubulcus illudens: 'Atqui,' inquit, 'bovatim loqui nescio. Tute, si scis, potius moneto.' Non cunctatus, Ipse accessit propius, et in aurem bovi illi diutule locutus, impetravit non modo ut in praesens sed ut etiam in perpetuum pabulo fabacio abstineret. Itaque bos ille Tarenti deinde molliter consenuit, in Iunonis fano sacer habitus cibisque hominum vesci solitus quos illi obvia turba offerebat" (Celenza 2010: 11–12).

These traditional attributes of Pythagoras, as well as the miraculous tales, would have struck chords in Poliziano's Florence. There is, first, the satirizing of his friend and friendly rival for cultural capital in Florence, Marsilio Ficino (1433–99).[57] Ficino had done much to make a certain variety of esoteric Platonism appealing to Florence's ruling elite in the 1460s and 1470s; in this "Platonism" Pythagoras was seen as one among many mystically important links in the chain of eternally evolving wisdom.[58] Yet during that time and after, there were other figures on Florence's cultural landscape, all of them competing for prominence and recognition. In 1473, for example, Lorenzo "the Magnificent" de' Medici had refounded the Florentine University, hiring among others a good number of Aristotelian scholars for the arts faculty (some of whom would be Poliziano's later antagonists).[59] The 1480s saw the emergence also of Pico della Mirandola, who hoped in 1486 to have a public open forum in Rome to debate nine hundred propositions related to religion and philosophy, many of them drawn from esoteric sources, the late ancient Platonic tradition, and the Cabala.[60] His hopes were dashed when Pope Innocent VIII found thirteen of them heretical, and the projected disputation was cancelled. After this event, Pico, previously Ficino's fellow traveler down esoteric byways, was chastened, finding solace in Aristotelian metaphysics and eventually, like many of Ficino's former followers (including Poliziano) becoming a follower of Girolamo Savonarola in the early 1490s.[61]

During this period, the 1480s and early 1490s, Ficino's Platonism grew ever more esoteric. He brought to the task of interpreting Plato a wide range of texts, including a number of late ancient Platonic ones, such as the *Lives* of Pythagoras by Porphyry and Iamblichus as well as Iamblichus's *Protrepticus*, which contain among other things the stories to which Poliziano alludes.[62] These and other similar Greek texts, lost to the west in the middle ages, presented mentalities that shared a family resemblance to Christianity. Miraculous wonder-working figures sent by the divine to aid humanity, the power of ritual to function almost sacramentally, parable-like approaches to wisdom: these and more features were shared both by members of the late ancient pagan tradition and by early Christians, visceral enemies though they might have been. Ficino's openness to esoteric styles of thought, within

---

57. See Kraye 2002.
58. See Hankins 1990: 1.265–366; Gentile 2002; Celenza 2007.
59. See Hankins 2003–4: 2.273–316.
60. See most recently Farmer 1998; Garfagnini 1997; Granada 2002.
61. See Polizzotto 1994: 100–17; Weinstein 1970: 185–226.
62. See Gentile 1990; Celenza 2002; for context and recent bibliography Celenza 2007.

which Pythagoras could indeed be seen as a wonder-working sage, was coming increasingly under suspicion in the early 1490s.

The two Pythagorean miracles that Poliziano reports represent criticisms that go well beyond Ficino and are directed at the perils of institutionalized learning. The first story, that of the meat-eating bear whom Pythagoras tames, represents the tendency of organized learning, and overbearing teachers in particular, to take away the natural energies, the spirit, of students. Once indoctrinated, like the formerly aggressive bear, they are tamed, happy not with bigger prey but with small, comfortable portions.

The second story, that of the bull of Taranto, has a similar resonance. Pythagoras persuades the bull not to do what comes naturally: eating the greens off of bean-plants. The bull ceases to act in accord with its natural inclinations, is venerated, and is thereafter able to live a life of relative leisure, as people, impressed by the bull's singularity, take care of it and feed it. Here it is difficult not to imagine that Poliziano was thinking of the vanity of the philosophy professors who had criticized him. They have ceased, in his view, to do what to Poliziano seems natural for a figure of intellectual integrity: reading widely, never excluding a text from consideration just because it is not part of a curriculum or established canon. Nevertheless, these figures actually achieve the veneration of students and an easy lifestyle, never needing to work authentically again. They gain a respectability they do not really deserve, as well as a kind of security; it is a security, however, that is precarious, as Poliziano argues in the fable that concludes the *Lamia*.

Poliziano is not done yet with Pythagoras, however, and the following section of his treatise displays a remarkable turnabout. Poliziano evinces a dialogical tendency in the *Lamia* to have the treatise keep turning in on itself, making it a worthy predecessor in that respect of Erasmus's *Praise of Folly*.[63] Poliziano, in retailing the origins of the word "philosopher," eventually accords a remarkable level of dignity to the figure of Pythagoras, which is surprising, given that Poliziano begins this section by describing Pythagoras as not only a (13) "professor" but as a "salesman . . . of such a revolting kind of wisdom."[64] The tone changes immediately thereafter, and though Poliziano's immediate source is Cicero's *Tusculan Disputations*, he goes beyond Cicero, moving eventually from Pythagoras to Plato, who, like Pythagoras, will go unnamed.

Poliziano's unwillingness overtly to name these two foundational figures,

---

63. Erasmus knew and cited Poliziano's *Lamia* (as an example of personification) in *De rerum copia commenatarius secundus*, in Erasmus, *Opera omnia* (Amsterdam, 1969–), 1.6.208, line 297, as cited in Wesseling 2002: 112, n108.

64. "Hic igitur Ipse, tam portentosae sapientiae professor ac venditator . . . " (Celenza 2010: 13).

Pythagoras and Plato, tells us something significant: Poliziano is emphasizing that the enterprise of philosophy (whatever the outward name) stands above any one individual. In addition, in an era before formal, eighteenth-century style histories of philosophy (in the manner of Johann Jakob Brucker), there were various ways to discuss the history of philosophy, or better, the various byways that the search for wisdom had embodied.[65] The *Lamia*, with its use of fable and myth and its nameless mentioning of Pythagoras and Plato, represents perfectly one genre of this style of thought: not a "formal" history of philosophy, since that sort of thing did not exist in the fifteenth century, it is instead a dialogical reflection on the search for wisdom. Pythagoras had his part to play.

After the sage from Samos invented the word "philosopher," having been asked what sort of man he was by Leon of Phlias, he went on, in Poliziano's retelling, to say that human life was like a festival (*mercatus*, which also has connotations of a marketplace), where people came to have contact with one another, to see and be seen, and to interest others in what they had to offer. One saw all types there, from discus-throwers to weightlifters, long-jumpers to wrestlers, tightrope walkers to lying poets (13–14). All sorts of people are present at the festival-marketplace competing for recognition, but there is one type of person who is set apart (15): "Afterward, he [Pythagoras] said, other more liberally educated people came together to those games to see places and contemplate unknown men, techniques, and talents, as well as the noblest artisans' works."[66] These true philosophers are essentially observers, (16) "eager to look at the most beautiful things, who gaze upon this heaven, and on the sun and the moon and the choruses of stars."[67] The ordering of the heavens possesses an originary beauty (16) "because of its participation in that which is the first intelligible thing, what He Himself understood as the nature of numbers and reasons."[68] Iamblichus, Poliziano's source here, uses a word for "participation" (the Greek *metousia*, which Poliziano renders with "participatus") that became popular in the late ancient commentary

---

65. For background and bibliography on the historiography of philosophy, see Celenza 2005; Celenza 2010; Catana 2005 and 2008.

66. "Postremo alios liberalius institutos coire ad ludos eos, aiebat, ut loca viserent, ut ignotos homines artesque et ingenia et nobilissimorum opera artificum contemplarentur" (Celenza 2010: 15).

67. "Sed inter omnis praecellere tamen eos et esse quam honestissimos qui rerum pulcherrimarum speculatione contenti sint, coelumque hoc spectent solemque et lunam et siderum choros . . . " (Celenza 2010: 16). Though Poliziano's most proximate source here is Iamblichus's *On the Pythagorean Life*, his astronomically-oriented comments would have taken on even more resonance given the two major Aratus-inflected poems by the "astronomicus poeta" Lorenzo Buonincontri (1410–c. 1491) on natural philosophy, one of which had been dedicated to Lorenzo de' Medici; for an expert edition of these works, see Buonincontri 1999.

68. "Qui tamen ordo pulchritudinem habeat ex illius participatu quod intellegibile primum sit, quodque Ipse numerorum rationumque naturam interpretabatur . . . " (Celenza 2010: 16).

tradition to reflect the general sense of participation's importance in Platonic philosophy: phenomenological things are "good" or "beautiful" in so far as they "participate" in what is eternally good or beautiful.[69] Here Poliziano, like Iamblichus, indicates that this sense of participation's importance is precisely what Pythagoras perceived when he said that number was the root of all things (16). It is a special type of knowledge whose possessors recognize and embrace the inner connectedness of all things, and the person pursuing this type of knowledge is the authentic philosopher.

Who is wise? In antiquity once, even experts in crafts could be thought of as wise. Then, however, there came a (17) "tall-shouldered" old man, whom people thought "full of Apollo." Without naming him, Poliziano thus brings Plato into the discussion, reported in various sources to have been physically large.[70] Poliziano takes as his point of departure the pseudo-Platonic *Epinomis*, where after running through crafts and expertises from flour-making to generalship, the interlocutors arrive at the importance of numbers. Once one understood the generative nature of number, one could understand astronomy, since the courses of the heavenly bodies represent nature's most perfect manifestation of number in action. Poliziano continues in his sequence of naming the various arts as he follows, alludes to, and reimagines the *Epinomis*. Geometry is necessary, since it shows us (19) "the likeness of numbers . . . progressing from planes to solids," which then allows one to discern "the harmonic ratios from which the entire science of sounds is brought about."[71]

The next step in the sequence is to place dialectic and rhetoric. The old Athenian man (Plato) (20) "also used to say that, first of all, that art by which the true was distinguished from the false was necessary, since it is the art by which lies are refuted. In the same way, on the contrary, that busiest of vanities is the art that does not follow this skill, but simulates it and belies its true color by means of trickery."[72] Dialectic, then, is necessary, whereas empty rhetoric should be shunned.

69. The *loci classici* are Plato, *Phaedo* 100c (where the verbal form is "*metechein*"), *Republic* 476a (where the interlocutors speak of a "*koinonia*"—a sharing, or holding in common between the phenomenological world and the world of Being), and *Parmenides* 133a (where the main verbal form is "*metalambanein*" and where the theory of participation is subject to refutation). For the late ancient usage of "metousia" see Liddell, Scott and Jones 1996 s.v. "metousia," II.

70. See Sen., *Ep. Mor.*, 58.30; Apul., *De Plat.*, 1.1; Diog. Laert., *Vit. Phil.*, 3.4; Olypiodorus, *Vita Plat.*, 2. Ficino, in his own *Life of Plato* (in Ficino's *Letters,* book four [Ficino 2000a: 764]), described Plato as "most impressive and robust of body."

71. "[geometria] . . . in qua numerorum similitudo conspicitur, a planis ad solida progrediens, ubi ratae cernuntur rationes, ex quibus tota sonorum scientia conflatur" (Celenza 2010: 19).

72. "Illam tamen in primis necessariam esse artem qua verum a falso dignoscitur. Mendacium refutatur, sicuti e diverso, esse occupatissimam vanitatem quae artificium hoc non sequitur sed simulat, verumque colorem fuco mentitur" (Celenza 2010: 20).

Here one sees the superficial convergence of opinion among Poliziano, his friend and colleague Pico, and Marsilio Ficino, refracted through the mirror of a close reading of a (pseudo-) Platonic dialogue. Their views, however, were different. Ficino understood dialectic in a Platonic fashion, as part and parcel of the philosopher's duty to raise himself up ontologically. Dividing and resolving terms and arguments represented a way to train the mind to realize the true unity in all things, so that one ultimately realized the divine love pervading the universe.[73] Poliziano's vision was different. As he reveals later in the *Lamia*, he understood dialectic as basic logical training that revealed language's thorny underlying structure. As such dialectic was absolutely necessary if language was to be correctly understood, and it pertained integrally to the basic competencies of the *grammaticus*.

Poliziano continues to paint his portrait of the ideal philosopher, for whom not only training is necessary but also good character. An ideal philosopher will have been born from a "consecrated marriage" and thus be both "well born" and "liberally educated" (22). A philosopher, preferably, realizes that the search for truth is like a hunt, so that at its best philosophy will be a social enterprise. The old Athenian man "used to say that the very same person who is zealously looking for truth wants to have as many allies and helpmates as possible for that same pursuit. . . . "[74] Here Poliziano refracts his own experience in his extended intellectual community, of himself, Pico, Barbaro, and others.

True philosophers, to continue with Poliziano's description of these exemplary figures, will also possess one distinguishing sign, whatever their differences: they are lovers of truth and haters of lying, even if it is permitted to the philosopher occasionally to feign ignorance of a specific point, as did Socrates, in order all the better to draw the truth out of his fellow philosophers (25). Uninterested in financial gain, true philosophers will also be unconcerned with the business of others. Poliziano alludes to yet another fable, which he attributes to Aesop, of a man with two bags. Each is full of vices, and one hangs from the front of his body, the other from the back. Poliziano adds: "would that these bags were turned around sometime, so that every man could scrutinize his own vices and not those of others!"[75]

---

73. One could not, for Ficino, teach this Promethean discipline to young minds not yet ethically ready for the explosive possibilities it contained. As Ficino wrote in his commentary to Plato's dialogue *Philebus*, Plato "shows that [dialectic] must not be given to adolescents because they are led by it into three vices: pride, lewdness, impiety. For when they first taste the ingenious subtlety of arguing, it is as if they have come upon a tyrannous power of rebutting and refuting the rest of us" (Ficino 2000b: 230). In general on dialectic see Allen 1998.

74. "Porro hunc et ipsum veritatis indagandae studiosum esse et habere quam plurimos eiusdem studii socios adiutoresque velle . . . " (Celenza 2010: 24).

75. "Atque utinam obverterentur aliquando hae manticae, ut sua quisque intueri vitia posset,

Listening carefully to Poliziano's list of all of the authentic philosopher's attributes, one learns something crucial, which Poliziano himself articulates as he sums up his own arguments: persons such as these are exceedingly unusual to find. They are, Poliziano tells us, echoing Juvenal's seventh satire, rarer than white ravens.[76] Poliziano even tells his listeners that he himself doesn't measure up (28): "After all, I have only barely come in contact with those disciplines that mark the philosopher's competence, and I am just about as far as can be from those morals and virtues that I mentioned."[77] Through this entire section describing the ideal philosopher, Poliziano engages in a delicate back and forth. As Nietzsche would do much later, Poliziano marks the fact that the enterprise of wisdom-seeking can be seen to have changed radically in the generation of Socrates, a direction then continued and solidified by Plato, the "tall-shouldered" Athenian (17): "Now, once, in the ancient era, men were customarily called wise who cultivated even the mechanical crafts."[78] Yet, as Poliziano moves on, it becomes ever clearer that this idealized philosopher is no bad thing . . . on the level of the ideal. The problem is that it is well nigh impossible to find anyone who measures up to the ideal.

Having used one method of approach to define the ideal attributes of the philosopher, Poliziano moves on to ask whether it would be a bad thing if he himself were a philosopher (which he concedes he is not; 29). To answer that question, he cites ancient incidents in which philosophers were banned from cities or condemned, and then he mentions respectable ancient figures who mistrusted philosophy (29–32). Even still, condemnation proves nothing, as different people have different tastes; so Poliziano moves on to a more positive account of philosophy's benefits, still echoing Iamblichus's *Protrepticus*. Poliziano suggests that one cannot live well without philosophizing, since philosophizing is living according to the virtue of the soul, a process that allows us to use our possessions wisely, in a way that reflects the power of human reason to gain knowledge (37).

It is true that philosophy can seem difficult, and yet: "wherever you are, the truth is right there."[79] Truth can be found anywhere, and the love of wisdom and the hunt for truth can always be pursued. The real problem, again, is a lack of self-knowledge, "For philosophy presses her favors on those

---

aliena non posset!" (Celenza 2010: 27).

76. Juvenal, *Sat.*, 7.202, and Wesseling in Poliziano 1986: 62.

77. " . . . nam et disciplinas illas vix attigi quae philosopho competunt, et ab his quos dixi moribus ac virtutibus absum longissime" (Celenza 2010: 28).

78. "Olim autem, apud saeculum priscum, sapientes appellari consueverant etiam qui sellularias quasdam callebant artes . . . " (Celenza 2010: 17).

79. "Ubi ubi enim fueris, praesto erit veritas" (Celenza 2010: 41).

who are awake, not sleeping."[80] The notion that philosophy was for those who were "awake" recalls Poliziano's earlier praise of Pico in the *Miscellanea* of 1489, where he had named Pico as his real stimulus to philosophy. Pico, Poliziano had written, "trained me to look at philosophy with eyes that were not sleepy, as they were before, but rather that were alive and awake, as if he were giving me life with his voice serving as a kind of battle-trumpet."[81]

Poliziano goes on: "we are so laughable that, for the sake of the lowest form of greed, we go beyond the pillars of Hercules, as far as the Indies, whereas to achieve the mission of philosophy, we are not prepared to shoulder the burden of even a few wakeful hours, not even in winter."[82] Yet for Poliziano philosophy itself offers us the ability to gain knowledge, something which all seek and the lack of which induces fear in everyone (43–48). It is our soul, that "tiny bit of divine breath" in us, that is truly worthy of extended meditation, since it alone is divine.[83] Pecuniary advantages are few for someone who practices this intense study of the soul, Poliziano admits. Yet those who are seeking financial gain really do not understand what philosophy is about (50–51).

Again, Poliziano's delicate examination probes positively and negatively all at once. Hindsight allows us to see him anticipating the Ludwig Wittgenstein of the *Philosophical Investigations,* who wrote there that philosophy cannot interfere in the use of language, cannot offer language any real foundation, and ultimately "leaves everything the way it is," including mathematics.[84] Much later in the history of philosophy, in other words, Wittgenstein would come to the conclusion that philosophy was in no way like a natural science. Practitioners of philosophy could observe, but their discipline had no active effect on the world.

Poliziano is not so pessimistic. He had not, of course, lived through

---

80. "Vigilantibus enim se, non dormientibus ingerit" (Celenza 2010: 42).

81. "Is [i.e., Picus] igitur continuo me, cum quo partiri curas dulcissimas et nugari suaviter interdum solet, et quem sibi studiorum prope assiduum comitem (qui summus honor) adlegit, is me instituit ad philosophiam, non, ut antea, somniculosis, sed vegetis vigilantibusque oculis explorandum, quasi quodam suae vocis animare classico" (Poliziano 1498: K iii[r]).

82. "Nos autem ita ridiculi sumus ut vilissimae aeruginis gratia etiam trans Herculis columnas, etiam ad Indos navigemus, philosophiam vero ut adipiscamur ne per hyemem quidem vigilias saltem pauculas toleramus" (Celenza 2010: 42).

83. "Nihil igitur in rebus humanis studio curaque dignum praeter illam quam pulchre vocat Horatius 'divinae particulam aurae,' quae facit ut in hoc caeco rerum turbine tamen vita hominum tuto gubernetur" (Celenza 2010: 49). Poliziano's allusion is to Horace, *Serm.*, 2.2.77–79.

84. Cf. Wittgenstein 1963, sec. 124: "Die Philosophie darf den tatsächlichen Gebrauch der Sprache in keiner Weise antasten, sie kann ihn am Ende also nur beschreiben. Denn sie kann ihn auch nicht begründen. Sie läßt alles wie es ist. Sie läßt auch die Mathematik wie sie ist, und keine mathematische Entdeckung kann sie weiterbringen. Ein 'führendes Problem der mathematischen Logik' ist für uns ein Problem der Mathematik, wie jedes andere."

the death of metaphysics that marked late nineteenth-century thought. Yet Poliziano, a thinker intensely interested, as was Wittgenstein, in problems of language, phrases the mission of philosophy as observational, not active: "I mean, philosophy doesn't *do* anything. It only frees one for contemplation. So be it. Philosophy, nevertheless, will show each the right way to do his duty."[85] This language-oriented strain of the history of philosophy leads its practitioners to the conclusion that philosophy is not something that can be as definitive in its conclusions as a natural science; it cannot serve as a "handmaiden" of science. It can, instead, serve an ethically therapeutic function.

For Poliziano true philosophy allows people, through intense self-examination, to understand their duty. Philosophy, again, is like sight: "although sight itself does not perform any work, it none the less points to and judges each type of work. . . . "[86] The practice of philosophy is like an Aristotelian virtue: a *hexis* or *habitus*, that is, an inborn capacity that all possess but that one can only bring from potentiality to actuality by repeated practice. And as Aristotle had noted at the outset of his *Nicomachean Ethics*, this fundamentally ethical, practice-oriented variety of philosophy does not allow the same sort of precision as do the other branches.[87] The philosopher, Poliziano goes on, does not respect traditional social categorization. He will laugh at people who take excessive pride in the amount of land they own, or who vaunt their nobility and ancestry: " . . . there is no king not born from slaves and no slave who does not have kings as ancestors."[88]

To sum up his portrait of the authentic philosopher, Poliziano retells the Platonic myth of the cave. He does not use what might seem the standard source, Plato's *Republic* (7.514a–517c). Instead Poliziano informs his audience that he will bring before them (58) "the most elegant image of that Platonist, Iamblichus, whom the consensus of ancient Greece is accustomed to call 'most divine.'"[89] This choice on Poliziano's part is noteworthy for at least three reasons. First, Poliziano has before him Iamblichus's *Protrepticus*, a text from which he had drawn the lion's share of the Pythagorean sayings of which he had earlier made sport. Second, again one sees the shapes of

---

85. "At nihil agit philosophia, tantum contemplationi vacat. Esto, modum tamen cuiusque praescribit officio" (Celenza 2010: 51).

86. "Sic autem et visus in corpore, quanquam ipse opus nullum peragit, dum tamen aut indicat unumquodque aut iudicat . . . " (Celenza 2010: 51).

87. Aristotle, *Eth. Nic.*, 1.3.1094b11–1095a13.

88. "Cum sciat . . . nec esse regem quemquam qui non sit e servis natus nec item servum cui non origo sint reges" (Celenza 2010: 57).

89. "Sed imaginem volo vobis elegantissimam referre Iamblichi illius Platonici, quem veteris Graeciae consensus vocare divinissimum solet" (Celenza 2010: 58).

Florentine intellectual life emerging before one's eyes, as this text, the *Protrepticus* of Iamblichus, was important to Ficino.[90] Third, Poliziano is intent on using a recondite source of which many of his targets (the "philosophers" teaching at the Florentine university) would most likely have been unaware.

The story's details are not significantly different from those in the *Republic*.[91] There are those who live bound in a cave. Outside a great fire burns, and in between the fire and the entrance of the cave, there is, adjoining a wall, a road that others traverse, carrying utensils and images of various animate beings. The things being conveyed are above the wall and their shadows, cast by the fire, can be seen by the cave dwellers. Since they are bound, the cave dwellers cannot see themselves or their fellow inhabitants, and they assume that those shadow-images represent reality. If one of them were freed from his chains and compelled to go up and out to see the world beyond the cave, he would be incredulous. The long force of habit would compel him to think that the experience closest to him, remote from reality as it might be, itself represented reality. He will experience perforce much new data, given his newly liberated condition. Even still, he will long for the comfort and familiarity of the cave, of his chains.

Little by little the now liberated cave dweller will realize that he is experiencing a more authentic, if less familiar reality, and "he will pity the lot of his companions, whom he left in such evils."[92] Still, this level of possible habituation to a better life will be difficult to attain depending on the conditions in the cave:

> However, let us say that back in the cave they had been accustomed to offering praise, prizes, and honors to those who made more precise observations about the images or to those who remembered with greater facility what, from these images, came along earlier, what later, and what at the same time, or again who almost predicted what would come next. If all this were the case, do we think it would ever happen that our friend would want those honors, praises, or prizes? Do we think, finally, that he would envy those who had pursued them? I don't think so.[93]

---

90. See Celenza 1999 and 2002.
91. Poliziano recounts the tale at *Lamia,* 58–66.
92. " . . . dolebitque vicem sociorum, quos in tantis reliquerit malis" (Celenza 2010: 64).
93. "Quod si etiam in spelunca laudari praemiisque affici et honoribus consuevissent quicumque simulacra illa acutius viderent, aut qui facilius meminissent quae priora ex his, quae posteriora, quaeve simul excucurrissent, aut item qui quasi addivinarent quae proxime subitura his forent, an eventurum putamus unquam ut honores illos, ut laudes, ut praemia noster iste concupisceret, aut his denique invideret qui consecuti illa fuissent? Non puto . . . " (Celenza 2010: 65).

That is, if those who are living in the cave (we can easily substitute "university enfranchised intellectuals") reward each other for pursuing what Thomas Kuhn would have called "normal science" and offer no inducements to think fundamentally differently about the patterned and secure life to which they are habituated, the cave dweller has few incentives to leave the cave.[94] What happens if the liberated cave dweller then returns to be among people of this sort? Poliziano continues:

> But let us say the status quo were restored and the same man returns to that unpleasant and blind home. Won't he see poorly, now that he has come from the sun into the darkness? Is it not the case, perhaps, that if a contest were held there, someone who sees the shadows of all things most acutely will triumph over our friend? Is it not the case that our friend will then become an object of ridicule to all, to such a point that, with one voice, all of those who were bound in chains would cry out that their colleague, who had come back to the cave, was blind and that it was dangerous to go outside? And so, if anyone tried to release anyone else ever again and lead him to the light, he (whoever it might be) would resist hand and foot and, if he could, would attack their eyes with his fingernails.[95]

The habitual self-selection that intellectuals in groups often pursue becomes, in Poliziano's reading, a brake on innovative thinking, it engenders resistance to new and unfamiliar sources of wisdom, and it represents nothing so much as the cancellation of individual human identity. Poliziano is careful to say that, once habituated to the comforts of the cave, anyone ("whoever it might be"—"quisquis fuerit") will succumb to its easy coziness. Engaging one's human individuality means occasionally defamiliarizing oneself with one's background by taking an untrodden path. For a philosophically inclined scholar this process entails a willingness to read noncanonical sources and, in modern terms, to cross disciplines.

This crossing of disciplines is precisely that to which the lamias, according to Poliziano, object. Poliziano takes for granted that his audience will understand his message of the myth of the cave in his retelling, to wit, that

---

94. See Kuhn 1996: 10–51.

95. "Verum redeat iam hic idem, quasi postliminio, ad illam ipsam sedem inamoenam et caecam, nonne ipse iam caecutiet a sole profectus in tenebras? Nonne si certamen forte ibi ponatur quis omnium acutissime umbras easdem cernat, superabitur hic noster et erit omnibus deridiculo, sic ut uno ore vincti illi clament caecum revertisse in speluncam socium, periculosumque esse iter foras? Tum si qui solvere iterum aliquem ex ipsis tentent atque ad lucem producere, resistat ille scilicet, quisquis fuerit, manibus ac pedibus et trahentium sese etiam, si possit, in oculos involet unguibus" (Celenza 2010: 66).

the cave-dwellers represent "the crowd and the uneducated, whereas that free man, liberated from his chains and in the daylight, is the very philosopher about whom we have been speaking for a time." Poliziano goes on: "I wish I were he!"[96] Poliziano's subtle ironic sensibility is foregrounded here. After he has finished enumerating all of the benefits of philosophy and the characteristics of the authentic philosopher, he avers that he could never claim to be a philosopher. Who, indeed, could possess all of those qualities? Poliziano seems to defend the ideal mission of philosophy and to endorse all the qualities that an ideal philosopher should possess, even as he implies strongly that such a figure cannot in reality be found.

It is unsurprising that among Poliziano's scholarly projects had been a translation of Epictetus's *Encheiridion*, the *Handbook* of Stoic philosophy.[97] For the Stoics, the notion of the sage was an ideal. According to Zeno, the sage (the *sophos* or *spoudaios*), lived *homologoumenōs,* which is to say in a state of perfect coherence, matching his own reason with the universal reason permeating the universe. The sage, in this ideal sense, might not even exist.[98] The *philosopher* was someone who trained himself to achieve that ideal, whose relentless self-scrutiny provided a way of life that might, indeed, stand in contrast to what he saw around him, but would nevertheless better serve the purpose of living coherently.

These Stoic sensibilities manifest themselves decisively in Poliziano's *Lamia*. He has gone through all the positive aspects of philosophy. Now he states his opponents' core objection: in their view, his decision to switch disciplines and teach Aristotle seems unwarranted, since he knows nothing about philosophy (68). Poliziano brings his opponents' opinions into the treatise by putting a speech into their mouths (ibid.): " . . . for three years now you've been calling yourself a philosopher, even though you had never before paid any attention to philosophy. This is the reason we also called you a 'trifler,' since for a time you have been teaching things you don't know and never learned."[99]

---

96. "Nunc illud tantum admonebo: vinctos in tenebris homines nullos esse alios quam vulgus et ineruditos, liberum autem illum clara in luce et exemptum vinculis, hunc esse ipsum philosophum de quo iamdiu loquimur. Atque utinam is ego essem!" (Celenza 2010: 67).

97. Epictetus's *Encheiridion* had been cobbled together from Epictetus's *Discourses*, themselves gathered by a faithful disciple, Arrian of Nicomedia, in the second century c.e. See Hadot 1998: 59–66. For Poliziano's 1479 defense of Epictetus, see his letter to Scala in Garin 1952: 912–25; his translation is in Poliziano 1498: S i(r)–S viii(v).

98. Hadot 1998: 73–77.

99. "'Sed illud indignabamur, facere te (ne graviore utamur verbo) subarroganter, qui triennio iam philosophum te profitearis ac nunquam scilicet ante id tempus operam philosophiae dederis. Ob id enim 'nugatorem' quoque te diximus, quod illa diu iam doceas quae nescias, quae non didiceris'" (Celenza 2010: 68).

Poliziano addresses his critics by highlighting the notion that he has never in fact called himself a philosopher. His self-identification is quite different, he avers, and herein lies Poliziano's most cogent statement of the mission of the *grammaticus*. One can observe Poliziano extending the traditional province of the *grammaticus* to include all disciplines, and in the end to be representative of the only true way of seeking wisdom. The *grammaticus*, the "philologist," in Poliziano's telling, becomes the true "philosopher," even if he abjures the title, believing as he does that it has been irremediably corrupted by its practitioners, who have allowed themselves to slide into intellectual complacency.

It may seem to be a leap to translate Poliziano's "grammaticus" as "philologist," yet the translation seems justified, given the modern resonances of the words "grammarian" and "philologist." A bit later in the treatise he distinguishes the word *grammaticus* from *grammatista*, leaning on Quintilian and Suetonius's *De grammaticis et rhetoribus* (70–71).[100] The latter word, *grammatista*, is the word properly used to denote either an elementary grammar teacher or someone who has not yet attained the level of the *grammaticus*. Second, and more important, is Poliziano's description of the *grammaticus:* philologists do it all. The result of their practice (their reading habits, in other words) is that "they examine and explain in detail every category of writers—poets, historians, orators, philosophers, medical doctors, and jurisconsults" (71). Mordantly, he continues: "Our age, knowing little about antiquity, has fenced the philologist in, within an exceedingly small circle. But among the ancients, once, this class of men had so much authority that philologists alone were the censors and critics of all writers."[101]

Poliziano's opinion is that ancient *grammatici* were ultimately responsible for ordering the knowledge that written culture embodied, and he cites a passage from Quintilian to make this point:

> It was on this account that philologists were called "critics," so that (and this is what Quintilian says) "they allowed themselves the liberty not only of annotating verses with a censorious mark in the text, but also of removing as noncanonical books which appeared to be falsely written, as if they were illegitimate members of the family. Indeed they even allowed themselves to

---

100. See Quintilian, 1.4.1–5; Suet. *De grammaticis et rhetoribus,* 4; and Wesseling in Poliziano 1986: 102.

101. "Grammaticorum enim sunt hae partes, ut omne scriptorum genus, poetas, historicos, oratores, philosophos, medicos, iureconsultos excutiant atque enarrent. Nostra aetas, parum perita rerum veterum, nimis brevi gyro grammaticum sepsit. At apud antiquos olim tantum auctoritatis hic ordo habuit ut censores essent et iudices scriptorum omnium soli grammatici . . . " (Celenza 2010: 71). For an examination of this passage, see Bravo 2006: 141–42.

categorize those authors that they deemed worthy or even to remove some all together."[102] For "grammatikos" (philologist) in Greek means nothing other than "litteratus" in Latin.[103]

Poliziano's passion for dialectic becomes more understandable. It is owed not only to a desire for recognition in the intellectual economy of the Florentine university world. It is also related to his belief about the proper function of the *grammaticus:* the *grammaticus* is a canon-maker whose main obligation is to sort through knowledge, to divide the diverse expressions of human wisdom into categories, and to delineate the "families" in which so many different varieties of human intellectual activity properly belong. Philology becomes the regulative discipline *par excellence,* since those calling themselves "philosophers" simply do not possess the breadth of vision suitable to confront human intellectual activity in all of its variety.

Poliziano says that his age has "fenced in" the *grammaticus,* and indeed it is this "fencing in" to which Poliziano objects most determinedly.[104] He has, he tells his opponents, been commenting on texts of law and medicine for some time, yet no one thought he considered himself a jurist or medical doctor (73). Even still, his opponents continue in their criticism: "We admit that you are called a philologist and that, nonetheless, you are not also called a philosopher. How could you be a philosopher when you have had no teachers and have never even cracked open any books of this sort?"[105] Their most telling objection, for Poliziano, is his lack of some sanctioned affiliation. Who were his teachers? With whom did he study? What has he read?

To respond Poliziano uses the rhetorical device of the *praeteritio,* "passing over" the fact that he has not only been in close and intimate contact with "the most learned philosophers" (by which he must mean at least Argyropoulos, Ficino, and Pico; 75). He has also consulted numerous commentaries, including those of the Greeks, "who usually seem to me to be the

---

102. Poliziano is citing Quintilian, *Inst.,* 1.4.2–3.

103. " . . . quos ob id etiam criticos vocabant, sic ut non versus modo (ita enim Quintilianus ait) 'censoria quadam virgula notare, sed libros etiam qui falso viderentur inscripti tanquam subditicios submovere familia permiserint sibi, quin auctores etiam quos vellent aut in ordinem redigerent aut omnino eximerent numero.' Nec enim aliud grammaticus Graece quam Latine litteratus" (Celenza 2010: 71–72).

104. "Nostra aetas, parum perita rerum veterum, nimis brevi gyro grammaticum sepsit" (Celenza 2010: 71).

105. "'Euge,' inquiunt Lamiae, 'concedimus ut vocere grammaticus, non tamen ut et philosophus. Quomodo enim tu philosophus qui nec magistros habueris nec id genus unquam libros attigeris?'" (Celenza 2010: 74).

most outstanding of all learned men."[106] Poliziano refers immediately here to the late ancient Greek commentators on Aristotle, whom he had listed in an earlier *praelectio*. Yet, Poliziano's real question is: What does all of this—background, citations, and so on—really matter? Instead he wishes to be judged by what he has produced. Epictetus comes up again: "'Sheep who have been sent to pasture,' so says Epictetus the Stoic, 'don't boast to their shepherd in the evening just because they have fed on a lot of grass. No, they offer him the milk and wool that he needs.'[107] So too should no one proclaim how much he has learned. Instead, he should bring what he has learned forward."[108]

Poliziano wishes to be judged on what he has written and on the list of texts on which he has lectured publicly. He therefore offers an impressive list of authors: "Quite some time ago I lectured publicly on Aristotle's *Ethics*, and recently I lectured on Porphyry's *Isagoge*, the *Categories* of Aristotle himself along with the *Six Principles* of Gilbert of Poitiers, Aristotle's little book called *On Interpretation*, then (out of the usual order) the *Sophistical Refutations*, which is a work untouched by the others and almost inexplicable."[109] Poliziano, in short, has been delving not only into the *Ethics* but also into works of the logic canon. Porphyry's *Isagoge*, the "Introduction" to logic, was popular throughout the middle ages, after having been translated into Latin by Boethius in the early sixth century.[110]

Even more interesting is Poliziano's attention to the *Six Principles*, which he attributes to Gilbert of Poitiers (the standard attribution until the mid-twentieth century).[111] Gilbert (c.1085–1154), a highly respected member of the School of Chartres, had been accused of heresy in the twelfth century because of his positions on the Trinity, as these were expressed in his commentaries on Boethius's *De trinitate* and *De hebdomadibus*. Gilbert retracted

---

106. "Nec autem allegabo nunc vobis familiaritates quae mihi semper cum doctissimis fuere philosophis, non etiam extructa mihi ad tectum usque loculamenta veterum commentariorum praesertimque Graecorum, qui omnium mihi doctores prestantissimi videri solent" (Celenza 2010: 75).
107. Epictetus, *Encheiridion*, 46.
108. "'Oves,' inquit Stoicus Epictetus, 'in pascua dimissae minime apud pastorem suum gloriantur vespere multo se pastas gramine, sed lac ei affatim vellusque praebent.' Ita nec quisquam praedicare ipse debet quantum didicerit, sed quod didicerit afferre in medium" (Celenza 2010: 77).
109. "Quare, quoniam libros Aristotelis *De moribus* iampridem, proxime autem Porphyrii *Quinque voces* et Aristotelis eiusdem *Praedicamenta* cum *Sex* illis Gilberti Poretani *Principiis*, libellumque qui dicitur *Perihermenias*, tum velut extra ordinem *Sophisticos elenchos*, intactum ab aliis opus et pene inenodabile, sum publice interpretatus . . ." (Celenza 2010: 78).
110. See Porphyry 1998.
111. See Heysse 1953 for the text, and 3–5 for difficulty of attributing the text to Gilbert; Ebbesen, Fredborg, and Nielsen 1983; Gammersbach 1959: 28–29; a portrait of Gilbert's philosophy is in Rovighi 1956.

some of his views but remained admired as an authority on logic throughout the history of medieval and Renaissance philosophy. The *Liber de sex principiis* to which Poliziano refers was early on attributed to Gilbert; it had a long medieval history after its composition, finding its way on to a number of high and late medieval university curricula. The University of Paris allotted it the same amount of time as Aristotle's *Ethics,* and a number of well known medieval philosophers (including Walter Burley, Albert the Great, Thomas Aquinas, and John Buridan) commented on it.[112] The treatise had a reputation as a difficult text. John Buridan went so far as to say that its teachings were "strong enough to kill dogs," and that "those who were trapped by them had no more hope of escaping than fish caught in a net."[113]

Poliziano's interest is worth noting primarily because it forms a small part of a long medieval tradition. In the *Liber,* "Gilbert" studies Aristotle's ten ontological categories in a way that reduces them fundamentally. This move (to reduce Aristotle's ten categories in number, finding some under which others could be subsumed) found its best-known humanist expression in Lorenzo Valla's *Repastinatio totius dialectice.*[114] As earlier medieval attention to this issue indicates, the problem was an old one. Poliziano's *Lamia* can be seen as an independent contribution to a long-standing debate in which complaints can be heard about the rigidity of institutionalized approaches to seeking wisdom. The fact that Poliziano devoted significant attention to teaching this complicated text indicates that, like Valla, he attempted to understand Aristotelian philosophy on its own terms. Given the difficulty of the *Prior Analytics* (which, he says, he is now ready to interpret), Poliziano openly wonders how anyone can blame him if he relinquishes the name "philosopher" to others (79). More than the name, what concerns Poliziano is how to achieve the mission of philosophy, since names do not matter. Poliziano suggests that his critics can call him whatever they please: a *grammaticus,* a dilettante, or nothing at all (ibid.).[115] In effect, Poliziano has

---

112. See Wieland 1982: 659–60.

113. See Buridan 1983: 145. (Quaest. 18, 35–37: "Talia enim mihi apparent satis fortia ad interficiendum canes, et capti in eis non plus possunt evadere quam ex reti pisces.") See also ibid., 129 and 149. Buridan was a harsh critic; in his Commentary on Aristotle's *Physics,* he says that the author of the *Six principles* would have done better not to have written the book at all (In *VIII Physicorum libros* [Paris, 1509, repr. Frankfurt 1963], 3.q.13, f.55vb, cit. Schneider, at Buridan 1983: 149n15): "Ad auctoritatem auctoris *Sex principiorum* dico quod ut mihi videtur melius fuisset, quod numquam illum librum fecisset."

114. See Valla 1982: 44–55 and Nauta 2009.

115. "Qui quanquam libri spinosiores alicubi sunt et multis rerum verborumque difficultatibus involuti, tamen ob id eos etiam libentius, alacrius, animosius aggredior quod fere in omnibus gymnasiis a nostrae aetatis philosophis, non quia parum utiles, sed quia nimis scrupulosi, praetereuntur. Quis mihi igitur iure succenseat, si laborem hunc interpretandi difficillima quaeque sumpsero, nomen

transferred what the Stoics saw as the attributes of the sage—an ideal figure who cannot really be found in this world—to the "philosopher;" and he has transposed the Stoic meaning of "philosopher"—self-scrutinizing, unafraid to ask the question "Why?"—to the philologist.

The oration began with a fable, and Poliziano chooses to end his speech with another one (80). Again, birds come under discussion, and this time there is an interspecies confrontation: "Once, almost all the birds approached a night owl and asked her if, instead of nesting henceforth in holes in houses she might not rather nest in the branches of trees, among leaves, for merry-making is sweeter there."[116] They point out a newborn oak tree to the owl as a possible home. The owl demurs, maintaining that the tree will produce dangerous sap as it grows, within which the birds are likely to become entangled. The birds do not heed the owl's advice, and they realize only too late that the owl was right, as they become further entangled in the sap. As a result, birds ever since "admire her as wise, and they surround her in a dense throng, for the express purpose of learning something from her at some point." Yet they do this to no avail, Poliziano suggests. The treatise ends bitingly: "In fact, I think they do so sometimes to their greatest detriment, because those ancient night owls were *really* wise. Today, there are many night owls who, to be sure, possess the plumage, the eyes, and the perch. But they don't possess wisdom."[117] It is not too much of a leap to take the "owls" as the colleagues who criticized Poliziano, and the "birds" as the students who surround the professors. Again, however, the ideal figure of wisdom, here the owl, is absent from the contemporary world, like the Stoic sage, even though there are many who falsely lay claim to wisdom.

Poliziano's project in the *Lamia* is to reclaim the search for wisdom and to do it in the only way that is appropriate in the circumstances in which he finds himself: through philology. Throughout the *Lamia*, Poliziano makes a number of arguments in favor of this broad-based conception of philology. The arguments are implicit, as he shows his erudition by close readings of recondite sources that he then transforms into a lively, almost chatty Latin

---

vero aliis philosophi reliquero? Me enim vel grammaticum vocatote, vel, si hoc magis placet, philosophastrum, vel ne hoc ipsum quidem" (Celenza 2010: 79).

116. "Aves olim prope universae noctuam adierunt rogaruntque eam ne posthac in aedium cavis nidificaret, sed in arborum potius ramis atque inter frondes; ibi enim vernari suavius" (Celenza 2010: 81).

117. "Etenim consilii illius memores admirantur eam nunc ut sapientem stipantque densa caterva, ut videlicet ab ea sapere aliquando discant. Sed, opinor, frustra, immo vero etiam interdum cum magno ipsarum malo. Nam veteres illae noctuae revera sapientes erant; nunc multae noctuae sunt quae noctuarum quidem plumas habent et oculos et rostrum, sapientiam vero non habent" (Celenza 2010: 82).

idiom; and they are explicit, when he lists all the competencies to which philologists can and should lay claim, provided they are willing to accept the obligation of reading widely and never remaining content within the walls of an artificially constructed discipline.

Doing so, in conclusion, Poliziano wound up claiming for philology the very sorts of regulative, critical attributes that would be usurped by philosophy only in the eighteenth century. For Poliziano, the philologist was the *true* philosopher, since only the philologist could examine all evidence, be unimprisoned by disciplinary shackles, and go on to pass dispassionate judgment on the problems life presents. Poliziano made this case in a social context of give and take among humanists, from his interactions with his friend Pico and their epistolary exchanges with Barbaro to the more immediate circumstances of conflict at the Florentine university. The *Lamia*'s complex social and textual genealogies remind us that pre-modern intellectual discourse was as much social and involved with the search for distinction as it was intellectual, even as it impels us to look for "philosophy" in places we are not always expecting to find it.

CHAPTER 4

Philology and the Emblem

Bradley J. Nelson

My contention in these pages is that philology displays a surprising but close family resemblance to the early modern emblem. To be more precise: just as emblems are philological, so too is philology emblematic. In fact, it may be legitimate to ask which discourse exerts more genealogical influence on the other. In order to substantiate this claim, I follow a three-part argument. First, I consider an emblem from Juan de Borja's *Empresas morales* (1581) with an eye to the way Borja's reader is guided towards a performance of the presence of Spanish linguistic and cultural hegemony and universality.[1] In the second section, I comment on how the aesthetic and theological witticisms of sacramental theater in Baroque Spain enact a similar if not identical performance of presence. In the last act, I turn to a recent philological study of this theater, in the form of Ana Suárez Miramón's 2003 edition of Pedro Calderón de la Barca's *El gran mercado del mundo,* in which the editorial commentary configures a universalizing emblematization of both Calderón and seventeenth-century Counter Reformation ideology.

My argument rests on three suppositions: (1) that what is most often at stake in the theoretical definition and concrete deployment of both emblematic and philological practices is the performance of presence; (2) that the performance of presence comes into play in early modernity when power is both articulated and questioned; (3) that the best way to study the ideological functions of the emblem is to focus on those strategies that realize or

---

1. I cite from the 1680 edition.

block the performance of presence and the ideological power it constitutes.² This relationship between the performance of presence and ideological force is grounded in Hans Ulrich Gumbrecht's definition of power, which he offers as an alternative to the Foucauldian insistence on institutional and discursive power structures: "Unlike Foucault, I think that we miss what is distinctive about power as long as we use this notion within the Cartesian limits of the structures, production, and uses of knowledge. My counterproposal is to define power as the potential of occupying or blocking spaces with bodies."³

Gumbrecht's groundbreaking work on the ritual dramatization of presence in the Middle Ages informs his "anti-Cartesian" understanding of power, which makes it very useful for studying the ritualistic framing of words and images in early modernity.⁴ Following Jan Assmann's distinction between the *semantic* and the *material* sides of the linguistic sign, a distinction also found in early modern emblem theory in the division between a verbal *soul* and hieroglyphic *body*, I argue that the way emblematic structures block access to the material circumstances of their articulation represents a particularly potent form of power.⁵ This argument necessitates a certain *rapprochement* between Gumbrecht and Foucault in that the visual or emblematic sign is equated with Gumbrecht's understanding of the 'body,' a move permitted by early modern emblem theory. The exemplary case of a body/sign that becomes ritualistically saturated by presence is of course the sacramental body of Christ, which is germane to all of the literary artifacts considered here and which also lends a particularly clear illustration of Gumbrecht's concept of power. Finally, it also serves to show how Foucault's definition of power cannot leave the body behind, any more than Gumbrecht's could consider the body as completely distinct from the world of the sign. The movement between the two theories and semiotic variables is in fact analogous to the movement between presence and meaning.

Emblem, Philology, Emblematic Philology

We begin with the "canonical" tripartite definition of the emblem, in which an *inscriptio*, or titular motto (fragmentary soul), is combined with an equally

---

2. When I was revising this essay, my book, *The Persistence of Presence: Emblem and Ritual in Baroque Spain*, was in press; it covers some of the same issues in greater detail.
3. Gumbrecht 2003: 5.
4. See Gumbrecht 2004.
5. See Assmann 1994: 24. The landmark studies of José Antonio Maravall and Fernando R. de la Flor (Maravall 1972; R. de la Flor 1995) on the ideological power and conservative deployment of the emblem in Counter-Reformation culture are fundamental to the discussion to follow.

fragmentary visual image (body), and framed by a *subscriptio* (commentary) that guides the reader towards the solution of the verbal-visual enigma. According to emblem theorists, the meaning of the emblem is not found in any one component but rather arises from the combination of the three, wherein the whole is greater than the parts. Emblem theory thus draws the reader's attention away from the individual, material parts of the emblem, each of which could serve as an object of philological inquiry, in favor of a unifying meaning: it is, in other words, allegorical. The reason most often given for the enormous success of Andrea Alciato's *Emblematum liber*—the first and exemplary collection of emblems—is that "*Alciato* brought together on a single page previously dispersed if widely disseminated discursive and cultural practices of the late Middle Ages and early Renaissance" (my emphasis).[6] Although established traditions in the creation and use of heraldic devices, manuscript illumination, the glossing of classical epigrams, and any number of courtly and religious pageants preceded the publication of Alciato's epigrams, his is the first work to exhibit what Karl Ludwig Selig calls the "perfect fusion of all the component parts of the emblem: motto, device and verse, together expressing the intent of the author."[7]

I would like to take a closer look at the moment and process of production of Alciato's book by questioning one of the philological assumptions underpinning what is understood to be its foundational role in emblematics. This presupposition might be glossed as follows: "although the theoretical rationalization of the emblem's form lagged several decades behind the publication of his book, Alciato purposefully and self-consciously combined its elements with a clear vision of their meaning." Setting aside the obvious temporal paradox, the problem with this statement is that this is not at all how the first emblem book was produced. Sagrario López provides an elegant summary of how the *Emblematum liber* came to publication:

> Inspired by the *Greek Anthology*, Andrea Alciato . . . composed 99 epigrams, each of which he gave a title. As luck [*Fortuna*] would have it, thanks to the imperial adviser Peutinger, the work would end up in the hands of the printer Steyner, who, thinking of the market, considered how appropriate it would be to add an illustration to each epigram. This task was given to the engraver Breuil, and the book was published in 1531 in Augsburg with the title *Emblematum liber*.[8]

---

6. Selig 1990: 5.
7. Selig 1990: 5.
8. López 1999: 31.

I will return to López's description in a moment: what matters for now is that although Alciato is responsible for the epigrams and titles, according to this account he cannot be considered the progenitor of *the emblem,* a form that requires a visual image. Alciato's manuscript, which as far as we know contained no images nor any mention of images, passes through the hands of a royal bureaucrat, who makes sure that the work is well received by a printer in Augsburg, who in turn decides that the epigrams would be more reader-friendly—sell more quickly?—if they were accompanied by visual images. So he hands the manuscript over to the engraver Breuil. There is no evidence that Alciato was involved in the discussions concerning which images should go with which epigrams, nor in the actual making of the engravings; nor did he participate in the design of the page. According to Stephen Rawles, as late as 1534, by which time multiple editions and translations of the book had already appeared, "there could be no generic expectation of a 'tripartite emblem.'"[9] The "meaning" of the emblem as a discursive protagonist of the first order lagged far behind its "invention," in which multiple, noncommunicating agents were directly implicated. From a logical point of view, there can be no question of authorial intent if the main criterion for the genre in which he is supposed to have expressed his intent, the visual image, is conceived and produced by other cultural agents. A more careful appraisal of the historical context and social role of each of the participants involved necessarily upends received scholarship concerning the emblem, which has tended to reify the importance given to the authority of Alciato by emblematists and other allegorical writers later in the sixteenth and seventeenth centuries. It will be my contention that the responsibility of philology is to move in the opposite direction to that of the predominant tendency of literary culture in early modernity, which has tended to amplify the role of authorial intent at the expense of social and historical "materialities of communication." The permutations and interventions that Alciato's manuscript undergoes on the road to publication place the question of authorial intention in a largely hypothetical frame of reference.

None of this has ever been particularly secret, and yet there seems to be an insistent, if unrecognized, desire to occlude the messy and almost accidental circumstances surrounding the creation of the first emblem book, which makes the emblem a compelling test case for all early modern publications, few of which passed directly from the genius of the author to the receptive gaze of the educated reader. Alciato is often made the single intentional source for the whole book and, consequently, the progenitor of the

---

9. Rawles 2001: 68.

emblematic form itself. And if Alciato is not used, then something equally metaphysical takes his place. In the original Spanish, López (cited above) uses *Fortuna* to embody the historical agency, or lack thereof, behind the convergence of artistic, political, economic, and technological (self-) interests and circumstances that converge on the *Emblematum liber:* according to this view, Peutinger, Steyner, and Breuil become unwitting and subrogated agents of an impersonal and overarching historical intentionality. Would it not be more accurate, more philologically responsible, to recognize that the founding gesture of the tripartite emblematic form is tentative, contingent, and multiple? Institutionally informed, commercially driven, and artistically imitative, it is better understood as an intersection of diverse and even contradictory practices than as a unified and "natural" discursive structure. Of course, the risk that one runs in admitting entrance to such material contingencies is the multiplication of the number and nature of authorial intents. Perhaps most damaging of all, however, is the weakening of the structural integrity of the very notion of authorial intent itself. The intransigent contradictions produced by López's narrative bear witness to the fact that the very attempt to contain the meaning of Alciato and his book inevitably produces uncontainable lines of escape once historical materialities are admitted entrance. It could be stated that the science of philology unravels the integrity of the philological fabric of meaning from the inside out.

The occlusion of the messy materialities of emblem production can itself be read as emblematic. According to Peter M. Daly, the emblematic mode of representation became a dominant discourse at the onset of modernity when the efficacy of medieval rituals of presence was destabilized.[10] What Daniel Russell has called the "age of the emblem"[11] came about as the result of the "the crisis of representation, the collapse of the distance between representation and world . . . [which] brought back the desire for presence."[12] The emblem appears in a world that has become multiple and conflictive and in which the traditional hierarchy between the word and the sign has become

---

10. Daly settles on this broad definition in an attempt to embrace the many forms and expressions of what is in fact an incredibly diverse collection of literary, artistic, and architectural discourses. In doing so he follows the pioneering theoretical work of Dietrich Jöns: "[Where Albrecht Schöne] insists on the 'potential facticity' and inherent thing-meaning relationships as *the* characteristic of the emblem. . . . Jöns . . . .emphasizes that with its allegorical roots in the middle ages the emblem is an instrument of knowledge, a way of interpreting reality, the basis of which is the Christian medieval belief in the significance of the qualities of things" (Daly 1979a: 52).

11. Russell 1995: 8.

12. Gumbrecht 2003: 13. Gumbrecht is actually talking about modernity proper, but the statement also holds for early modernity.

unstable; and it reacts to this emerging cosmic vacuum by projecting a unified meaning from a constitutively hybrid form. In a world characterized by movement and instability, the visual is put into play with the verbal, and the vernacular is framed by classical epigrams and religious verses all in an effort to fill the irreversible appearance of epistemological and ontological breaches in the organicist medieval world view.

But if the emblem embodies a desire for presence in the face of a world of disintegrating certainties, the dispersed and confused nature of its material production also embodies and enacts the disintegration itself. Even as the emblematist sets himself apart from the past in order to select and make present those signs deemed most communicative because of their proximity to the supposedly primordial origins of language, the emblem, in its multiple and contradictory materiality, points to the absence of certainty symptomatic of the increasing fragmentation and relativization of the unified world view that characterized the Middle Ages. Likewise for philology.[13] It may seem odd to link Selig's philological analysis with metaphysics, but according to Gumbrecht, philology is implicated in just such a search for epistemological certainty on which to ground its editorial practices and establish its scientific legitimacy:

> [A]ll philological practices generate desires for presence, desires for a physical and space-mediated relationship to the things of the world (including texts), and . . . such desire for presence is indeed the ground on which philology can produce effects of tangibility (and sometimes even the reality thereof).[14]

What Gumbrecht calls the presence effect of allegorical and philological discourses both arises from and reproduces the void at the heart of modern symbolic edifices.[15] Like the emblematist's attempt to fix the meaning of signs and words by pointing the reader towards a singular, allegorical meaning, philology uses the structure of authorial intent to block access to the contingency, multiplicity, and ambivalence of modern literary dissemination in the effort to fix the meaning of the literary text. It thus stands to reason that the emblem and philology appear and become dominant

---

13. Said points out that philology is an eminently modern practice, whether we are talkig about early modernity or modernity proper, due to the peculiar relationship between the philologist and the past: "Philology is a way of historically setting oneself off, as great artists do, from one's time and an immediate past even as, paradoxically, one actually characterizes one's modernity by doing so" (Said 1978: 132).

14. Gumbrecht 2003: 6.

15. See Bell 1992.

modes of social practice in the same historical moment. As historians and philosophers from José Antonio Maravall to Slavoj Žižek have argued, the founding moment of modernity is not the affirmation of transcendental certitude based on rational categories of thought by self-present Cartesian subjects, but rather the experience of the abyss out of which reason, like the emblem, dramatically arises as a gesture of symbolic power, all the while harboring an unconscious symptom of its constitutive limitations. The role of the emblematic body is to block or fill this empty space with an ineffable and therefore transcendental presence of mysterious origins and meaning.

The interaction of emblematic and philological presencing-effects is illustrated by an emblem (or *empresa*) from Juan de Borja's *Empresas morales*. Borja, the third son of San Francisco de Borja—the Captain General of the Jesuits in sixteenth-century Spain—assembled his collection of emblems while he was a Spanish diplomat in Lisbon and published it in 1581 after he had taken up a similar post in Prague. Borja's philological sophistication can be observed in an *empresa* whose inscription reads "SATIABOR CUM APPARVERIT" (I will be satisfied when it appears) (see p. 114). This legend appears above an image in which a "hieroglyphic" sign, the Coptic *letter* TAU, is sculpted on the face of a perspectivally rendered pyramid, which, itself, has been lifted out of any identifiable frame of reference and placed on a pedestal for our inspection.

The second part of the subscription reads as follows:

> That which Christ our Lord won for us with his Cross, which the Egyptians signified in their Hieroglyphic Letters with the Cross as can be seen on the Obelisks, which they made with the Letter: TAU. Which signifies the Cross, by which they understood the life which was to come, as very serious Authors declared it, and so with reason we should work and hope for relief from this life, which is to come, which with so many travails he won for us.[16]

The "hieroglyphic" fragment selected by Borja is the image TAU, which the author illuminates by writing a commentary that alludes to "serious Authors" in its attempt to teach the reader about the history and meaning of the sign in question. There are several strategies here which display the power of the emblematist/philologist as he leads the reader towards a "cor-

---

16. "La qual nos ganó Christo nuestro Señor con su Cruz, como lo significavan los Egipcios en sus Letras Hieroglyphicas por la Cruz como se vee en los Obeliscos, que hizieron con Letra: TAV. Que significa la Cruz, por la qual entendían la vida que havia de venir, como lo declaran Authores muy graves, y assi con razon devemos trabajar, y esperar el descanso de la vida, que està por venir, que con tanto trabajo se nos ganò en ella" (Borja 1981: 442–43).

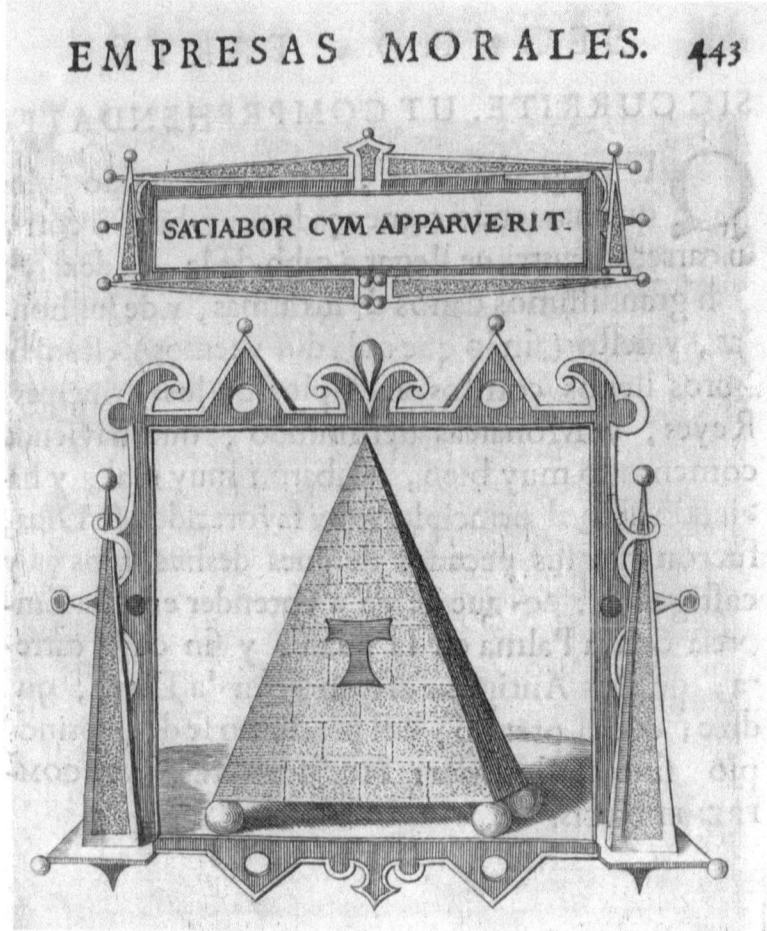

rect" interpretation of the emblematic riddle (the meaning of *tau*). In the first instance, the letter is placed in relief on an Egyptian pyramid, which visually projects the image back to the limits of historical time and space. In fact, it is probably more accurate to say that the way in which the image is constructed—an iconic image sculpted into the face of a geometric shape that seems to exist in a vacuum—removes both the sign and its material support from time altogether. Similarly, this ingenious assemblage converts a letter, albeit a foreign one, into a pre-alphabetic sign: a hieroglyph. The stubborn silence of the sign, in fact, is the space into which Borja's commentary will enter in order to satisfy the reader's desire for knowledge. Moving to the legend, the reader is entrenched in an already "weak" position through a two-pronged movement: on the one hand, if the reader does not know Latin, he will once again have to defer to Borja's commentary; if he knows Latin, he is now confronted by the grammatically passive *satiabor*. According to the syntax, the sign and its meaning will self-consciously "appear," suddenly becoming present to the patient reader as if he were witnessing the denouement of an epic story, which in fact he is, as the teleological pull of Fortune or Providence saturates the *inscriptio*. Most striking is the way Borja's etymology turns on a visual pun that misconstrues the Egyptian alphabet by reading the letter *tau* as a hieroglyph,[17] confusing alphabetic and ideogrammatical signs, not only by interpreting a Greek-derived alphabetic letter as an Egyptian hieroglyph but by appropriating this hieroglyphic symbol and its ideal knowledge in the name of Spanish Catholicism. Put another way, the accidental, material similarities between *tau* and the Christian cross are read through the lens of historical necessity. Finally, Borja positions his own authorial practice in relation to unnamed but nevertheless "very serious" authors, thus establishing his own legitimacy in a way that understates his authorial choices and overdetermines their authoritative pedigree.

The result of this strategic positioning of signs and authority is that the knowledge and signs of Egypt become legible and profitable through their placement within the symbolic network of Spanish Counter-Reformation values or *costumbres,* wherein the aura that emanates from their resistant iconicity and otherness is linked to a concrete semiotic and political project through what Jesús Maestro calls *transducción:* "The problem of transduction . . . is generated and resolved in the evolution of language, as a formal and functional medium that (empirically) permits the (intersubjective) normalization of (ontological) difference."[18] The ontological differences that Borja so elegantly cancels, or transducts, include, first and foremost, the difference between alphabetic and hieroglyphic signs, which stands in as a metaphor for the differentiated relationship between modern and primitive, Christian and pagan, Spanish and other.[19] Borja's emblematic choices dem-

---

17. Pedro Mexía's *Silva de varia lección* contains a similar interpretation of TAU: "Of the sign and figure of the cross; as before Christ suffered on it, it was revered and prized by the Arabs and Egyptians, and since it is a most perfect figure in itself" (qtd. in Selig 1990: 66).

18. El problema de la transducción . . . se genera y se resuelve en la evolución del lenguaje, como medio formal y funcional que permite (empíricamente) la normalización (intersubjetiva) de la diferencia (ontológica)" (Maestro 2004: 45).

19. R. de la Flor describes this process as one of a number of "methods of operatory approximation between the letter and the icon. . . . Everything worked towards indicating the existence of the signified, the only *via regia* for penetrating the sanctuary of signification. In this way the order of signs is diffracted and complicated at the same time, since an iconic observation is superimposed over the linguistic reading, with the latter providing a decisive sense to the complex relation that unites them" (R. de la Flor 2002: 347).

onstrate that the Golden Age emblematist is free to redefine symbols according to his strategic objectives as long as their meaning is contained within a linguistic and cultural universalism consonant with Counter-Reformation ideology. The presencing of Catholic universalism, channeled through the apparatus of the emblem, blocks both the reader's and the philologist's path to the material practices and effects of Borja's philological machinery, thus achieving what Žižek calls the dialectical turn from the other to the same, as the meaning of *tau* becomes what it "always-already was."[20] Whether or not the Egyptians were consciously aware of it, they nevertheless participated in a linguistic drama of universal proportions. Put another way, what the Egyptians actually took as the meaning of *tau* is irrelevant to the correct identification of the meaning of the sign. In this scheme, *tau* functions like a cipher, which, though it represents different meanings to different audiences, only has one true meaning.

(I realize that my emphasis on Borja's choices moves in opposition to my previous discussion concerning authorial intent. That being said, although there is considerable evidence that Borja worked in consultation with painters, engravers, and printers in the production of his work,[21] I have attempted to place the choices he and his collaborators made within a broader ideological context, a strategy whose objective is the simultaneous recognition of Borja's authorial activity and the outlining of the material context within which those choices are possible and probable.)

Emblematic Theater: The *auto sacramental*

The most emblematic literary and cultural practice of early modern Spain is theater. In the case of the *auto sacramental*, a one-act religious allegory situated at the doctrinal and celebratory heart of the annual Corpus Christi festival, the spectator is confronted by nothing less than a public performance of emblematic modes of representation.[22] The *auto* is in essence a theatrical transduction of the Catholic mass, in which the Eucharist—the hypostatic marriage of flesh, sign, and spirit—is the fundamental trope, dramatic climax, and liturgical *razón de ser* of the dramatic plot. I will look at one example of the emblematic nature of Pedro Calderón de la Barca's *El gran mercado del mundo*, before turning to how the text itself has received emblematic treatment in a recent philological commentary.

---

20. See Žižek 1991a.
21. Mahíques 1998.
22. For a more in-depth study of the emblematic nature of the *auto*, see Nelson 2005.

The plot of *El gran mercado del mundo* configures a contest of reception in which the character who interprets the confusing appearances, or merchandise, of the *Great Marketplace of the World* more emblematically ultimately wins the day. At issue is not just a way of reading or interpreting polyvalent signs, but a normative way of desiring meaning which pits two semiotic regimes against each other: a playful discourse of immanence, or earthly love of material existence, embodied by one brother, *Mal Genio;* and a discourse of deferral in which the relation between the subject and his reality is mediated by a third, imagined, authoritative gaze, represented by the other brother, *Buen Genio.* This narrative structure illuminates the historical situation of the *auto sacramental* itself, in that the theatrical representation of Eucharistic presence is structurally dependent on the internal threat posed by a diabolical semiotic regime of fragmentation and multiplicity. The real presence of Christ's sanctified body requires that the allegorical or metaphorical presence of the ethno-religious other first appear as a threat and then be annihilated during the climax of the play. This other, be it the Jew, the Muslim, the Protestant, or the colonial idolater, comes to embody the materialistic discourse of immanence mentioned above. The theatrical performance of divine presence thus becomes a metaphor for the Counter-Reformation struggle against the religious and political other, as the audience witnesses a contest between two competing norms for interpreting and moving through an ambivalent space. In the play's ritual and violent movement from chaos to order, the actions of the protagonist *Buen Genio* correspond to what Pierre Bourdieu calls "structural exercises" in the "projection of mythico-religious oppositions," as he traverses the marketplace and emblematically interprets the spiritual value of the merchandise displayed.[23] His "evil twin" *Mal Genio*, on the other hand, is the source of all transgressive desire, becoming the central protagonist in what Catherine Bell calls the ritual "motivation of bias."[24]

The difference between the interpretive paradigms of Buen Genio and Mal Genio is emblematized by the conflict between two allegorical figures, *Apetito* ("Appetite") and *Fe* ("Faith"). Both characters are blind, but their asymmetrically framed maladies symbolize the perspective that each brother projects onto the stage of the world. Appetite embodies a desire for material objects in the here and now, in the historical time of the subject, and judges them for what we might call their immediate use value on the plane of immanence. Appetite is completely blind to the allegorical significance

---

23. Bourdieu 1977: 89–96.
24. Bell 1992: 172.

of the material world, bent instead on a search for knowledge and pleasure of and in the market itself. Faith, on the other hand, is blind to all but the extensive, or hypostatic, meaning of material reality on the plane of transcendence. Through this dialectic of being and meaning, all material existence is converted into changeable and disposable signs of something else: the material world fades so that the meaning of Eucharistic icons may become present. Appetite and Faith demonstrate that the occupation of a point of view is constitutive of one's relationship to sin or salvation. If the presence of the *intended* meaning of the Eucharist absorbs the entirety of your gaze (and its desire), you are saved; if your gaze goes awry, resisting the ritual blocking of desire, you are *other*, the enemy, the heretic.[25]

Like Borja, the use of ritual structures and doctrinal nodal points creates the impression that Calderón's art and theology proceed from another more permanent and perfect place, rather than from the crisis-ridden and politically driven historical reality of baroque Spain. A more materialist inquiry would necessarily place the critic in the position of the antagonist/other in the sense that the material letter and its material circumstances of production would be valued in and for themselves rather than transducted into accidental and superficial figures for more permanent and *present* meanings. As with Borja, the historical author's intent becomes melded to the Godhead character in the play, which directs interpretive and editorial decisions towards the firmament of metaphysical intentionality.

Perhaps the most problematical historical circumstance with respect to traditional and conservative readings of the *auto* is that the vital role given to the heretic in the play is completely out of proportion to the actual threat posed by religious and ethnic minorities in early modern Spain. Recent studies on *Morisco* populations (Childers 2006) and the so-called Crypto-Jews (Contreras 1991; Silverman 1991) present convincing evidence that the apocalyptic picture painted by Spanish theater, both secular and sacred, is not a trustworthy portrayal of the actual historical relations between religious minorities and the Christian hegemony but reflects instead a highly scripted theatrical ruse designed to bring the desire for the other and its annihilation into the gaze of the spectator. The aesthetics of presence in the *auto sacramental* are better understood if we recognize that the author and the prodigious technological and social apparatuses that frame his choices actually serve to bring the diabolical threat of the other into existence in the social imaginary of early modern Spaniards. If the philologist remains tied

---

25. Slavoj Žižek (1991b) connects the 'other,' anamorphic gaze with the subversion of ideological fantasies of historical necessity and transcendence. See also Castillo 2001.

to a transcendental intentionality in these texts, s/he runs the risk of reifying a fabricated world view that substantially deforms our appreciation for the complexity of the historical reality and, more importantly, the complexity of the relationship between the literary artifact and its specific circumstances of production. As we have seen with the deployment of "Egyptians" in Borja's emblem, whatever the historical *Morisco* or new Christian/crypto-Jew might have to say about Catholic beliefs is irrelevant in the sacramental play.

Philological Emblematics

The emblematic and metaphysical operations of philology where Calderón is concerned are exemplified by a recent study by Ignacio Arellano and J. Enrique Duarte, members of a Golden Age research group (GRISO) based at the University of Navarra in Pamplona, Spain. They state that the main objectives (intentions) of the *auto sacramental* are "to provoke the emotive wonder of the spectator—which provokes an adherence *without fissures* to the dogmatic exaltation—and to pedagogically fix the imparted doctrine" (my emphasis).[26] This positing of a lack of fissures between the ritual creation of divine truths and their reception by what can only be called a participatory practicant is reminiscent of Borja's emblematic strategies, and it is typical of much philological criticism on Calderón. Arellano's and Duarte's study, which includes as complete a synthesis of the institutional history of the *auto* as one is likely to find, effects a noticeable divorce of the text of the *auto* from its communicative materialities. Of particular interest is the marginalization and eventual bracketing-off, or blocking, of one of the central characteristics of the *auto,* at least according to the "inventor" of modern Spanish theater, Lope de Vega: I am referring to the aforementioned privileging of the politico-religious war on error. Only a complete separation of the aesthetic form from the historical context can sustain such a sanitized reading of Calderón's sacred theater, which Arellano and Duarte achieve by guiding readers away from the material contingencies and circumstances of institutionalized theater towards the world of allegory, that "traditional mode of expression in the Bible and in religious tradition [of] those truths that are incomprehensible."[27] The blocking effect so central to Gumbrecht's definition of power is elegantly staged by the GRISO critics through the placement of paradox, and especially religious paradox, in the space where a

---
26. Arellano 2003: 72.
27. Arellano 2003: 35.

more rigorous consideration of textual materialities might produce concrete knowledge concerning the role of ideology and epistemology in Calderón's theater, and vice versa. As in the case of emblematics, the insistence on a divinely inspired intentionality fills the abyss of doubt and doctrinal contradiction evidenced in the plays themselves and effectively closes the question concerning the antagonistic role of the ethnic and political other in the representation of divine presence.

Similar procedures can be observed in the GRISO edition of *El gran mercado* by Ana Suárez Miramón. Her commentary stages an emblematization of Calderón within a universal framework of literary genius that includes figures such as Nietzsche, Edgar Allan Poe, Lewis Carroll, Berthold Brecht, Ibsen, and Pirandello. "There is no doubt," she writes, "that Calderón is the first link in the great chain of writers who have been conscious that creation is language and it creates itself through the created and creating word."[28] It is no accident that the medieval concept of the Great Chain of Being and the religious privileging of the word (the *logos* of philology) resonate in this celebration of Calderón's founding role in the literary patrimony of modernity. In fact, the commentary brings us back to the founding rift of modernity. Where Borja marries the "hieroglyphic" to Spanish imperialism, and where Calderón creates a substantive link between one's judgment of the material world and salvation, Suárez Miramón links her reading of Calderón to a series of universalizing propositions designed to turn our attention away from the "distractions" posed by verbal and theological contradictions as well as the discursive violence at the heart of these politico-religious spectacles. In one instance she states that "the two brother protagonists [are] living examples of the dualism rooted in the Nature and allegory of the same antinomy of the human being split into body or material and soul or spirit."[29] This phenomenalization of a seventeenth-century Catholic point of view through the marriage of Nature and allegory mirrors the gesture of Arellano and Duarte concerning the inability of human language to penetrate divine truths. In both cases, the dehistoricization of Calderón and Counter-Reformation thought pave the way for the universalization of Calderón's drama as well as the placement of writers with very distinct aesthetic and ideological programs within Calderón's and the critic's reach.

A particularly illuminating example of this practice is the conversion of Miguel de Cervantes into the source and inspiration for Calderón's play. It is worth noting that this philological turn actually places Cervantes, and

---

28. Suárez 2003: 42.
29. Suárez 2003: 61.

not Calderón, in the role of modernity's progenitor; more importantly, no literary figure from the Spanish Golden Age is more resistant to the type of orthodox militancy out of which Calderón's art arises than Cervantes, and his rehabilitation into an orthodox, Counter-Reformation Catholic merits special attention. The emblematization of Cervantes is built on three similitudes, or analogies. In the first instance, Suárez Miramón finds a "total correspondence" between Calderón's Buen Genio and Cervantes's Don Quixote in the motif of the "voyage towards an ideal walking together with an ingenuous material man."[30] Evidently, the comparison also rests on the identities of Mal Genio and Sancho Panza, which is problematic given the dramatic downward turn of Mal Genio's fortunes in the *auto*. Secondly, "the withdrawal of Don Quixote to the mountains [and] the return of Buen Genio through the desert are reminiscent of the Lenten period that Christ spent in the desert."[31] Finally, what might be called the *materialistic impasses* represented by Mal Genio and Sancho Panza are channeled through a depoliticized and dehistoriziced application of Mikhail Bakhtin's concept of carnival, a move which ignores the theological dialectics at play in Calderón as well as the corrosive irony of Cervantes.

Suárez Miramón's comparison of Buen Genio and Don Quixote rests on two religious doctrines of the Counter-Reformation: free will and Providence. In the first instance, the conflation of the desires of Alonso Quijano and Buen Genio to test their mettle in a search for love and transcendence must strategically overlook important differences between the characters, the works in which they are situated, and their chosen objects of desire. The object of Buen Genio is the hand of Gracia, an allegorical representation of divine will who requires that he reject the truth effect of what appears before his gaze, in other words, the material significance of the world and its objects in the here and now. As a result, his freedom is completely inscribed within the doctrine of *desengaño,* a theological sleight-of-hand that converts historical existence into a phantasmatic experience and, consequently, places it completely under the power of the allegorist. In Benjamin's words, "it is now quite incapable of emanating any meaning or significance of its own; such significance as it has, it acquires from the allegorist."[32] Here, freedom is not consonant with the drive for self-realization but rather with a process of self-annihilation under the punishing gaze of the Father. R. de la Flor summarizes this melancholy philosophy: "this infinite order of things and the emptiness and mystery that surround them, forces one to characterize

---

30. Suárez Miramón 2003: 87.
31. Suárez Miramón 2003: 89.
32. Benjamin 1977: 183.

the human knowledge that one has of them as useless, empty, lacking in capacity and fallen, even ridiculous."[33] It is no wonder that Buen Genio must search for allegorical meaning in such a wasteland.

In the case of Don Quixote, the freedom to realize his quest to bring knight errantry to the mundane plane of La Mancha is constantly undone, not by any wavering on his part but rather by the often violent encounters with a material landscape which shows itself to be infinitely more substantial and resistant (and rich) than the doctrine of *desengaño* allows. What is most sublime about the knight's quest is the abject failures to which it leads, failures that are often exacerbated and even orchestrated by his erstwhile foil Sancho Panza. A case in point is the scene cited by Suárez Miramón as an analogy to Christ's allegorical pilgrimage through the desert. If Don Quixote's will is tested on the Sierra Morena, it is certainly not due to any demonic figure offering earthly riches and power. Rather, his own demons, arising from his miserly existence on the lowest rung of a decadent aristocracy and channeled through the romanticized penitence of figures like Amadís of Gaul, will drive him to leap from rock to rock dressed in nothing but a nightshirt, while Sancho alternately looks on and looks away, as it is too much even for him to glance at his master's withered genitalia when Don Quixote takes a header on the rocks. The carnivalesque inversion effected by Cervantes here is devastating in the way master and servant are separated and resituated in terms of decorum and rationality. In this case, the knight's abject materiality obstructs any transcendental meaning we might want to project onto the scene.

This brings me to Bakhtin. In discussing the socio-aesthetic aspects of the *auto,* Suárez Miramón writes: "Its novelty arises from having synthesized all previous tendencies in a multiple-thematic synopsis to which it adds its peculiar vision of the world in which the mythic and the popular are melded together in a perfect carnivalization of the world."[34] Putting aside the fact that one of the two protagonists in the play must be annihilated in order to unify the great marketplace of the world, the main problem with this statement from a theoretical point of view is that if there is any one thing that characterizes Bakhtin's concept of carnival, it is the emphasis he places on the imperfect, unfinished, and excessive nature of the carnivalesque mode of discourse which directs any imposition of order, synthesis, or harmony toward the ironization of its constitutive violence: in short, carnivalization is never anything like perfect, finished, or whole. Indeed, the ideological constructs

---

33. R. de la Flor 2000: 346.
34. Suárez Miramón 2003: 125.

that carnival subverts are precisely the kinds of power that philologists exert when they extract authors and texts out of their disharmonious and problematic contexts and emblematize them according to universal axioms and genealogies. By redirecting Calderón's contingent symbolic practice away from the chaotic marketplace of Counter-Reformation history, Arellano, Duarte, and Suárez Miramón avoid the complex relationship between the dramatic representation of Apostasy, Heresy, the Jew, the Lutheran, the nonbeliever, and the sophist, etc., and the cultural commodification and political violence that convert baroque religious spectacles into such a powerful and effective practices of ideological containment. No substantive attempt is made to explore how Calderón plays with history in the same way that he plays with allegorical meaning: through a sophisticated semiotic regime that emblematically uproots and reconfigures historical actors and their material relations according to a historically situated religious and political frame of reference.

Conclusion

In chapter 52 of the second part of Cervantes's *Don Quixote,* our intrepid hero strides into a printing press in Barcelona. As he enters the shop, the knight observes that different textual operations are taking place in different cubicles ("cajones"): some of the laborers are cranking pages out of the press; others are correcting the plates that others have just composed; and still others are emending what their colleagues have done.[35] No order is established for these distinct forms of literary praxis, as they all seem to be happening simultaneously and largely independent of each other. After this initial survey, Don Quixote strikes up a conversation with an "author" who happens to be supervising the publication of his own book. I place the designation *author* in quotation marks because it turns out that the book whose publication he is financing is a translation of a Tuscan work titled *Le Bagatele*. Don Quixote, it so happens, has some knowledge of Tuscan, and he initiates a discussion with the author-translator concerning the relationship between an original work and its translation. The knight's statement, that reading a translation is like "seeing a Flemish tapestry from the back; although one sees the figures, they are full of threads that obscure them, and they cannot be seen with the clarity and colors of the face," is well known. What is not often commented on is how he also recognizes that a good translation

---

35. Cervantes 1978: 518–19.

can surpass and even substitute for the original: "they felicitously put into doubt which is the translation or which is the original."[36] Cervantes does not stop his inspection of the integrity of the artistic act here, as the final question his protagonist poses concerns that most sacred of all philological cows: the motivation of the artist. In the words of the independently minded author-translator: "I do not print my books to achieve fame in the world, since I am already known for my works; it is profit I seek; since without it a good reputation isn't worth a wooden nickel."[37] With this brief side trip to a printing press, Cervantes manages to place into question every assumption that drives philology towards making ever more present the insistently problematic, not to say absent, voice and figure of the author, and leaves us instead with a number of nagging doubts and questions.

What is lost when we assume that Alciato is solely responsible for inventing a new literary genre? What is gained by positing a Calderón whose art reaches into postmodernity? We might contend that philology comes into being before literature itself is a recognizable institution; it might even be said that philology frames literature as a recognizable social practice and, by doing so, creates its own object of inquiry while, at the same time, containing and domesticating both the work's and the author's potential as a social force. As Gumbrecht suggests, philology does not study the literary object; it brings it into being, and not as what Heidegger would call an "in itself," but rather as a "for itself." The separation of the work and the author from their material contexts of production and reception is perhaps the *sine qua non* of philology, a cut which necessitates the labor of the philologist. This literary "for itself" is thus more properly understood as "for the philologist," since it is the philologist who decides the nature of the object s/he is studying before getting to work, which is merely saying that philology is like any other scientific endeavor wherein the results of the experiment can only be read through the apparatus that brings about the perceived change in the object of analysis.

Mindful of this, I have surreptitiously mimicked Barthes's call for a literary criticism that would "liberate what may be called an anti-theological activity . . . [which would] refuse God and his hypostases—reason, science, law" by demonstrating how the form of the author used by Selig and then López obscures the material processes at the origins of emblematic discourse; or, perhaps better stated, it performs an emblematization of that same form, in which a multiplicity of actors and discourses are arranged through an

---

36. Cervantes 1978: 519–20.
37. Cervantes 1978: 520.

equation that produces a sum that is both greater and less than the parts themselves.[38] I next looked at an emblem by Juan de Borja in which the historically situated, allegorical operations performed on a symbolic artifact, the hieroglyphic/letter *tau*, are projected into the sign by the emblematist-philologist. The authorial form in question here is either God himself or a messianic intentionality through which the transhistorical meaning of *tau* "appears" before us in all its universal plenitude. After Borja, I moved to Calderón's theatrical emblem, in which an authoritative performance of divine presence is produced through the dramatic conflict between opposed semiotic regimes and then made more present through the staged annihilation of one of the protagonists. What I have tried to underline in this movement from emblem to emblem is that what is recovered is also obscured by the tools at the emblematist's, or philologist's, disposal. These practices, including the form of authorial intentionality, are our own materialities of communication, and our resistance to scrutinizing their impact on the object of study and the communication of our findings places us in a similar position to Don Quixote in the Sierra Morena: hopelessly exposed to the critical and discerning eye of the materialist.

I have chosen to close with this carnivalesque image because the multiplication of meanings that arise once we admit entrance to historical accidents and contingencies, as well as the inevitable upending of canonical interpretations, are closely analogous to the topsy-turvy world of Bakhtin's carnival. As such, I propose an alternative critical practice which might be called 'carnivalesque philology.' As Don Quixote moves from cubicle to cubicle in the Barcelona printing press, our assumptions concerning the easy movement from creative genesis to printed page are annihilated and reborn according to the demands of the marketplace; the creative act is, in short, subjected to the processes of mechanized fragmentation, standardization, and correction consistent with commodification and the modern marketplace. Moreover, the figure of the author becomes occluded by the translator's labor to such an extent that the one competes on equal ground with the other. In the end, the motivation for literary creation is grounded in that most banal, yet true, capitalist ethic: profit. It should be clear that the concept I am offering here, *carnivalesque philology,* is neither original nor innovative for early modern authors. It is in fact the most appropriate posture to take with respect to authorship in early modernity. I have merely attempted to provide some of the general contours of what such a practice might look like in the way I have framed this discussion of the emblem. In

---

38. Barthes 1977: 143.

fact, a first step in assembling a carnivalesque philology would be to recognize the emblematic structure of author-driven philology. If we accept the premise that literature, especially modern literature, is embedded in institutional matrices of production, including the marketplace, then we must make room for a significant multiplication of literary actors, too numerous to mention here. A carnivalesque approach would necessarily admit entrance to actors and forces not visible in current critical practices (even though they are clearly visible to Don Quixote and Sancho), concentrating on what Gumbrecht has called "the materialities of communication" and, ultimately, reinvigorating historical artifacts in unpredictable ways.

CHAPTER 5

On the Road
Travel, Antiquarianism, Philology[1]

Jonathan Sachs

In an edited volume on the history of philology it should come as no surprise that so many of the contributors ask what "philology" is. Do we all agree on just what it is we are recovering? Absolutely not: that is what makes the endeavor exciting. Philology is a slippery concept, one that seems simple and perhaps even discreet, but which has developed a broad range of meanings and implications. The concept of philology and its potential recovery becomes even more complicated when we begin to consider the complex relationship between philology and history, between the rigorous text-oriented procedures of philology and the material practices that surround these procedures. If philology is, as Nietzsche described it, a "magic potion" mixed "from the strangest liquids, metals, and bones,"[2] and if these liquids, metals, and bones can be likened to codicology, palaeography, stemmatics, and papyrology, then we are confronted with a set of practices whose rigor derives from its engagement with the concreteness of language and what Paul de Man called "the materiality of the letter."[3] And yet even as we acknowledge the material techniques on which the foundations of philology rest, we must also consider the desire of philology to abandon itself, to deliver itself over to modes of exposition that would elide its material bases.

This, it seems, is exactly what Hans Ulrich Gumbrecht has in mind when, in *The Powers of Philology*, he describes philological practices as containing "a type of desire that, however it may manifest itself, will always exceed the

---

[1]. Research for this essay was made possible by the generous support of the Paul Mellon Centre for British Art in London.

[2]. Nietzsche 1988: 2.1.247.

[3]. de Man 1986: 86.

explicit goals" of those practices. Gumbrecht characterizes this desire as a desire for presence, for "a physical and space-mediated relationship to the things of the world," and he suggests that this desire for presence, when it is "conjured up by the philological practices, bring[s] into play the energy of the philologist's imagination."[4] The result is a tension between what Gumbrecht calls "mind effects and presence effects" that he likens in structure and impact to contemporary definitions of aesthetic experience. Such an analogy, as Gumbrecht acknowledges, is a far cry from the traditional image of philology. It clashes with our understanding of the constraints of philological method, with, in short, philological rigor. Nonetheless, by reintroducing imagination to philology, Gumbrecht's emphasis on presence-effects opens a space to ask about the relationship between the rigorous text-based procedures of philological inquiry and the extra-textual factors—material, imaginative, and historical—that aid and abet that process.

This essay will explore this relationship between the textual and the extra-textual at a moment before F. A. Wolf, the *studiosus philologiae*, but a moment critical for what Wolf himself would achieve. It asks about the relationship between an eighteenth-century tradition of antiquarianism and grand tourism and the focus on empirical evidence and textual interpretation that characterizes the history of modern classical philology, and indeed, the philological endeavor more broadly. Scholarship by Joseph Levine, Rosemary Sweet, Peter N. Miller, and others has underscored the importance of antiquarianism for contemporary ideals of civic life (Miller), for the formation of national identity (Sweet), and for the development of modern historiography (Levine).[5] These studies point the way for questions about the extent to which the sophisticated, methodologically rigorous approach to classical antiquity found in *Altertumswissenschaft* may owe a debt to the material practices and imaginative speculations of amateur travelers and part-time scholars of the eighteenth century. In response to these questions, I will consider the case for understanding Homer as an oral poet made by Robert Wood in *An Essay on the Original Genius and Writings of Homer* (1775). Wood is an important figure because he was an amateur classical scholar and traveler through the regions of antiquity whose published work nonetheless elaborates a sophisticated historical approach to the problem of Homer's language. If, following Gumbrecht, we understand philology as "a configuration of scholarly skills that are geared toward historical text curator-

---

4. Gumbrecht 2003: 6–7.

5. Levine 1987; Miller 2000; Sweet 2001. On British antiquarianism more generally, see also Piggott 1976; for a sense of the range of historical writing and method in the eighteenth century, and the place of the antiquarian within it, see Momigliano 1966.

ship" (Gumbrecht 2003: 2), then Wood, who had no interest in establishing a correct text of the Homeric epics, would hardly seem to qualify. Nonetheless, Wood may fit aspects of our more narrow understanding of philology if we recognize that virtually all of his published work reads like a long and sustained gloss on Homer's corpus, a prolonged attempt to fill the empty margins surrounding Homer's text—a text from which it seems he never parted.

Today, if Wood is remembered at all, it is largely for his understanding of Homer as an oral poet, a view that places him in an interpretive tradition running from Vico to Wolf and beyond. Wood was not the first to posit that Homer composed orally or that he was, in effect, illiterate. In antiquity, Cicero claimed that the works of Homer were not formally written down until Pisistratus, while Josephus asserted that Homer could not write as part of his argument for the superiority of literate Hebrew culture over Greek culture. In postclassical thought, we can trace this argument for Homer's illiteracy from Vico's assertion that Homer must have lived in a time prior to the invention of the alphabet through Wood to Wolf's theory that certain textual problems in Homer can be explained by recognizing that none of the Homeric texts were written down until Solon or Pisistratus, and, ultimately, to Milman Parry's groundbreaking account of Homeric style, which suggested that the economy of Homer's verse was imposed by oral methods of composition.[6] Eric Havelock then expanded the arguments for orality and oral epic narrative made by Parry and Alfred Lord into an account of the oral basis of Greek culture more broadly to explain how the origins of Greek philosophy can be linked to the restructuring of thought imposed by the invention of writing.[7] As Adam Parry, Walter Ong, and others acknowledge, Wood's contribution to this line of interpretation is important. Parry credits Wood with developing a new theory of Homer as an entirely different kind of poet from later, literate writers. According to Parry, "No scholar had succeeded in imagining any better than Robert Wood in 1767, or even so well, the kind of poet who would sing the kind of song we have in the *Iliad* and *Odyssey*,"[8] and Ong confirms that Wood "was apparently the first whose conjectures came close to what Parry finally demonstrated."[9] What seems to me distinctive about Wood, however—and what scholarly accounts

---

6. For an excellent account of the transmission of the so-called Homeric Question, see Parry 1971. On the connection between the Homeric Question and more general theories for the importance of orality, see Ong 1982.

7. Havelock 1963.

8. Parry 1971: xxi. Parry is referring to an earlier, privately printed version of Wood's essay: see below.

9. Ong 1982: 19.

have been slow to recognize[10]—is the central importance of Wood's travels in working out both his specific ideas about Homer and his more general emphasis on the need to read classical texts in an elaborate political, social, and material context. In other words, for Wood, in all of his thinking about antiquity, the experience of place is crucial and the logic by which he works out Homer's orality is deeply indebted to his experiences traveling through Ionia on two occasions.

Robert Wood was a British traveler, politician, and member of the Society of Dilettanti. He first visited Greece in the 1740s when he traveled among the Aegean islands and also to Syria and Egypt. At some time after this, he settled in Rome, where he met the young and wealthy James Dawkins and the connoisseur and collector John Bouverie. While walking from Rome to Naples to see classical ruins there, the three set upon the idea of exploring antiquities in the Mediterranean region. This, the voyage that made Wood's reputation, began in May of 1750 when, accompanied by Dawkins, Bouverie, and the Italian engraver/sculptor Giovanni Borra, Wood set out from Naples for the Troad. Travel in the East was certainly difficult, but the voyage has been described as a "scholar's dream,"[11] and the travelers had every feasible convenience, including their own 160-ton ship, the SS *Matilda*. Wood notes that this boat "brought from London a library, consisting chiefly of all the Greek historians and poets, some books of antiquities, and the best voyage writers. . . . "[12] Upon landing, the men explored the entire region of the Troad, then moved on to the coast of Syria, where they visited Palmyra and Balbec before setting out for Athens in May of 1751. After assisting James Stuart and Nicholas Revette on the project that would become the *Antiquities of Athens* (1762), Wood returned home to prepare his two great folios, *The Ruins of Palmyra* (1753) and *The Ruins of Balbec* (1757). Wood returned once more to Europe as the tutor to the Duke of Bridgewater, before the reputation established by the Palmyra volume resulted in a lucrative appointment to a position in public affairs when the elder Pitt made Wood undersecretary of state in 1756. Wood subsequently held various appointments through several changes in government, and was an MP from March 1761 until December 1770. He died in September 1771.[13]

---

10. One notable exception here is Constantine 1984.
11. Spencer 1957: 75.
12. Wood 1753, in the letter "From the Publisher to the Reader": n.p.
13. A detailed account of Wood's expedition to Palmyra and Balbek can be found in Hutton 1927. Further details of Wood's early life and later political career can be found in the *Oxford Dictionary of National Biography*.

Wood's work on Homer, though begun just shortly following the publication of *Palmyra*, took over twenty years to complete. Public service left him little time to continue with his classical studies or to accomplish his professed design of describing the insights gained from reading the *Iliad* and the *Odyssey* in the lands where Homer wrote. A rough sketch of this work was proposed initially in a letter to the ailing Dawkins, likely written in 1755 when Wood was in Rome with Bridgewater; seven copies of this letter were privately printed in 1767 as *A Comparative View of the Antient and Present State of the Troade. To which is prefixed an Essay on the Original Genius of Homer.* An enlarged anonymous edition appeared in 1769, without the *Comparative View*, again in a small print run of six or seven. This was the edition sent to J. D. Michaelis in Gottingen, where it was reviewed by C. G. Heyne in March 1770, and translated by Michaelis's son in 1773. Goethe, Herder, and other lesser writers can all be shown to have read Wood's essay in its German translation, and Wood's thinking about Homer also influenced F. A. Wolf in his seminal *Prologomena ad Homerum* of 1795.[14] Only after Wood's death in 1771, however, was the whole scheme edited by Jacob Bryant and published as *An Essay on the Original Genius and Writings of Homer* in London (1775).

The hypothesis of Homer's illiteracy, for which Wood is today best known, did not originate with him. In the postclassical tradition, Vico made Homer's lack of writing prominent as early as the first edition of the *New Science* in 1725. Vico argued that there was no single, true "Homer"; the Homeric epics were, rather, a collective endeavor, "composed and revised by several hands in several ages."[15] Vico does not idealize Homer, and he is keen to deny that Homer was in any way a philosopher or the possessor of esoteric wisdom. Homer, for Vico, is savage. If a central quality of wisdom is the taming of savagery, then Homer could not have been wise because his epics fail to curb or tame savagery. They do, however, represent for Vico a particular kind of truth. Vico reasons that since primitive people have no power of reflection and, therefore, no possibility of falsehood, their first, heroic poets must sing the unvarnished truth, and their songs, in turn, represent a collective memory of their earliest history. But because this early history is preserved as a collective memory, it precedes vernacular script, and Homer must not have written:

---

14. On the transmission of Wood's work in Germany, see Constantine 1984: 66–84; Fabian 1976; On Wood's influence on Wolf, see Anthony Grafton's comments in Wolf 1985: 104, 110.
15. Vico 2001: 363.

> By a necessity of nature, the first nations spoke in heroic verse. Here too we must admire divine providence. In an age when popular letters had not yet been invented for writing, the nations expressed themselves in verses; and their metre and rhythm, by aiding the memory, helped preserve the histories of their families and cities.[16]

As evidence for his claim that the early Greeks lacked a written vernacular, Vico observes that Homer never refers to letters. Thus, for Vico, not only is there no one, true Homer, but in addition whatever works the collaborative "Homer" produced were the product of an oral tradition and therefore not written. Homer, according to Vico, "was an idea or *heroic archetype of the Greeks who recounted their history in song.*"[17]

Wood's account of Homer is similar to Vico's in a number of respects. Like Vico, Wood reads Homer as history. In a section on Homer's travels, for example, Wood suggests that we owe our knowledge of early Greek shipbuilding and navigation to Homer. Because Greece has such an extensive sea coast, Wood notes,

> And considering how much the various occupations of high and low life were then confined to one rank and order of men, it is not extraordinary, that we should find the Poet so conversant in the language and manners of the sea, and so knowing, as well in the business of the ship-wright as of the sailor. Indeed, it is only by following him through each of those arts, that history is furnished with the earliest account of them.[18]

Just as Vico refused to idealize Homer, Wood also insists that Homer is fundamentally distinct from later associations of Greece with philosophy and refinement. Whereas for Vico Homer was the specific archetype of the early Greek people, for Wood, Homer's lack of refinement brings him closer to nature, by which he becomes representative of human nature more broadly. Finally, Wood, like Vico, builds his case for Homer's orality around textual details, specifically the lack of any reference to writing or letters in Homer's corpus. Wood acknowledges the mention of a written text in *Iliad* book 6, but he suggests that it contained not letters but a pictogram, a "Symbolical, Hieroglypical, or Picture Description, something of that kind . . . no doubt known to Homer" (Wood 1775: 250).

---

16. Vico 2001: 372.
17. Vico 2001: 381.
18. Wood 1775: 36. Further page references to this edition will be provided parenthetically in the text.

Wood differs from the author of the *New Science,* however, in that while Vico denies that Homer was a single author and suggests that there were multiple Homers, Wood firmly insists on a single Homer and he sees the two epics as the unified composition of a particular historical figure. While Vico suggests that we do not know where Homer was from,[19] Wood asserts that he was from Ionia in the region of Troy, and this geographical specificity forms a crucial aspect of his reading. Indeed, Homer was, for Wood, a real person whose work reflects mimetically and transparently the customs, manners, and geography of his time. His orality, far from being a hindrance, meant that he worked all the more closely to nature, thus making his poems more accurate mimetic reflections of transcendent natural truths.

All of Wood's publications contain hybrid qualities that make them difficult to categorize. The volumes on Palmyra and Balbec, for example, combine travel narrative, specimen book, archeological record, and treatise on how to read classical literature. But they all share a locative understanding of classical texts. For Wood, the writings of antiquity are best understood in the landscapes that produced them. As he puts it in the introduction to *The Ruins of Palmyra,* "The life of Miltiades or Leonidas could never be read with so much pleasure, as on the plains of Marathon or at the streights [*sic*] of Thermopylae; the *Iliad* has new beauties on the banks of the Scamander, and the *Odyssey* is most pleasing in the countries where Ulysses traveled and Homer sung."[20] For Wood and his traveling companions, in their ship with its full library of Greek classics, such combinations of text and place were routinely possible. As a result, reading for Wood was more than the abstracted encounter of mind and page; it manifested a desire to be present at the site of an event, a desire that we could compare to the desire for presence, for "a physical and space-mediated relationship to the things of the world" that Gumbrecht characterizes as a result of philological practices (Gumbrecht 2003: 6). At the base of Wood's locative understanding of classical texts sits the belief that one cannot trust textual descriptions or even pictures; one must be present at the site of the description. This is why, in Katie Trumpener's words, "Wood's travels in Homer's footsteps inaugurate a new mode of literary tourism."[21] But Wood, I want to insist, was himself more than simply a literary tourist. He was an experienced traveler, and travel lies at the heart of his practice as a reader. We can, I think, see glimpses of Wood himself when he characterizes Homer as "a traveller of curiosity and observation" (Wood 1775: 34), and continues to note that "an important

---

19. Vico 2001: 359.
20. Wood 1753: iv.
21. Trumpener 1997: 103.

thirst after knowledge was in those days only to be satisfied by travelling" (Wood 1775: 35). His locative hermeneutic joined reader, writer, text, and travel in what sometimes seems a seamless unity as he uses his travel experience to place himself at the site of a Homeric episode and then uses Homer to make sense of his own travel experiences.

Travel illuminates Homer in a manner that makes the scene of reading simultaneously a scene of remembering, looking, and re-narrating. We can see this clearly when we examine how Wood evaluates Homeric episodes which recount an experience of travel. At such moments we are reading a travel narrative that is itself reading a kind of travel narrative. Consider, for example, the third book of the *Odyssey* in which Telemachus, having set sail in search of his father, seeks news of Odysseus from Nestor, who recounts the dispute over how to proceed home and the eventual disaster that so many of his companions encountered. The passage, in Pope's translation, begins:

> But when (by wisdom won) proud *Ilion* burn'd,
> And in their ships the conqu'ring *Greeks* return'd;
> 'Twas God's high will the victors to divide,
> And turn th' event, confounding human pride [. . .] (lines 159–62)[22]

As the passage continues, it tells of a dispute between Agamemnon and Menelaus over whether to depart immediately home (Menelaus) or to wait in order to sacrifice to Athena (Agamemnon). The army splits into two camps and Nestor and Diomede join Menelaus to sail for home. At Lesbos, another dispute arises over how best to sail back:

> If to the right to urge the pilot's toil,
> (The safer road) beside the *Psyrian* isle;
> Or the strait course to rocky *Chios* plow,
> And anchor under *Mimas'* shaggy brow? (lines 205–8)[23]

The group chooses the most direct route and, with the aid of a favorable wind, reaches Geraestus point from which they follow the coast home. The episode, for Wood, evokes his own immediate experience:

> I was present at a consultation on the same sort of question, near the same place, and under the same circumstances, as far as they concern the illustra-

---

22. Pope 1967: 93.
23. Pope 1967: 95–96.

tion of our present inquiry. It was in the year 1742, that I happened to be on board His Majesty's ship the Chatham, then escorting the Turkey trade from Constantinople to Scanderoon. (Wood 1775: 40)

Again, the dilemma turns on whether to pursue the more secure route along the coast or the more direct route across the sea. Like Nestor, Wood's group chooses the sea route. "If we compare our situation with that of Nestor, Diomede, and Menelaus, who had the ablest pilot of that age on board," Wood continues,

we see, that though our destinations were different, our point under deliberation was so far precisely the same, that we both doubted between the shortest and the surest way. They ventured to sea, though it was most dangerous; we chose it, because it was most safe; and this constitutes one of the great differences between ancient and modern navigation. (Wood 1775: 41)

Although Wood's provisional conclusion here concerns the manner in which antiquity differs from the modern age, he continues his analysis of the passage to argue for Homer's "historical accuracy" (Wood 1775: 42) in the face of commentators who, according to Wood, "by their different constructions of part of the passage here alluded to, deviated from the plain sense of the Poet" (Wood 1775: 41). The argument here resembles many other moments throughout the *Essay* in which Wood resolutely insists on the accuracy and truth of Homer who is, for Wood, the most mimetic of poets. In each case, Wood uses his travel experience to clarify what he considers to be misinterpretations of the Homeric text by critics who attend "more to grammatical criticism than to the genius and character of the Poet, and of the age when he wrote" (Wood 1775: 46). Clarifications of this sort occur not only in Wood's published work, but also in the marginalia of Wood's *Iliad*, which reads like a sustained dialogue between Wood's travel experience and his Homeric reading. Both Wood's published and his unpublished works, in other words, underscore a theory of literary interpretation that requires travel for proper textual understanding.

The *Essay on the Original Genius and Writings of Homer* is Wood's effort to establish the "true Homer" much as he hoped to find the "true" site of Troy. In the *Essay*, Wood offers a series of reflections on Homer's Country, Homer's Travels, Homer's Navigation and Geography, Homer's Winds, Homer's Manners, Homer as an Historian and Chronologer, Homer's Language and Learning, and Homer as a Philosopher. Taken together, all these categories show what Wood calls "Homer's original genius." For someone like Vico, Homer's errors were, as Anthony Grafton suggests, "historical clues that revealed the differences of feeling and expression that had grown up between Homer's time and his own."[24] In contrast, Wood routinely denies that Homer, that faithful copier after nature, could have made any errors.

Throughout the *Essay*, Wood consistently examines any perceived errors in Homer in an effort to suggest that the mistake lies not with the poet, but with the commentator. In a section titled "Description of Pharos and Alexandria," for example, Wood discusses lines from book 4 of the *Odyssey*, where Menelaus describes Pharos as a day's sail from Egypt. A footnote reprints the lines in Greek and in Pope's translation, which reads as follows:

> High o'er a gulfy sea, the Pharian isle
> Fronts the deep roar of disemboguing Nile:
> Her distance from the shore, the course begun
> At dawn, and ending with the setting sun,
> A galley measures; when the stiffer gales
> Rise on the poop, and fully stretch the sails. (cited in Wood 1775: 93)

Wood notes that the lines have drawn criticism from commentators, who object that since Pharos is only a mile from Alexandria, Homer's description must be inaccurate. But, according to Wood, the commentators themselves are mistaken and "this passage has been misunderstood, for want of due attention to the changes which have happened, both in the situations and names of places, in that part of the world, since the building of Alexandria" (Wood 1775: 99–100). Wood explains that Alexandria was made possible only by the canals built well after the time of Homer in a "more commercial age," and thus what we take to be a vital part of Egypt was "in Homer's days" of no importance, it was "too insignificant to deserve a boundary or to be claimed by any country. . . . It made no part of Egypt at that time, when the extent of the Nile marked the natural limits of that country" (Wood 1775: 102). Wood here emphasizes the importance of his own travel experience in making this claim, for such an insight "could not escape the observation of those who have seen and considered that country with the least degree of attention" (Wood 1775: 103). He further underscores the relevance of his own experience when he recounts how perilous it was for him to sail the Egyptian coast on his 1743 voyage in order to defend the accuracy with which Homer renders the difficulty of the voyage. Wood therefore seems

---

24. Grafton, introduction to Vico 2001: xxi.

justified in his claim that the long-standing dispute over this passage can be solved "not from books, but from the face of the countries which Homer describes" (Wood 1775: 95–96). Nevertheless, we should note that even here, Wood's point depends on what we might call a philological turn. Wood suggests that when Homer describes Menalaus's voyage, it is from Pharos to the Nile, "or, as he calls it, the river Ægyptus, Αἴγυπτος; and not from Pharos to the land of Egypt" (Wood 1775: 100). The dispute, in other words, hinges on the interpretation of a word. Wood continues to claim that even if Homer used the word Αἴγυπτος to indicate the country, it would still have been thirty miles away because, for the reasons detailed above, most of what we think of as lower Egypt did not exist in Homer's time and the distance from Pharos to the south angle of the Delta "would make above fifty leagues, which may be called a day's sail, agreeably to the general proportion, which Homer observes between time and distance in navigation" (Wood 1775: 108–9).

Wood's explanation is suggestive for two reasons. First, his emphasis on accuracy reveals the fundamental standard for Wood's judgment of Homer's excellence: mimesis. Wood consistently praises Homer for the most faithful, mimetic representation of the age in which he lived. Homer's "great merit," Wood claims, "seems to be that of having transmitted to us a faithful transcript or . . . a correct abstract of human nature . . . which belonged to his period of society" (Wood 1775: xiii). Indeed, Wood explains that his inquiry will be limited to Homer's "Mimetic Powers":

> For whether we consider him as a Geographer, Traveller, Historian, or Chronologer, whether his Religion and Mythology, his Manners and Customs, or his Language and Learning . . . in these several views his Imitation alone is the great object of our attention. We shall admit his antient title of Philosopher only as he is a painter. (Wood 1775: viii–ix)

This fundamental belief in the accuracy of Homer's work as representative of the manners of his age extends also to Wood's sense of Homer's geography. We have seen this clearly in the above explanation of the distance from Pharos to Alexandria. Indeed, Wood believed that Homer was so accurate in his geographical descriptions that he could use the text of the *Iliad* to find the site of the original Troy on the Scamandrian plain.

My second reason for noting Wood's use of his own experience to substantiate Homer's accuracy is to underscore the close relationship between Wood's travels and his reading of Homer. Again, the example of the Pharos-Alexandria dispute suggests the close proximity of travel experience and textual analysis for Wood, and we can see this proximity further detailed throughout Wood's published and unpublished writings. Homer, Wood claims in one of his notebooks, "has left us a picture as well as a Map of Greece."[25] As I mentioned earlier, when Wood traveled through the Mediterranean on his 1750–51 tour, the wealth of one of his traveling companions, James Dawkins, enabled them to outfit a ship stocked with a full classical library. Referring to this in the same notebook, Wood declares, "Of all the books in the collection that we made for our ship none was so universally useful & necessary as Homer, while others served particular provinces or particular parts of our voyage he was always in our hands as Poet, Geographer, Historian & antiquarian, by Sea he was our pilot, by land our Guide."[26] Homer, then, was a kind of tour guide for Wood and his companions, and they used the text not only as a guide to Homeric geography, but also as a source of insight into the manners of contemporary inhabitants as they toured the Mediterranean. In the ninth book of the *Iliad*, for example, during the embassy to Achilles, Patroclus orders a bed to be made up for Phoenix. Next to these lines, Wood writes:

> This bed is made in the turkish manner but the turks only take of(f) their outward garments commonly, whereas we see Agamemnon dresses in ye morning; Achilles had we see another lady in the absence of Briseis and Patroclos had also his mistress, but I am not certain whether women are employed at present in ye east to make men's beds.[27]

Like the *Lonely Planet* and other such contemporary guidebooks, Homer's texts served both as a map and as a guide to the manners and morals of the near East.

Wood traveled with Samuel Clarke's *Iliad*. This edition was first published as a folio in London in 1729; each page was set around a generously laid out portion of Greek text, next to which sat a Latin translation in smaller font, with a space below reserved for notes and commentary. Wood's copy, however, was a reprint of Clarke's translation published by J. Wetstenium in Amsterdam in 1743.[28] This printing dropped the notes and commentary of the 1729 edition and printed the Greek on the left page with an equally-sized Latin translation on the page facing it. Because this

---

25. Wood Collection, MS 18: 98.
26. Wood Collection, MS 18: 99.
27. Wood Collection, MS 22: note opposite book 9, lines 655ff., p. 222.
28. Clarke 1743. Measuring 17 by 10 cm and bound in vellum with a flap, this is item 22 in the Wood Collection.

left little space for marginalia, Wood arranged for his binder to interleave blank pages for his extensive handwritten notes.

In her groundbreaking study of readers writing in books, H. J. Jackson categorizes the marginalia produced between 1700 and 1820 under three headings: critical (e.g., evaluative); personal in the sense of registering "the judgment and artistry of a named, living critic, and thereby implicitly convey[ing] an impression of his individual character"; and, finally, as designed to be shared and thus fulfilling a social function.[29] Wood's marginal notes in his *Iliad* would seem to confirm this broad pattern. They regularly evaluate the work at hand, they routinely establish Wood's own positions on the text, especially when it differs from other Homeric scholars like Pope or Madame Dacier, and they were clearly designed to be overseen by others.[30] Reading through Wood's marginalia shows considerable overlap with the comments of his published work on Homer, and one has the sense that marginal notes provided the preliminary material used by Wood for the longer and more formal *Essay*.

Particular aspects of Wood's marginalia, however, distinguish Wood's commentary from that of others in the period. To facilitate his notes, Wood designed an elaboratley categorized key as follows:

A: environs of Troy
B: geography in general
C: criticall remarks
D: beautys
⊕: winds
Δ: women and marriages
⊞: particular customs
S: similie
X: days of ye poem[31]

Jackson observes that such systems are common, but she also notes that "schemes like these are devised for particular occasions and seem not to last. Every time you invent a custom-made system, you have to explain it somewhere, so that it is liable to be more trouble than it's worth. There may

---

29. Jackson 2001: 60.

30. Consider, as an example, Wood's note opposite line 341 of book 14: "I must take the liberty of begging that the Lady's who take the trouble of reading Pope or Dacier's Homer (particularly the latter) would observe that in this most ancient account of a lady's dressing room (very different indeed from that of a modern poet whom they may have read) the first & principall attention is to cleanliness and then to ornament" (Wood Collection, MS 22).

31. Wood Collection, MS 22; code found on the verso of the page at end of Preface.

be annotators with private codes that they used over and over again, but I have not come across them."[32] Wood's system appears only in his copy of the *Iliad* and thus might be seen to conform to the letter of Jackson's comment, but the consistency with which Wood applies his symbols throughout the text suggests that, unlike the systems considered by Jackson, Wood uses his private code over and over again as he reads and rereads his Homer. Similarly, Jackson notes the common practice of interleaving and comments that "There is something premeditated about this convenient arrangement, however, that is at odds with the spirit of impulsive marginalizing, and I have found few examples in which interleaved pages are not used for work-related purposes such as authorial revision, editing, or lecturing." Interleaved volumes, she concludes, "often go this way: annotators begin enthusiastically, but after a while the prospect becomes discouraging—all those blank leaves still to fill—and unless the book is very important to them, or the task quite imperative, they give up."[33] Homer was clearly very important to Wood, because his interleaved pages continue throughout his edition in a manner suggestive of continuous rereading and reannotating; admittedly, they are thickest in the first twelve books, but there are extensive notes in book 24. In this way, Wood's use of his Homeric text distinguishes him from the broad survey of other annotators covered by Jackson.

Wood's marginalia are also distinct from those left by others in Clarke's edition of Homer. Of the numerous copies of Clarke held by the British Library that contain marginal notations, the most common type of marginalia are glosses that add comparative references to other passages or other classical texts.[34] Also prevalent are small corrections to the Greek text,[35] and, sometimes, marginal notes show readers working out the tenses and cases of Greek words.[36] One reader left a small sheet of ledger paper on which are written Greek words next to their Latin translation.[37] Only a single reader's markings are concerned with identifying contemporary locations and names

---

32. Jackson 2001: 29.
33. Jackson 2001: 34.
34. British Library shelfmark 995.d.10, Clarke's *Odyssea,* 2nd ed. (London, 1753), for example, is full of marginalia of this sort; see pages 86 and 183 for examples. Similarly, 995.h.1, Clarke's edition of Homer, *Opera Omnia,* which the catalogue suggests contains marginalia from Charles Burney, also makes comparative references throughout.
35. See British Library shelfmark 995.d.10, p. 82 and 183; also British library shelfmark 995.h.1, p. 7.
36. See British Library shelfmark 1349.c.14, Clarke's *Iliad,* 2nd ed. (London, 1735).
37. See British Library shelfmark 11315.0.18, Clarke's *Iliad,* 5th ed. (London, 1754), between pages 480 and 481.

for ancient references.[38] Finally, all of the comments found in these margins are written in Latin or Greek.

Wood's marginalia, however, are entirely in English; furthermore, while they do contain commentary on the text, and responses to other critics and commentators, Wood's notes are dominated by comparative analysis linking Wood's reading of Homer with his travels. They suggest a process of continuous rereading and comparison. As he explains on one of the interleaved pages, "The following notes which are interleaved are not wrote from having regularly read Homer from the beginning, but I generally carry this book with me in my travels as containing the most inexhaustible fund of entertainment of any I know, so after one regular reading over, I often open him and read any part which first occurs marking such things as strike me. . . . "[39] A separate note further explains,

> Having now compared Homer's pictures of the inanimate materiall world with the originals which he copy'd and found a perfect conformity to truth and nature let us read him over again with a view to collect his different sketches of the human mind. As it was necessary to travel through Greece to make a first comparison so it will be necessary to place ourselves near 3000 years backwards to make this and to make allowances for the state of religion, laws, and manners of that age.[40]

These comments suggest the importance of travel for Wood's project. He emphasizes that only through travel in the region can one see just how perfectly Homer copied nature, with the implication that travel in the regions of which Homer sang affords a familiarity with Homeric geography that illuminates the Homeric text.

In addition, Wood's mention of the need "to place ourselves near 3000 years backwards . . . to make allowances for the state of religion, laws, and manners" of the Homeric age, suggests a kind of Homeric anthropology by which Wood aims to understand Homeric manners through what he sees to be their contemporary analogue—the manners of the Turks and other inhabitants of the contemporary near East. In his marginal notes to his text of Homer, in his notebooks, and in his published texts, Wood repeatedly likens the manners of the contemporary near East to those of the ancient Greeks. We have seen this above in his marginalia to *Iliad* 9. As a further

---

38. See British Library shelfmark 995.d.10, p. 212, 233, 278.
39. Wood Collection, MS 22: note opposite page 2, n.p.
40. Wood Collection, MS 22: first page, n.p.

example, on the subject of the exchange of gifts in *Iliad* 24 Wood comments next to the text, "In severall places through the poem we see how the ancient Greeks and Jews and present Turks agree in the custom of making frequent presents besides which we may observe they agree a good deall in the things presented which was in the old testament change of raiment here for the most part garments of different sorts."[41] Similarly, in his marginalia to *Iliad* 3 on the subject of veils and head coverings, Wood comments "I have in several places observed the agreement between the ancient Jewish & Greek customs & also those used still in the levant, the women did not eat with the men, had no portions, were veiled & had separate apartments."[42] Wood is most explicit about this in his published work on Homer, where he notes that a comparison between the Arabs and Homer will show how accurately Homer sketched the rude state of manners in earlier stages of society. Indeed, Wood notes that the difficulty of reading Homer comes from the need to reconcile ourselves "to usages and customs so very opposite our own," and he explains that "we found the manners of the *Iliad* still preserved in some parts of the East" (Wood 1775: 145). He later notes that the interior of Arabia provides "a perpetual and inexhaustible store of the aboriginal modes and customs of primeval life" (Wood 1775: 155).

James Porter has described this process of comparison between the manners of antiquity and those found amongst the inhabitants of certain present-day classical sites as "a kind of Homeric ethnography,"[43] and these sorts of comments pervade Wood's published work on Homer. Throughout his long chapter on manners, for example, Wood draws a series of comparisons between ancient Greek and present Arabian manners to explain what he perceives as the prominence of dissimulation; the reign of cruelty, violence, and injustice; the virtue attached to hospitality; the unnatural separation of the sexes; rough humor, and so on. What Wood suggests here, then, is that while one cannot travel back to the age of antiquity to experience antique manners and thus better understand the Homeric text that offers a faithful representation of them, one can at least get a sharper sense of those manners through travel among present-day Turks and Arabs, all of whom are seen to share the rude manners of the ancient Greeks. Travel, then, provides Wood compensation for his inability to travel back in time to antiquity. There is, however, a kind of reciprocity in the reverse direction, whereby just as Homer provided Wood and his companions with what they thought to be an accurate geographical map of the region, so too, Homer becomes a

---

41. Wood Collection, MS 22, note opposite bk. 24, line 228.
42. Wood collection, MS 22, note opposite bk. 3, line 140.
43. Porter 2004: 333.

kind of guidebook for the manners of the East. At one point, for example, Wood draws an explicit comparison between heroic and Bedouin manners, both of which he claims lack respect for one's word of honor. "Ulysses," he concludes, "would form a perfect model for those, who wish to make their way in it with security and respect" (Wood 1775: 159).

Up to this point, then, the importance Wood places on travel to the original sites of antiquity, his emphasis on Homer's mimetic skills in describing the geography and manners of these regions, and the very categories of his analysis mark him out as part of what we might call an amateur, tourist tradition of classicism—a tradition that we commonly see as distinct from a more methodological, text-based tradition of philology. Indeed, we often see this more professional rigorous tradition of philology as a response to and vanquishing of exactly this sort of amateur classical scholarship. It is curious to note, however, that Wood uses the same sort of analysis, one based on a treatment of the text as a historical and anthropological document, with its emphasis on the manners and cultural forms that accompany certain stages of society, to support his suggestion that Homer was illiterate. This, I think, complicates our distinction between an amateur, creative tradition and a critical scholarly approach to antiquity,[44] and shows, further, how a more empirical, archeological account of antiquity may, as Joseph Levine has suggested, owe significant, sometimes unacknowledged, debts to a more generically unclassifiable tradition of antiquarian knowledge and insight.[45]

The sharpness and academic logic of Wood's understanding of Homer are certainly apparent in his comments on Homer's language. Wood makes clear that Homer could not possibly have used a Greek "dialect." Why? Wood reasons that when Homer wrote, there was no settled Greek language, and therefore there could have been no standard form against which variations could be considered as dialect: "the distinction of dialects can be only known to a cultivated, and, in some degree, settled state of language, as deviations from an acknowledged standard" (Wood 1775: 238). The same goes for the distinction between Greeks and barbarians and that between poetry and prose. It would be wrong, Wood claims, to grant Homer poetic license because there was no possibility of prose standards from which license to deviate could be granted.

Comments like these suggest that, unlike many of his eighteenth-century contemporaries, Wood was clearly aware of a distinction between the times

---

44. This rather artificial distinction would seem to be Gumbrecht's target in *Powers of Philology* (2003), and we can see further how it might also translate into a division in classical studies between archeology and philology. On this, see Vermeule 1996.

45. See Levine 1987.

of Homer and later ideas of classical Greece, and that he resisted attempts to associate Homer with an idealized notion of Greek classicism. Wood's approach to Homer's language is historical and not grammatical. For him, Homer is primitive poetry. Having thus begun to break down the claims of those "who have affected to discover so perfect a system of morals and politics in Homer" (Wood 1775: xii), Wood continues and asks "How far [was] the use of writing . . . known to Homer?" (Wood 1775: 248). He replies, in what must have been a striking claim to his contemporaries, "Homer could neither read nor write" (Wood 1775: 248).

How does Wood support this claim, and what insights into Homer's work does he gain by it? Like Vico, Wood begins his claim for Homer's illiteracy by noting that there is no reference to writing in Homer. He finds it "remarkable, that, in so comprehensive a picture of civil society, as that which he left us, there is nothing, that conveys an idea of letters, or reading; none of the various terms, which belong to those arts, are to be found in Homer" (Wood 1775: 249). There is the letter carried by Bellerophon to the king of Lycia in *Iliad* book 6, but this, Wood claims, was similar to "Picture Description" and did not use letters. In keeping with the lack of reference to writing, there is much evidence that writing came late to Greece. Wood observes that all contracts and treaties were verbal (Wood 1775: 251), that heroes were buried with a mound but with no inscription (Wood 1775: 252), and that there are no allusions to written laws in Homer, in whose work the word νομός does not occur (Wood 1775: 253).

The Greeks, then, must have gotten their alphabet late, and it must have come from elsewhere. But without an alphabet, how could Homer construct the elaborate, perfect poetry that Wood so loves and praises? Here, Wood reasons that the astonishing power of Homer's poetry arises from the way that lack of writing must have enhanced the powers of memory at a time when less was known so there would have been less to remember:

> As to the difficulty of conceiving how Homer could acquire, retain, and communicate, all he knew without the aid of Letters; it is, I own, very striking. And yet, I think, it will not appear insurmountable, if, upon comparing the fidelity of oral tradition, and the powers of memory, with the Poet's knowledge, we find the two first much greater, and the latter much less, than we are apt to imagine. (Wood 1775: 259)

In other words, while the extent of Homer's knowledge must be lesser, he had a remarkably sharp memory with which to recall fewer things. Wood adds that "in a rude and unlettered state of society the memory is loaded with nothing that is either useless or unintelligible" (Wood 1775: 260). The problem with this, of course, is that Homer, Wood's great hero, becomes something of a barbarian. Here, Wood himself acknowledges that the state of Greece when Homer wrote was such that the Arts were unfamiliar, and the times were barbaric: "Without letters, it may be said, there could be no effectual method, either of ascertaining or promulgating the sense of law; but this corresponds exactly with the wretched state of government, which we have described under the article of Manners" (Wood 1775: 263).

Homer would thus seem to lose from Wood's insights and claims. But this, Wood is at pains to point out, is not the case. "Poetry," Wood declares, "is found in savage life," and it is precisely because Homer writes before the cultivation of modern manners that his poetry is so essential and mimetic, so "true." As Wood explains:

> The simplicity without meanness or indelicacy of the Poet's language rises out of the state of his manners. There could be no mean or indelicate expression, where no mean or indelicate idea was to be conveyed. There could be no technical terms, before the separation of arts from life, and of course no pedantry, and few abstract ideas before the birth of Philosophy; consequently, though there was less knowledge, there was likewise less obscurity. As he could change the form without changing the meaning of his words, and vary their sound without altering their sense, he was not tempted to sacrifice Truth and Nature to Harmony and Numbers. (Wood 1775: 291–92)

Homer, by this account, is not "classical," as many idealizing Greece had insisted, rather he is a barbarian. But this, for Wood, places him closer to the essence of human nature.

With Wood, in other words, we have a clear example of a pre-twentieth-century primitivist: he looks at non-Western cultures and sees Homer. His gaze is not classicist but historicist, although in this sense, Wood's understanding of Homer must be distinguished from that of German thinkers like Schlegel, Schelling, and Schiller, all of whom insist that modernity is defined by the absence of the Hellenic ideal. In the sixth of his *Letters on the Aesthetic Education of Man,* for example, Schiller claims that

> Closer attention to the character of our age will, however, reveal an astonishing contrast between contemporary forms of humanity and earlier ones, especially the Greek. The reputation for culture and refinement, on which we otherwise rightly pride ourselves vis-à-vis humanity in its *merely* natural state, can avail us nothing against the natural humanity of the Greeks. For

they were wedded to all the delights of art and the dignity of wisdom, without, however, like us, falling a prey to their seduction. The Greeks put us to shame not only by a simplicity to which our age is a stranger; they are at the same time our rivals, indeed often our models, in those very excellencies with which we are wont to console ourselves for the unnaturalness of our manners. In fullness of form no less than of content, at once philosophic and creative, sensitive, and energetic, the Greeks combined the first youth of imagination with the manhood of reason in a glorious manifestation of humanity.[46]

Schiller's distinction between his age and earlier ages marks his thinking as historicist. His historicism, here and elsewhere, however, is tied to a classicizing idealization of what he calls the "wholeness of being" of the ancient Greeks. Wood, as we have seen, is also a historicist, but in contrast to Schiller, he does not link his historicism to a classical impulse. Indeed, Wood's understanding of Homer is the opposite of Schiller's: Wood defines the Hellenic through the primitive, through the absence of the ideal.

In this sense, Wood's association of poetry with savage life can be compared to Rousseau's claim in the "Essay on the Origin of Languages" that figurative language preceded literal language and that "at first men spoke only poetry."[47] Rousseau explains that:

> A savage meeting others will at first have been frightened. His fright will have made him see these men as larger and stronger than himself; he will have called them *Giants*. After much experience he will have recognized that since these supposed Giants are neither bigger nor stronger than he, their stature did not fit the idea he had initially attached to the word Giant. He will therefore invent another name common both to them and to himself, for example, the name *man,* and he will restrict the name *Giant* to the false object that had struck him during his illusion. This is how the figurative word arises before the proper [or literal] word does, when passion holds our eyes spellbound and the first idea which it presents to us is not that of the truth.[48]

Both Wood and Rousseau would agree that poetry appears before written language and thus marks "savage" life. For Rousseau this is a problem because he associates poetry and figurative language with lies, or at least with

---

46. Schiller 1995: 97–98.
47. Rousseau 1997.
48. Rousseau 1997: 254.

untruth. Wood, in contrast, celebrates the connection. For Wood, Homer is pure art, but he is also pure life because he lacks artifice. And this lack of artifice is only possible by associating Homer with an earlier stage of social development.

Significant here is the association between language and manners. All of Wood's insights into Homer's language arise from the close association that Wood makes between the state of Homer's language and the state of Homer's manners, and Wood suggests that he has insights into Homer and his manners by virtue of his travels. His dismissal of the supposed "rude manners" of the Turks and Arabs that he encountered on those travels certainly appears culturally insensitive, but the error allowed Wood to develop a sophisticated and influential account of Homer's language. This, in turn, has implications for our understanding of the relationship between the materiality of the letter considered as the concreteness of the text and the material practices that surround the understanding of that text. It would be an exaggeration to claim that without Wood there could be no Wolf, and I have no desire to argue that point. Still, Wood was influential for Wolf, and Wood's combination of Homeric ethnography with the proto-philological analysis of Homer's language stands as an important event in the history of philology. In this context the example of Wood shows that the imagination and the presence-effects so important to Gumbrecht's account of philology are not simply an inevitable result of the philological endeavor, but a necessary precondition to it. Wood shows further how the sort of antiquarian production that we would not ordinarily recognize as philology helps to produce philology, and in this hybrid we can perhaps also recognize the ludic quality that James Porter notes at the heart of the most serious philological endeavors, a tension related to that between parody and positive philology that he describes as the constitutive essence of philology.

CHAPTER 6

What is Philology? Cultural Studies and Ecdotics

Nadia Altschul[1]

In 1982 Paul de Man wrote "The Return to Philology," bringing to the stage, at least within much modern literary scholarship, a term that many would have found difficult to define with any measure of confidence. In Paul de Man's wake, Harvard organized a conference in 1988 on the topic "What is Philology?" It was published in 1990 as both a special issue of the journal *Comparative Literature Studies,* and as the book *On Philology.*[2] Around 1990 discussions about philology and medieval studies had also started to flourish, particularly through a special issue of *Speculum* on *The New Philology* edited by Stephen Nichols.[3] The aftereffects of this publication galvanized medieval studies, producing further self-questioning on the past and future of medieval studies as well as on the significance of philology for medievalists and literary scholars in general. Among these engagements are Seth Lerer's *Literary History and the Challenge of Philology,* William Paden's *The Future of the Middle Ages,* and John van Engen's *The Past and Future of Medieval Studies.*[4] The place of philology in literary and medieval studies henceforth became a very active field of inquiry, and many of its engagements explicitly echoed the title of De Man's by now famous essay. Lee Patterson, for instance, added his own "The Return to Philology" in 1994, and in 1997 David Greetham published "The Resistance to Philology" as a conflation of de Man's "The

---

1. This essay is a revised version of Nadia Altschul, "Terminología y crítica textual," which appeared originally in Altschul 2005. By permission of Editorial Pliegos.
2. Ziolkowski 1990a, 1990b.
3. Nichols 1990b.
4. Van Engen 1994; Lerer 1996; Paden 1994.

Resistance to Theory" and "The Return to Philology."⁵

That there are returns in philology might seem a commonplace, yet it should not be taken for granted that what returns is "the same." A 2004 essay by Marie-Rose Logan on the meaning of the term philology as used by Guillaume Budé (1468–1540), for instance, ratifies that for Budé *philologia, litterae* and *philosophia* were not disciplines or genres but broad semantic fields. Indeed, *philologia* underwent a momentous shift in the late eighteenth and nineteenth centuries, leading it to become an institutionalized discipline. Thanks to this new disciplinary garb, it changed meaning so much that Friedrich Nietzsche's *Wir Philologen*—literally "we philologists"—is more appropriately translated as *We Classicists*. Tellingly, however, Logan also points out that "the range of inquiry in philology was never, it appears, to be defined with any precision."⁶ Fraught by constant returns, never defined with any precision—how may we approach what is philology?

The present essay dwells on the question concerning philology by concentrating on vernacular medieval studies, particularly after the "return" of Paul de Man and the 1990 *Speculum* issue on *The New Philology*. Focusing specifically on the study of medieval vernaculars, I will examine philology as an interplay between its potential range and the specific disciplinary uses in which it is concretized. In order to negotiate this interplay I will compare the Castilian tradition and the Anglo-American tradition in the United States, two very different language traditions whose confrontation will force us to broaden our sense of philology's meaning and range of application.

"Philology" in the Castilian and Anglo-American Traditions

Differences between the Spanish and Anglo-American academic traditions have been observed in the past. Karl Uitti traces the distinction to Yakov Malkiel, and ratifies his opinion that while "philology" in the Anglo-American tradition tends to be understood as the critical study of texts, "the conservatism inherent in the Hispanic tradition" has tended to associate the Spanish "filología" and "filólogo" with "humanities" and "humanist."⁷ Differences may also be revealed in the respective dictionary definitions, which also make apparent the difficulty of giving "philology" a unified sense. The dictionary of the Royal Spanish Academy (*DRAE*) defines *filología* under three headings:

---

5. Both published in de Man 1986. See Greetham 1997; Patterson 1994.
6. Logan 2003: 1148.
7. Uitti 1982: 6.

1. Science that studies a culture as it is manifested in its language and its literature, primarily through written texts.
2. Technique that is applied to texts in order to reconstruct, fix and interpret them.
3. Linguistics.[8]

The *Oxford English Dictionary* (*OED*) organizes these meanings differently and in the pertinent entries defines philology as:

1. Love of learning and literature; the study of literature, in a wide sense, including grammar, literary criticism and interpretation, the relation of literature and written records to history, etc.; literary or classical scholarship; polite learning. Now *rare* in *general* sense except in the U.S.
[. . .]
3. *spec.* (in mod. use) The study of the structure and development of language; the science of language; linguistics (Really one branch of sense I.).[9]

The *OED* does not explicitly mention a sense equivalent to *Textkritik* or the "technique that is applied to texts in order to reconstruct, fix and interpret them," as we find in the second entry of the Spanish dictionary. Thus in order to better approach the meanings in the Anglo-American tradition, and following on the footsteps of Ziolkowski's published recap of the Harvard conference, we shall turn to the entries of the *Webster's New World Dictionary of the American Language*. Despite its relative vagueness, especially when compared to the *DRAE*, *Webster's* presents a rough equivalent to the Spanish dictionary by way of a tripartite definition that includes the reconstruction and interpretation of written texts. Its three headings for "philology" are:

1. Originally, the love of learning and literature; study; scholarship.
2. The study of written records, especially literary texts, in order to determine their authenticity, meaning, etc.
3. Linguistics: the current use.[10]

The association between philology and linguistics is particularly intriguing.

---

8. Real Academia Española 2001. Translations from Castilian to English are my own.

9. *Oxford English Dictionary*, 2nd ed. s.v. "philology." The second entry is deemed obsolete, rendering from Greek the meaning "love of talk, speech, or argument" as opposed to "love of wisdom, philosophy."

10. *Webster's New World Dictionary of the American Language*, s.v. "philology."

While the Royal Spanish Academy sends the reader to a new entry (by printing "Linguistics" in bold face), the *OED* and *Webster's* emphasize that in its modern and current meaning philology is a branch of linguistics. One reason for this is that when the term linguistics was starting to make an impact in the first quarter of the twentieth century, the British academy did not accept the neologism and continued to use "philology" for what became established in other traditions as "linguistics."[11] But Ziolkowski reports that the equation between linguistics and philology was soundly rejected at the Harvard conference and, more significantly, that most of the encounter "was spent in assessing the utility of philology in determining what *Webster*'s so amusingly and evasively designated the 'authenticity, meaning, etc.' of written records."[12] Thus in the oral discussion of the Harvard conference "philology" was closely associated with the *DRAE*'s second entry: the "Technique that is applied to texts in order to reconstruct, fix and interpret them"; or, in different words, to *Textkritik*.

For those present at Harvard in 1988, then, *Textkritik* was the primary meaning of philology. This meaning has been traced by Suzanne Fleischman to one of the works of Erich Auerbach: the *Introduction aux études de philologie romane,* where Auerbach maintained that many scholars consider that the most noble and most authentic facet of the philological enterprise is the making of critical editions.[13] Fleischman concluded that "history seems to have upheld Auerbach's assertion about the centrality of textual criticism to the philological enterprise; so much so, in fact, that for many in the humanities today, philology *is* textual criticism."[14] Fleischman's equation of philology with textual criticism is not laudatory, but we may point out that the relationship with *Textkritik* has stood its ground well enough to be the structuring definition of, for instance, Hans Ulrich Gumbrecht's 2003 *The Powers of Philology.*[15]

---

11. Bolling 1929: 30. I want to thank Boncho Dragiyski for bringing this essay to my attention.
12. Ziolkowski 1990a: 6.
13. Auerbach 1949.
14. Fleischman 1996: 93. As pointed out to me by Sean Gurd, dismissive gestures associating *Textkritik* with philology are also found at the beginning of Ferdinand de Saussure's *Cours de linguistique générale* (Saussure 1916; translated in Saussure 1986). In a maneuver to legitimize linguistics as an independent discipline Saussure states that "early philologists sought especially to correct, interpret and comment upon written texts" (Saussure 1986: 13). Interestingly, considering the observations below, he notes that philological studies "also led to an interest in literary history, customs, institutions, etc." (Saussure 1986: 13–14).
15. "In the title of my book and throughout its chapters, the word *philology* will always be used according to its second meaning, that is, as referring to a configuration of scholarly skills that are geared toward historical text curatorship" and whose other side is the "study of language or, even more generally . . . almost any study of any product of the human spirit" (Gumbrecht 2003: 2).

While this might seem to answer the question "what is philology" in an apparently simple manner, a clearer consideration of non-English language traditions complicates matters. While in US English "philology" elicits connections with punctiliousness and textual reconstruction, in Spanish the term continues to be fruitfully used in a much broader sense. This may be observed in the names of many academic departments. While in the US a typical nomenclature will be *Department of Portuguese* or *Department of Romance Languages and Literatures,* the equivalent in Spain will commonly be known as *Filología francesa* or *Filología italiana*. Moreover, many departments of *Filología* in Spain contain graduate students who see themselves as linguists, while graduates of US Departments of Language and Literature are in most cases still predominantly trained in literary criticism or literary theory. This state of affairs does not equate *filología* with linguistics in Spain, nor does it disqualify an equation of *filología* with textual criticism, but it does point to a different semantic range. Indeed, despite its close connection with linguistics, we can glimpse the broader meaning of *filología* in many Spanish scholarly publications. To provide one significant example, a book by José Portolés on *Half a Century of Spanish Philology* does not mention the field of textual criticism, and is concerned primarily with the history of Spanish literary scholarship.[16] At first sight, a simple explanation would be to accept Uitti's and Malkiel's statements and place Spanish *filología* as part of a more "conservative" scholarly tradition that uses the term in the broad sense of humanistic studies. But the Spanish, British, and US English dictionaries all show that the different facets of "philology" cannot be explained with reference simply to conservative or innovative intellectual traditions. While it might be comforting to set aside the Spanish case as "conservative" while enhancing a more "innovative" English usage, the duality of philology can also be approached as integral to the term itself. In his contribution to *Speculum,* Lee Patterson observes a distinction between "philology as *Textkritik* and philology as *Geistesgeschichte.*"[17] A few years later, in his 1994 essay on "The Return to Philology," Patterson advanced that philology has always been in a constant struggle between these two aspects, and separates a "history of culture" or *Kulturgeschichte* from the erudite and punctilious practices that he had earlier aligned with *Textkritik.*[18]

---

16. Portolés 1986. Among the many essays that work within a similarly broad sense we can mention "The Humanism of Menéndez Pelayo from the Perspective of Modern Philology" by Manuel Muñoz Cortés (1956–57) or "Positivism and Idealism in the 'Spanish School' of Philology" by Francisco Abad (1990).
17. Patterson 1990: 91.
18. Patterson 1994: 233.

In the Castilian tradition, where common usage has maintained the conceptual validity of philology's broader sense, medieval studies handles the ambiguities by making explicit the way the word is used. As examples, we may observe two articles on Hispanic textual editing first published in the journal *Romance Philology*, forming part of the 1991 issue that has been perceived as a response to the 1990 *New Philology* issue of *Speculum*. Due to unexpected circumstances these two essays had the unusual privilege of being translated into English and published in 1995 in a volume on *Scholarly Editing* edited by David Greetham for the Modern Language Association of America. In these essays the Spaniard Alberto Blecua explains that the book by José Portolés mentioned above traces the trajectory of the masters of Spanish Philology "in the broad sense of the term," while the Argentinean Germán Orduna refers to the "philological labors of Ramón Menéndez Pidal . . . at the editorial level."[19] A second striking example of the duality and the *difficulties* of negotiating it—even in the more literal Castilian tradition—is in Pedro Sánchez-Prieto Borja's discussion of "[t]he place of textual criticism in 'philological' studies."[20] Paired with textual criticism, the quotation marks around the word "philological" are used to indicate the broad "humanistic" sense of the term; we are to understand that the use of the word without quotation marks would indicate textual criticism. However, a few pages later, showing indeed how difficult it is to keep a lid on the term, he will write that the lack of rigorous editions in Castilian "is the consequence of a way of conceiving humanistic studies, of understanding philology."[21] In this case, the word denotes a direct equivalent of humanistic studies.

What is important for us here is the dislocation produced by the Castilian tradition in the established equation of philology with *Textkritik* within the Anglo-American sphere. Indeed, the very literal level of engagement found in the Castilian tradition not only clarifies that philology cannot be unequivocally equated with *Textkritik,* but also confronts the reader with a different—and larger—set of terminological alternatives for their intersection. In the following section I will examine one of these terms—Ecdotics—and propose it as an option for conceptual change within the field of editorial philology.

---

19. Blecua 1995: 459; Orduna 1995: 486.
20. Sánchez Prieto-Borga 1996: 19.
21. Sánchez Prieto-Borga 1996: 21.

"Philology" as Ecdotics

In a handbook on Castilian textual criticism published in 1983, Alberto Blecua argued that "the goal of the art of textual criticism is to present a text purified as much as possible of all the elements that are extraneous to the author."[22] To Blecua, however, the terminological disparities within the field were noticeable enough to deserve mention, and he thus provided an extensive footnote on available terms that refer in one way or another to his main topic:

> Dom Quentin coined in 1926 a new term, *Ecdotique* ("Ecdotics"), which some critics use as a synonym for *textual criticism*. . . . [O]thers . . . give to this term a broader meaning, since it would include besides its purely philological nucleus—textual criticism—all aspects of editorial technique. . . . On occasion the term *stemmatics* is also used as a synonym of *textual criticism*, since the so-called Lachmannian method, based on the construction of the *stemma*, is the most widely used. In relatively recent times a new art has emerged under the name *Textology*. The term . . . is common in Slavic philology.[23]

English language readers of medieval vernacular topics commonly encounter "stemmatics" and "textual criticism," but "textology" and "ecdotics" are a lot rarer if they surface at all. In the Castilian case, among the different options presented by Blecua—and despite the use of "textual criticism" in his title—the medieval Castilian field has in great measure chosen "ecdotics." In other words, if in English philology is textual criticism, in Castilian textual criticism is ecdotics.

Ecdotics however is not an "autochthonous" term but one that was incorporated from the Italian editorial school. Dom Henri Quentin coined it to characterize his work in editing the Vulgate, and in time it came to be widely used by the Italian *Nuova Filologia* or neo-Lachmannian school of editing.[24] When the Castilian editorial tradition adopted this tradition in the last quarter of the twentieth century, the term "ecdotics" was also made available within medieval Hispanism.[25] Because of its connection to

---

22. Blecua 1983: 18–19.
23. Blecua 1983: 18–19n5.
24. Quentin 1926.
25. The close connections between the Italian and the Castilian fields have been expressed by neo-Lachmannian critics like Germán Orduna, who traced the disciplinary history of Castilian rigorous editing as an Italian affair: the rigorous neo-Lachmannian method was introduced in Hispanic scholarship through the works of mid-twentieth-century Italian critics such as Giorgio Chiarini, Se-

the *Nuova Filologia,* ecdotics is closely linked with the methodological crisis created by Joseph Bédier when he challenged the appropriateness of the traditional Lachmannian method for the study of medieval vernaculars. After the shock of Bédierist skepticism, Quentin proposed a more "objective" use for common-error analysis in the accurate filiation of witnesses. Quentin's propositions did not succeed in renewing criticism in Lachmannian stemmatics, and it was left to one of his students, Gianfranco Contini, to revitalize ecdotics by positing that editors do not provide a true authorial text but a working hypothesis on the common ancestor of the extant tradition.[26] The term ecdotics as well as the Italian neo-Lachmannian school are therefore both closely related to the crisis provoked by Bédier's rejection of the stemmatic "Lachmannian" method for the editing of medieval vernaculars.[27]

It should be noted in this case that just as the *Nuova Filologia* was less than acknowledged in the apparent homonym of the Anglo-American New

---

bastiano Timpanaro, or Cesare Segre, and their work led to the further introduction of their predecessors, Giorgio Pasquali, Gianfranco Contini or D'Arco Silvio Avalle (Orduna 1995: 488).

26. Contini 1939 and 1986.

27. Although Bédier associated the stemmatic method of the common error with Lachmann, creating the dichotomy known as Bédierism and Lachmannism, Karl Lachmann did not strictly use this method in his editions of medieval vernacular texts. Bédier challenged what he called the Lachamnnian method—introduced in France by his teacher Gaston Paris—in two main venues (Bédier 1913, 1928). The problem centered on the impossibility of objectively recognizing an erroneous scribal reading. Bédier noticed that editors working with the common-error method tended to divide the tradition into only two branches. This implied that there was no objective way to separate between original and erroneous readings and that editors separated until only two irreconcilable options were left. Bédier also noticed that using the common-error method he was able to form four plausible *stemmata* of the *Lai de l'Ombre,* which would lead to four different critical texts. If the identification of error was not secure, and different *stemmata* were equally plausible, then no critical text could be deemed closer to the original. Quentin responded by trying to provide scientific ways of counteracting editorial subjectivity in the recognition of errors, noting that the logic underlying the practice criticized by Bédier was based on circularity and depended on editors' prejudices. He proposed changing the terminology to the neutral concept of "variant"—leaving "error" only for cases when a reading was confronted by an established original—and developed a statistical method that would bypass editorial subjectivity in identifying error (Quentin 1926). L. P. Schmidt, however, argues that there could have been no crisis of the common-error method at the time of Bédier and Quentin because the true formulation of this method only occurred in the aftermath of Bédier's and Quentin's interventions, in Paul Maas's 1927 reply to Bédier's methodological doubts in *Textkritik,* and Giorgio Pasquali's review of Maas's book in 1929 and his fuller reply in *Storia della tradizione e critica del testo* in 1934 (Schmidt 1988: 234). The beginnings of the Italian *Nuova Filologia* would then be placed in Pasquali's rehabilitation of the so-called Lachmannian method in the *Storia,* together with Michele Barbi's 1938 *La Nuova Filologia e l'edizione dei nostri scrittori da Dante al Manzoni.* For further discussion of this history of editorial philology see Altschul 2005: 73–97. For specific discussions of Lachmann's editorial practice, see Ganz 1968 and Schmidt 1988. Mary Blakely Speer's "In Defense of Philology" (1979) and Paola Pugliatti's "Textual Perspectives in Italy" (1998) are especially useful presentations and discussions of the Italian *Nuova Filologia.*

Philology, the term ecdotics is also generally unknown within the US.[28] For instance, when the translation of Orduna's "Ecdótica hispánica" was produced for Greetham's MLA volume on *Scholarly Editing*, his title was renamed "Hispanic Textual Criticism."[29] This situation is related to the history of the "Lachmannian" method in the United States, a revised form of which entered American English studies with the highly influential work of Walter W. Greg on the selection and manipulation of a copy-text for Renaissance compositions. It coalesced as an "eclectic" editorial school after World War II with the aid of Greg's continuators, forming a theoretical triumvirate with Walter Greg, Fredson Bowers, and Thomas Tanselle, and leading an existence somewhat independent from other language traditions.[30] The Italian revisions introduced into the stemmatic methodology starting in the 1930s were not a strong presence in the United States. Instead of presenting a common ancestor as a working hypothesis of the authorial text, the US school produces "eclectic" editions that incorporate textual elements from different available witnesses into a copy-text.[31] The eclectic school can also go as far as to propose that holographic copies in the author's hand also need editorial correction. In the case of modern authors, when the existing holograph does not match the editorial ideal, it may be posited that the editor should reconstitute the composition that the author must have had in his or her mind before writing it down erroneously on paper.[32] Eclectic editors could thus reconstitute not an actual composition—an ancestor or archetype—but the ideal composition that the author would have wanted to write.

In contrast, the term ecdotics and the neo-Lachmannian editorial branch adopted today in the Castilian tradition were both formed in reaction to the critiques of Joseph Bédier. Because of its intellectual descent, "Ecdotics" is therefore the editorial equivalent of the reformed stemmatics of the Italian Nuova Filologia. There is, however, despite this association of "ecdotics" with the reformed Lachmannian branch of *Textkritik,* a more suggestive range to be reclaimed for this term. I would thus like to rescue a proposal of the Spaniard Elisa Ruiz. Ruiz mentions the Greek etymology of ecdotics as the background for an expansion of this term. The etymological connection with ἐκδίδωμι and ἔκδοσις connects the word with the idea of "issuing forth," "sharing with friends," "bringing to light," and thus with the realm of edit-

---

28. In the 1990 *Speculum* issue Howard Bloch mentions the previous existence of the Italian *Nuova Filologia* and disparages the choice "New Philology" (Bloch 1990: 38).
29. Orduna 1991, 1995.
30. For a discussion of the history of editorial debates in the US see Myerson 1995.
31. For the eclectic school see, for instance, Bowers 1978; Greg 1950–51; and Tanselle 1996.
32. See in particular Tanselle 1996.

ing and publishing.³³ Based on these connotations, Ruiz proposed that even if many scholars use the term as a synonym for textual criticism, and even though this was the meaning Quentin conferred on it when he coined it, ecdotics can nevertheless be broadened according to its etymological value to "designate *in genere* the art of editing books."³⁴ We should consider Ruiz's expansion of the range of ecdotics as a valuable addition to the available critical vocabulary in English because of the restricted definition of *Textkritik*. "Textual criticism," despite its ample potential as a semantic field, has a precise meaning in medieval vernacular editing that associates it with the search for authorial texts.³⁵ Although Lachmannism and Italian neo-Lachmannism contend that the common-error method introduced from biblical and classical studies is trustworthy and applicable to medieval vernacular texts, and Bédierism holds that it is faulty, both posit a reconstructed common ancestor or a best-manuscript to stand for the lost authorial composition, avatars, we might say, of the lost authorial text.³⁶

Ecdotics introduces the possibility of breaking away from this emphasis on an authorial text. For instance, it was in confrontation with these two branches of *Textkritik* that the Anglo-American New Philology, consciously basing itself on Paul Zumthor's *mouvance* and Bernard Cerquiglini's *variance,* proposed to account for the constant non-authorial modifications of the linguistic code in vernacular manuscripts of the Christian Middle Ages.³⁷ Elsewhere I have called this third editorial position "scribal versionism" and I have argued for a distinction between it and the Bédierist field.³⁸ But the existence of scribal versionism as a third editorial option opens a particular terminological question. How are we to relate this discordant editorial position to textual criticism? What is the place of a non-authorial stance in a *Textkritik* defined by its interest in authorial originals? The editorial position of the New Philology cannot be subsumed under any of the rubrics available today: it is not a form of Lachmannism, and it is not a form of Bédierism.

---

33. It is worth pointing out that although related to the idea of "publishing," the meaning in Greek was indeed closer to the idea of sharing with friends a work that might not be finished, than to the current notion of releasing a finished work to a broad and unknown reading public. I want to thank Georg Luck for his assistance with this etymology, as well as Sean Gurd.

34. Ruiz 1985: 71.

35. "To present a text purified as much as possible of all the elements that are extraneous to the author" (Blecua 1983: 18–19).

36. I am referring to an avatar as an icon or representation. The word derives from the Sanskrit Avatāra and, tellingly, means the deliberate "descent" or incarnation of a Hindu god-like figure into the earthly mortal realm.

37. For Paul Zumthor's *mouvance* see Zumthor 1970: 325–27; 1972: 65–79; and 1981. For Bernard Cerquiglini's *variance* see Cerquiglini 1989 and 1999.

38. Altschul 2006.

When Bédierism stops positing that the best-manuscript is an authorial avatar and begins to consider that each manuscript is an individually valuable composition, it becomes something else. And this "something else" is not "neo-Bédierism" but a different philosophical take on medieval textuality. The same may be said of the relationship between Lachmannism and neo-Lachmannism. The Italian *Nuova Filologia* viewed itself as a continuation of the Lachmannian methodology and thus continued its attachment to authorial texts. It reformed some aspects of the common error methodology and became, in its own estimation, neo-Lachmannism. But if this reformed neo-Lachmannian methodology eventually separates itself from the search for an authorial *Urtext*, then it will also sever its connection with textual criticism and become something else.[39] The rubric of ecdotics as "*in genere* the art of editing" provides ample room for editorial endeavors that do not hinge on the recuperation of authorial texts. "Ecdotics" can include editorial methodologies such as neo-Lachmannism, the Eclectic school, and Bédierism, but it can also include philosophically contrary endeavors such as the *mouvance*-inspired editorial perspective of the New Philology. "Ecdotics" is also broad enough to include not just specific editorial methodologies but also the study of these methodologies, histories and historiographies, that is, the study and critique of their intellectual genealogies.

At this point, however, it becomes clear that philology is not, or at least not merely, textual criticism for the simple reason that *Textkritik* is only an authorial branch within an editorial world that must accommodate the propositions of the New Philology and the study of *mouvance*. Equating philology with textual criticism also represents a simplification of the editorial terminology, which includes at a minimum stemmatics and Slavic textology. But more importantly, this equation is an unfortunate reduction of the range of philology itself. Earlier we noted that philology includes the study of culture as well as text, a focus reflective of "older" terms such as *Kulturgeschichte*. At first sight, then, the cultural facet of philology may give it the same comprehensive extension it had in the nineteenth century. But it is here that we may find a philology *for the present*. In the section that follows, we will thus move away from the topics opened by philology-as-*Textkritik* and discuss philology as the study of culture.

---

39. I discuss these positions more fully in "The Genealogy of Scribal Versions" (Altschul 2006), where I also provide an example of an ecdotical non-authorial "neo-Lachmannian" enterprise. In an earlier article I had identified a fissure within the neo-Lachmannian authorial edifice in the theory of diasystems of Cesare Segre (Altschul 2003), and "The Genealogy of Scribal Versions" more openly proposes the 2004 edition of the medieval Castilian epic *Mocedades de Rodrigo* by Leonardo Funes—a former student of the neo-Lachmannian critic and theorist Germán Orduna— as an actualization of the editorial possibilities opened up by Segre's diasystems (Funes and Tenebaum 2004).

Philology and Culture

For Fleischman, Anglo-American scholarship has largely followed Erich Auerbach in understanding *Textkritik* as the highest rank of philological activity. Similarly, Stephen Nichols suggests that the Anglo-American literary field followed René Wellek and Austin Warren in their *rejection* of the cultural aspiration of philology.[40] In the highly influential *Theory of Literature* first published in 1942, Wellek and Warren maintained that philology's ambition to study "all products of the human mind" was excessive and, finally, that it would be better to exclude the term from the literary lexicon.[41] Considering that De Man's essay of 1982 was the first to reclaim philology in a noticeable measure for literary studies, and considering that he only recovered those punctilious aspects that closely echoed his own methodology of close reading, it could be argued that Wellek and Warren's injunction to "forget" philology was indeed successful.

Within medieval studies, two aspects seem particularly problematic in the apparent "forgetfulness" of philology's cultural interests. The first is that philology runs the risk of being constrained to meticulous erudition and characterized as a relic from the past, while its cultural facet becomes the property of "new" fields and disciplines. Despite Wellek and Warren's disavowal, it seems apparent that there is need for an analogous term that focuses on a cultural study of the past. Indeed, there are terminological alternatives available for philology as the study of culture, just as there are alternatives for the more reduced meaning of philology as textual criticism. One of the most successful terminological alternatives in the US has been in use since 1979. In this year a group of English-language bibliographers and textual critics founded *The Society for Textual Scholarship* (STS) based in New York City. The STS decided on an innovative term because they intended to bring together all scholars concerned with textual matters of all kinds and because, as Tanselle explained in 1981, "textual criticism" was too closely linked to the study of pre-modern textualities.

> A long tradition of what is usually called "textual criticism" exists, concerned primarily with the texts of classical and biblical writings, and more recently, with medieval manuscripts.... This Society has chosen the term "textual scholarship" rather than "textual criticism" not in any sense as a rejection of the latter term but only because the former is the more encompassing term.

---

40. Nichols 1990a: 2.
41. Wellek and Warren 1956: 38.

The great tradition of classical and biblical criticism forms but one branch of textual scholarship as a whole.[42]

The terminological innovation is not only more inclusive in its incorporation of post-medieval textualities but is also clearly a replacement for the disciplines that were once "philology." "Textual scholarship" is "cumulatively and collectively perhaps a field somewhat like the old 'philology' of an earlier dispensation, the technical and conceptual recreation of the past through its texts, and specifically the language of those texts."[43]

Note that "textual scholarship" seems to rely for its legitimacy on the disappearance of philology's ambition to study culture. So much is this the case that Greetham defines the range of textual scholarship in terms uncannily similar to one of the entries in the dictionary of the Royal Spanish Academy. (Recall that the DRAE defined philology as the field "that studies a culture as it is manifested in its language and its literature, primarily through written texts.") One thus wonders whether "textual scholarship" would have been needed at all if the "old" philology had retained its meaning as a "technical and conceptual recreation of the past through its texts, and specifically the language of those texts."[44] The return to an "old" style of studying culture, however, is not textual scholarship's aim. What alerts us to a more significant broadening is not its interest in including both premodern and post-medieval texts but more particularly a change of object of inquiry. Elsewhere Greetham argues that the difference between textual scholarship and "old philology" does not concern timeframes or even styles of scholarly editing, but the definition of *text* and the separation of textual scholarship from the realm of literature and letters. In Greetham's words: "While literary texts (or, at least, texts composed of words) are the most familiar objects of textual scholarship, the textual scholar may study any means of textual communication—a painting, a sculpture, a novel, a poem, a film, a symphony, a gesture."[45]

---

42. Tanselle 1981: 2. This quotation continues by positing that another branch is the "English-language tradition in the editing of Renaissance and post-Renaissance literature" that we associated with Greg, Bowers, and Tanselle and which figures prominently in the United States and in the STS. It is plausible that a terminological alternative was related to the need to place the US school on equal footing with the older tradition of "textual criticism." We may also point out that the STS posited an additional innovative term and called the editorial facet of philology by the name "scholarly editing."

43. Greetham 1994: ix.

44. In practice, nonetheless, the term textual scholarship has found acceptance as an accessible name that is not restricted by the temporal connotations assumed for textual criticism. This might therefore be a good time to mention that the full title of Gumbrecht's 2003 book is *The Powers of Philology: Dynamics of Textual Scholarship*.

45. Greetham 1992: 103.

Here, with Greetham's inclusion of the written, the aural and the visual as philological objects of inquiry, there arises a second problematic aspect of the "forgetting" of the broader cultural facet of philology: the status of literature as a privileged area of inquiry. We can observe philology's reliance on literature in the dictionary definitions cited above, but it serves us better to point to a more detailed discussion. So, for instance, when Patterson outlines a division within philology between *Textkritik* and *Kulturgeschichte*, the struggle between them is presented as a war between "philological pedantry and literary philosophy."[46] A similar example may be found in Nichols, who identifies a conflict within philology between "language study narrowly focused on textual study [and] literary language as a manifestation of culture."[47] Nichols links this division to the new comparative linguistics, which searched for models of language outside literature and thus "struck at the heart of philology's initial *raison d'être*."[48] He argues that *Kulturgeschichte* emerges from a textual realm limited to literary compositions; it is thus in "literary language" that philology would be able to observe a manifestation of culture. Let us underline that literature may be exceptionally important as a manifestation of culture. It is well posed to produce a living image of the past; it fictionalizes and makes available human interactions within a cultural realm; it is in itself part of the culture of a time and a place. But culture need not be "high culture," and written compositions need not be privileged over nonverbal artifacts, nor need literature occupy for the study of culture a position hierarchically superior to religious, philosophical, technical or other sorts of writing.

We have seen the weight that literary critical figures such as Auerbach, De Man or Wellek and Warren have had at different times on contemporary notions of philology. But a notion of philology as exceeding the realm of the properly literary can also be found in Edward Said's short introduction to Auerbach's "Philology and *Weltliteratur*." For Auerbach himself philology was significantly more than textual criticism, even in the handbook used by Fleischman to posit and critique a restricted meaning for the field.[49] But

---

46. Patterson 1994: 233.
47. Nichols 1994: 123.
48. Nichols 1994: 123.
49. Auerbach devotes a full chapter to "La philologie et ses différentes formes." He does specify that one of the oldest forms of philology—the "classical" form—is the critical edition of texts, and that it is considered by many as the most noble and most authentic form of philology (Auerbach 1949: 9). But together with *Textkritik* he provides other branches for philology: linguistics; literary study, including bibliography and biography, esthetic criticism and literary history; and "l'explication des textes." In "Philology and *Weltliteratur*" he further posits that philology is "a historicist discipline," and that its object of inquiry is the "inner history of the last thousand years," "the history of mankind achieving self-expression" (Auerbach 1969: 5).

Maire and Edward Said note that Auerbach's practice is concerned "with strictly literary philology"[50] and seek to counter this circumscription by re-opening inquiry into texts that are not "literary." "One is always to keep in mind," they write, "that philology's 'material' need not only be literature but can also be social, legal or philosophical writing."[51] Tellingly the Saids still circumscribe philology to the study "of all, or most, of human *verbal* activity,"[52] that is, to texts whose material is not literary but is still composed of words. Today it seems patent that philology can move further away from the realm of letters. As Greetham points out, it need not be circumscribed either to literature or to texts composed of words. Indeed, the field with which philology may have the strongest affinity is not "languages and literatures" but cultural studies. And this affinity, in turn, seems to resonate with earlier disciplinary spans, even with the older *Kulturgeschichte* which included written and visual artifacts as objects of inquiry.

Cultural studies is presently one of the liveliest areas of scholarly research, to the point that some contemporary scholars have identified this shift of interests in the humanities as a cultural turn.[53] The specific caveat presented by cultural studies is that the field is not particularly concerned with the medieval or classical past. In the straightforward words of Simon During, cultural studies can be defined "as the engaged analysis of contemporary cultures."[54] But why not have a cultural studies of the past? Or more properly, in what ways might the "cultural studies" of the medieval past cross-pollinate with the project of cultural studies? Unfortunately *Kulturgeschichte* suffers from the perception that it is extremely technical and absorbed by the nitty-gritty of sound changes, obscure etymologies, reconstructed fragments, and a long line of *etceteras*.[55] But a more yielding point of entrance might be to question what is the final *goal* of philology; and that might just be described as a cultural study of the past.[56]

It would be a mistake to assume that there are no differences between cultural studies and *Kulturgeschichte*. The nineteenth-century view of *Kul-*

---

50. Said and Said 1969: 2.
51. Said and Said 1969: 2.
52. Said and Said 1969: 1; my emphasis.
53. See for instance Grabes 2002 and Hansen 2004.
54. During 2005: 1.
55. During's definition of "engaged analysis" also takes us to a direction that I will not be able to discuss here. "Engaged" is used in three senses, as political or critical engagement, as celebration of different cultural experiences, and as aspiring to join everyday life instead of studying culture as an object (During 2005: 1).
56. The interested reader may peruse recent bibliography focusing on this confluence, such as two special issues of the *Journal of Medieval and Early Modern Studies:* Hahn 2001 and Lees and Overing 2004.

turgeschichte tended towards understanding it as a search for the "spirit" or essence of a collective. As explained by Patterson, *Kulturgeschichte* embodied a commitment to unity or wholeness characteristic of the Romantic beginnings of historicism, in which the aim was to understand "the spiritual radix of the historical period, the *diapason* . . . of which each individuality was but a partial and symbolic expression."[57] Cultural studies does not correspond with this search for a spiritualized and unified notion of culture, nor does it understand culture as a homogeneous whole. On the contrary, one of its main interests is a conscious separation from hegemonic cultural discourses and an attention to hitherto undervalued and underexamined groups and practices.

Interest in a cultural studies of the past is therefore not a reintroduction of the search for the "single radix" of nineteenth-century *Kulturgeschichte;* nor should it imply "doing" *Kulturgeschichte* under fashionable new keywords. One of the keys to the newness of a philology "for the present" is that it does imply a change in our materials as well as a change in the questions we ask of our materials. A philology for the present requires an acceptance of its worldliness, of its functions and effects in the world today, and this means accepting that the questions we have inherited from the nineteenth century need not have the same value that they had at their inception. Yet this should not be understood as meaning that interest in a cultural studies of the past, or in a philology for the present, is merely a retrospective application of questions and interests formulated in *Kulturgeschichte*'s twentieth-century "namesake." Philology as a cultural studies of the past must insist on a mutually engaged approach, where philology is not merely applying and echoing the interests and vocabulary of cultural studies, but carves out a space in which both fields may be pollinated and even redefined in the contact. In other words, while philology should be ready to change its materials and questions and expand its theoretical underpinnings, it is also in a position to modify core issues of cultural studies and thus to demand to be recognized as an active partner in disciplinary dialogues and a contributing member in the paradigm-setting realm of theory.

I hope to have clarified that the study of culture is not foreign but integral to the philological realm; and thus I hope that philology, conceived as a cultural study of the past, could dispel residual doubts that medieval studies "dwells in the past" or is merely a foreign guest at the table of the cultural turn.

---

57. Patterson 1987: 27.

CHAPTER 7

Nietzsche, Rhetoric, Philology

James I. Porter[1]

> Il s'agit du point irréductible extrême où le geste est un corps, un espace, une figure. L'extrême irréductible de tel point est son obscénité: ce point-là n'est ni physique ni géométrique; il est la mémoire de ce qu'est le mouvement dans tout corps. Mais ce dernier est aussi bien affecté de cette mémoire inverse: le corps est une limite dans le mouvement. Cette réversion est infinie.
>
> —J. L. Schefer, *La Lumière et la proie*, p. 29.

No inquiry into the problem of philology, its history, and its chances for recovery and a productive future can afford to overlook Friedrich Nietzsche, who perhaps more than anyone else in the nineteenth century helped to set the agenda for a critical and above all self-critical practice of philology. He paid for his act of daring, for his refusal of academic and cultural prejudices, with the ultimate price: rejection and exclusion, which ought to remind anyone who wishes to engage in a rigorous critique of philological practices that such a gambit is not a game, and if the establishment accepts and even rewards your findings, then this too is worthy of further inquiry. Have times truly changed? Has the establishment become liberal, tolerant, and soft? Or has it grown complaisant and indifferent? Perhaps philology is now irrelevant, a field in which anything can be said because nothing matters. Or perhaps one's findings are a bit *too* acceptable, not trenchant enough to draw

---

1. This essay is a revision of "Nietzsche's Rhetoric: Theory and Strategy," *Philosophy and Rhetoric* 27.3 (1994): 218–44, copyright 1997 by the Pennsylvania State University. Reproduced by permission of the publisher. Abbreviations: CW = *The Case of Wagner* (Nietzsche 1967b); BGE = *Beyond Good and Evil* (Nietzsche 1966); EH = *Ecce Homo* (Nietzsche 1967a); WP = *The Will to Power* (Nietzsche 1967c); GM = *On the Genealogy of Morals* (Nietzsche 1967a). Further abbreviations, as they appear, are explained below.

a rejection in turn. Or perhaps a critique of philology modeled after one like Nietzsche's is too calibrated in terms of the privileged stakes of classical culture to find any translatable returns in a postmodern world in which the classics no longer resonate—though I personally find this last theory doubtful, as a quick glance at the media attention over the new Acropolis Museum in Athens strongly suggests,[2] not to mention the unrelenting publications in classics and the swelling, not dwindling, undergraduate classical civilization majors in North America. Classics do matter, and a critique of classical philology ought to matter today as well. Nietzsche's example was never more relevant. What can be learned from it?

A great deal, as Sean Gurd's introduction to this volume makes crystal clear. For one, the mere inclusion of Nietzsche in any history of philology is obligatory, a natural first step in the recovery of philology's internal bearings. His erasure from the official histories of philology was a shameful disgrace. More shameful was the way in which philologists, usually German, secretly continued to visit the Nietzsche archive in Weimar, the better to be able to appropriate whatever gems they could from his brilliant but unpublished *paralipomena* without detection. They forgot that by signing the guest registers they left a paper trail that could be followed years later.[3] Then there is Nietzsche's own method, or rather example. Neither is exactly imitable or capable of being described in a few words. But Nietzsche was a master of philology in every sense. Scrupulously trained, fastidious in his attention to detail, fluent in the languages of his disciplines and intimate with the most arcane primary and secondary sources (albeit with clear predilections for some areas within philology and a disregard for other areas of classics, principally material and visual culture), he was well grounded in the fields he proceeded to unground. He knew whereof he spoke. Finally, he had both feet solidly planted in the present. His critique of philology was cultural, presentist (in the best possible sense), and viewed from the perspective of life and the living. Not only was philology *never enough* for Nietzsche, which meant that philology, while in ways an end unto itself, in other ways was a conduit through which larger questions from adjacent areas of inquiry could be explored (chiefly, philosophy, psychology, and culture, usually in this ascending order). What is more, there is nothing arid about Nietzsche's critique of philology: his writing is free of jargon, it is alive, it speaks to us today with a ferociousness and an urgency that he must have felt at the very moment he composed it; it is driven, it *howls,* even in his most pedantic-

---

2. See Hitchens 2009 and Konstandaras 2009.
3. For a partial list, see Cancik 1995.

seeming footnotes. It knows that no assumption is immune to criticism, and that every claim to knowledge is open to objection, above all claims to knowledge about a past that has been conventionally idealized since classical antiquity itself. Nietzsche further knows that, like their objects, all critiques of philology contain a history and a *habitus* that are embedded in their very appearance of contemporaneity and futurity—appearances that are therefore often the most suspect of all. This is perhaps what makes all philology rhetorical to the core, namely, the concealed historical operations and the habits of the mind and heart lurking in the deepest grammars of its statements. But in order to grasp this last point, one must turn to Nietzsche's critique of ancient rhetoric, an area which, as we shall see, opened up for him an entire field of speculation about the philosophy of thought and language beyond and through classics.

I. Listening to What Writing Says

In an essay from *The Responsibility of Forms* entitled "Listening," Roland Barthes writes, "*Hearing* is a physiological phenomenon; *listening* is a psychological act. It is possible to describe the physical conditions of hearing (its mechanism) by recourse to acoustics and to the physiology of the ear; but listening cannot be defined only by its object or, one might say, by its goal" (emphasis in original). Barthes goes on to identify three degrees of listening: pragmatic or indexical, hermeneutic, and finally a complex attunement to *signifiance* (as against "signification," following the distinction originally drawn by Kristeva). This third term of the aural Barthes polemically labels a modern faculty, and he uses John Cage as an example: "it is each sound one after the next that I listen to, not in its syntagmatic extension, but in its raw and as though vertical *signifying:* by deconstructing itself, listening is externalized, it compels the subject to renounce his 'inwardness.'"[4] Listening at this pitch is "a general 'signifying' no longer conceivable without the determination of the unconscious." As an externalization of the act of speech and hearing, with the intimacies of the unconscious raised to a surface level for inspection but barely audible nonetheless, the "grain" of the voice puts the subject in a pleasurable if precarious state between his or her faculties of comprehension, judgment, and engagement: the voice, sung or spoken, lies within and beyond reach, a double articulation, a sonority and a suggestion. Inflected with colorations, still body and material, the voice is also a site for

---

4. Barthes 1985: 245; 259; emphasis in original.

formation and hardening, for the ultimacy of a shape that shades off into the intangibility of ordinary meaning. Another name for this phenomenon, which contrasts with listening in the strictly phenomenological sense, is the *geno-song*, which provides an "image of the body" through the quasi-physical, quasi-psychological, and ultimately dispersive, intersubjective, and active event of listening.[5] With Barthes, compare the following:

> Once more: I become a better human being when this Bizet speaks to me. Also a better musician, a better *listener*. Is it even possible to listen better?—I actually bury my ears under this music to hear its *causes*. *It seems to me I experience its genesis*—I tremble before the dangers that accompany some strange risk; I am delighted by strokes of good fortune of which Bizet is innocent.—And, oddly, deep down I don't think of it, or don't know how much I think about it. For entirely different thoughts are meanwhile running through my head. (CW 1; second emphasis mine)

The words are now Nietzsche's, although we might nonetheless insist that the *voice* is that which will one day be Barthes's. Nietzsche, too, gives the phenomenon of the voice—of *style*—a kindly hearing. He listens to it with a "third ear," ever attentive to its sources in a "geno-text" (for *causes* above, the German gives *Ursachen;* for *genesis, Entstehung*), to "the rhythmically decisive syllables," to every "break with any excessively severe symmetry," "every *staccato* and every *rubato*," to "how delicately and richly" the "sequence of vowels and diphthongs . . . can be colored and change colors as they follow each other" (BGE 246). And again he notes:

> The most intelligible factor in language is not the word itself, but the tone, strength, modulation, tempo with which a sequence of words is spoken—in brief, the music behind the words, the passions behind the music, the person behind these passions: everything, in other words, that cannot be *written*.[6]

The language in all three passages is a direct descendent of Nietzsche's early lectures on rhythm, but especially his lectures on rhetoric, which will be the primary focus of this paper and to which we shall presently turn. But first, a small paradox: If Nietzsche's statements from *Beyond Good and Evil* are a commentary, not on listening to the spoken voice, but on *read-*

---

5. Barthes 1985: 255, 270, 276 ("it is not the psychological 'subject' in me who listens").
6. Nietzsche 1988 (henceforth, KSA): 10.89.

ing the voice legibly embodied in a text,[7] by the same token, which is to say, *for the same reasons,* so is the latter quotation about "everything that cannot be written," despite its apparent favoring of voice over text.[8] (If you have any doubts about this, just try reading the passage *aloud.*) What is this source and genesis of language, which would seem to underlie, and thus assume primacy over, both written texts and spoken utterances? And why does Nietzsche posit it, when to do so is to appear open to the charge of what he elsewhere calls *Phaenomeno-Manie* or "phenomenomania" (KSA 12.239)—of projecting causes where they are strictly unwarranted? Why assume that what "cannot be written" is *somehow more true,* more revealing, or even more intelligible, than what *can* be written? What is perhaps worse, why assume that the postulation of this dimension "beyond" or "behind" is any more valid than that of "the word itself," or the aspects of language that have to be registered in all their apparent immediacy and then progressively subtracted away, by layers, in order that their putative source might be reached? For there is nothing in principle to prevent the logic of subtraction from being extended *ad infinitum:* if we include not just the passions, but the person, why not go behind the person to the surroundings, the history, or the collective national, cultural, or racial histories behind (but informing) the personal history, and so on, indefinitely? With each step, intelligibility recedes farther away, as does any grasp on the "phenomenalities" to which intelligibility is apparently tied (how can I take it in? how does it appear to me?—and yet, somehow I must, and it does). Perhaps Nietzsche has no other purpose in mind than to provoke this tailspin of logic. In fact, he probably does have this purpose in mind, and several others as well.

Surely part of the problem is the way in which the issue has been framed. Nietzsche is isolating the dimension of language that ordinarily goes under the name of rhetoric or style, but he is clearly attributing to it an extraordinary significance and a rare privilege. Style is not generally considered the *cause* of language or its *source,* because it is an *effect* of words. Nietzsche's analysis is at the very least tendentious; more generously, we might call it hyperbolic. Let us assume that Nietzsche is aiming only at what *escapes* meaning so that meaning may be released—the uncodifiable elements of intelligibility, at the rich seam that lies between the body and discourse.

---

7. Compare the following from Raymond Williams, which reads like a paraphrase of Nietzsche: "The true effects of many kinds of writing are indeed quite physical: specific alterations of physical rhythms, physical organization: experiences of quickening and slowing, of expansion and of intensification" (Williams 1977: 156).

8. As in KSA 10.22: "Because a writer *lacks* many of the means used by one who practices oral delivery, in general he must take as a model a *very expressive* kind of delivery: the copy of that (the written text) will necessarily look much paler in comparison."

Even so, his position is far from clear. The body seems to be one of the instruments in this critical *démontage* of meaning; but then its serviceability is short-lived, for it too, must be jettisoned along with meaning, in favor of a greater, unknown intelligibility—one which, as we saw, may add up to no more than an insight into the contingency of meaning itself. *Could Nietzsche's affirmation of the rhetorical essence of language itself be part of a larger rhetorical strategy?*

So put, Nietzsche's position begins to look less guilty of projecting knowledge into places where this is strictly unwarranted, and still less like a positive theory about language or the body "behind" (even if it is only within) language. At the very least, Nietzsche's position seems to be a provocation and a challenge to common and even uncommon sense: his words seem to point to the opposite of what they seem to mean; yet he does mean what he says. The logic that drives meaning into its endless contingencies is both logically necessary and psychologically inescapable. We cannot prevent ourselves from construing language (any instance of "the word itself") as an utterance, as stemming from a source, not least because language always is an utterance, stemming from *some* source. This observation about language and our relation to it is a fixed feature of Nietzsche's critique of meaning at every stage of his writings. The critique is double-edged insofar as it acknowledges something like what we today would call the intentional fallacy, but implies something further: namely, that the greater fallacy is to imagine that one can escape from the fallacy of projection just by acknowledging it. Thus is Nietzsche able to offer us a phenomenology of reading and understanding and to take away its foundations in the same breath. Intriguingly, he locates the ever-elusive sources of meaning in the materiality of an utterance, but it is a materiality that is necessarily evanescent: here one moment, wherever meaning seems to crystallize, it is gone the next.

In what follows, I would like to concentrate on how the fates of the body's materialism and that of language (which is just another way of naming what rhetoric is) are joined together by their strategic importance in Nietzsche's assault on inherited and habitual ways of imagining the world. In demoting the concept of "the word itself" to incoherence, and in identifying rhetoric with the reason for this demotion, Nietzsche is anticipating Theodor Adorno, who in his *Negative Dialectics* views rhetoric, not as a formal technique, but as the birthright of all expression: it is, in his own striking words, "the body of language" and "the blemishing stain on thought." Rhetoric scandalizes thought and language because it brings them back to our senses, confronts us with all their historical and contextual contingency, and renders thought both materially present (this is perhaps a phenomenological proposition) and, we might say, *materially* intelligible—intelligible insofar as it has a material history, which is emphatically not the same as the abstract and ideal intelligibility that thought's expression would present by itself (this takes us beyond the phenomenology of meaning, in the direction of the more unwieldy contingencies of meaning). Rhetoric *situates* an utterance, radically and ineradicably, though not by referring it to some easily determined final instance. "In the qualitative character of rhetoric, culture, society, and tradition [actually] *bring thought to life*."[9] Both Adorno and Nietzsche are trading on the centuries-old hatred of rhetoric, what Adorno in the same place calls the *ressentiment* towards what rhetoric conjures in the minds of those who would disavow its relevance.

The argument has a special relevance today, not least owing to the prominence that rhetoric has received in poststructuralist circles in the guise of "rhetorical criticism." But rhetorical criticism had a different meaning prior to deconstruction: it was once connected to the classical (Greek and Roman) art of persuasion, oratory, and the analysis of language. Nietzsche, the philologist turned philosopher, has been implicated as a crucial hinge in this transfer of technology from antiquity to postmodernity. If there is any way to recover the philological basis of rhetorical criticism, surely our best bet is to look to Nietzsche. As it happens, returning to Nietzsche will require that we return to antiquity as well. Furthermore, it will require of us a different kind of reading of Nietzsche—less a rhetorical reading than a philological one, a close, scrupulous, and unflinching reading that is not preordained, that does not set out to establish some pre-established truth about the figural nature of all language and (hence) of all thought. Perhaps what a fresh approach to Nietzsche's theory of rhetoric will most of all expose is that such limiting readings of his writings are themselves simply poor instances of philology.

As will be seen from the present essay, Nietzsche tracks language back to its sources beyond language into the realm of the body and the senses, where he finds that the ultimate "rhetoric" lies. Such reductionism, in its voluble muteness, is fatal to all plenary theories of meaning but especially to all models of linguistic determination (the bread and butter of poststructuralist theory). In Nietzsche's hands, however, corporeal reductionism, with precedents in ancient rhetorical and philosophical traditions, is above all a way of disturbing modern paradigms of secure meaning: The very grounds on which this kind of materialism is premised are themselves in need of

---

9. Adorno 1973: 56; emphasis added. Adorno's writings contain, and exhibit, a rhetorical insight that very much deserves to be discussed.

endless and insatiable proof at every turn, a fact that Nietzsche is the first to point out. In this way, Nietzsche's philology of rhetoric leads back to a physiology of rhetoric, which in turn is premised on a historical inquiry in relation to which Nietzsche's own working on and through the matter of rhetoric remains deeply respectful. (At the risk of a slight contradiction, which is really not one at all, we might say that Nietzsche respects the *fact* of historical inquiry, even if he does not always respect the *facts* of history that such inquiry brings to light.) His writings are an encyclopedic encounter with this history. Their materiality just is, in the end, the materiality of this history. And so too, only a philology attuned to Nietzsche's language in all of its complication, perversity, and uncertain certainty will stand any chance of excavating its many and various layers of rhetoric.

RHETORIC ALWAYS invokes a repressed memory. Perhaps what characterizes Nietzsche's willingness to stir up these memories once again, and the same holds for Adorno in his wake, is less his interest in original *causes* (the fully embodied and originary voice of an utterance) than his attention to the persistent *effects* that symptomatically come associated with the disavowal of rhetoric and everything it has come to represent (its scandalous nature). In Nietzsche's case, this takes a peculiar turn, for he reads the disavowal of rhetoric in modern (if you like, bourgeois, or *bürgerlich*) society as a historical *decline* in rhetorical capacities—hence his blistering attack on the deafness of the German ear in the same passage from *Beyond Good and Evil.* In revenge, he does all he can to effect an untimely revival of rhetoric, be it in his own forms of writing or in his explicit theorizing of rhetoric. But the impression that Nietzsche tends to give is misleading, for, if we focus only on the resuscitation of rhetoric and not on that resuscitation *as a critical gesture,* we are missing the greater part of Nietzsche's meaning. This misperception is a calculated part of Nietzsche's purpose and a key element of his seductiveness. Coming to grips with these evasions is what makes reading Nietzsche so uniquely difficult and so hazardous an undertaking. Otherwise, rhetoric—the search for the "genesis" of significance, the "body" of language, or even its tropological system—risks becoming the postulation of a fetish-object that exists somehow independently of the rhetoric of Nietzsche's own language that conveys his ostensible theory of rhetoric. How can we read Nietzsche's theory of rhetoric and at the same time view it rhetorically? This is one of the greatest challenges of his writings, but as we shall see, only a philological approach can help to solve this problem.

II. Figures of Speech and Thought, Bodily Inscribed

Die Physiologie demonstrirt es ja besser! (KSA 13.338)

From even before his early lectures on Greek metrics (1870/71) to the late fragments, Nietzsche is generally given over to a theory of gestural language, language conceived of as corporeal inflection and "externality" (*Geberden, Leiblichkeit, Aeusserung;* cf. EH IV.4; WP 809). The concept of gesture covers without opposing vocality ("the whole reach of the consonantal and the vocalic"),[10] and both are intimately connected with what functions as a register of their material difference, *rhythmos*, "that force which reorders [*neu ordnet*] *all the atoms of the sentence*, bids one choose one's words with care, and gives one's thoughts a new color, making them darker, stranger, and more remote" (GS 84).[11] This "rhythming of speech" (*Rhythmisierung der Rede*) is an atomization, pulverization, and a reconfiguration of language. Gesture asserts itself at the level of the word—and indeed at all levels of discourse—as the *alternation* of stylistic differences, as a series of modulations and modifications. "Life betrays its variety in a wealth of gestures," and so does writing: "One must *learn* to feel the length and brevity of sentences, the interpunctuation, the selection of phrases, the pauses, the sequence of the arguments—as gestures" (KSA 10.22)—just as "all *movements* [of any kind whatsoever] *have to be conceived of as gestures*, as a kind of language" (KSA 12.16 [1885/6]). Rhythm, consequently, marks these differences with the non-mark of their own difference, as their *intermittence*, what Nietzsche elsewhere calls *Intermittenzformen*, "forms of intermittence" ("The Dionysian Worldview," KSA 1.574). And this rhythm is physiologically diagnosable.

At this point one could cite the description Nietzsche gives to the derivation of concepts from sensation in his essay "On Truth and Lying in an Extra-Moral Sense" (1872/3), or the parallel description in his lecture notes on Greek rhetoric, dating from 1874, but most likely resuming materials presented in an earlier course on the same topic, dating from 1872/3. The point of departure in the latter set of texts is in fact rhythm and the aural properties of language, particularly the contrast, which runs through all of Nietzsche's philology, between classical literary sensibilities and their modern correlative. The whole of ancient literature is *rhetorical* in the root sense of the term ("speech"-oriented); its focus is "the ear, in order to captivate it

---

10. "*Das ganze Bereich des Consonantischen und Vokalischen*" is said to be gestural (KSA 7.361 [1871]) somewhat along the same lines as those taken by Dionysius of Halicarnassus in his account of qualities of letters in terms of the mechanics of phonation (*De compositione verborum* chap. 14).

11. Cf. Nietzsche 1933–42 (henceforth BAW): 5.372.

[or 'corrupt' or 'bribe' it: *um es zu bestechen*]." The modern sensibility to rhythm, by contrast, has been worn thin by habituation to written forms of communication: "We are much paler and abstracter." Nietzsche goes on immediately to say, "It is not hard to show that those instruments of conscious art which we refer to as 'rhetorical' were always at work as the instruments of unconscious art [*als Mittel unbewusster Kunst*] in language and its engenderment [*Werden*]. There is absolutely no unrhetorical 'naturalness' to language to which one could appeal: language is itself the result of nothing but rhetorical arts" (R 20/1; trans. adapted).[12]

With this move, the material possibilities of language, its *rhythmos* and peculiar temporality, receive an amazing authorization: they are driven deeply into the very structure and form of language, running from expression down to its embedded grammar (itself a result of figuration [R 24/5]), and from there down to the basic level of sensations (*Empfindungen*) and their underlying neural stimulation (*Nervenreiz*), at which point "communication" no longer applies—although "rhetoric" continues to apply. This process, which trades one kind of naturalness for another, needs to be explored briefly.

What is a word? Nietzsche's answer strikes us as extreme: "The image of a neural excitation in sounds" (TL 248/878; trans. adapted). What is truth? Here Nietzsche's answer is, by contrast, reassuringly familiar: a massive and systematic falsification, "a mobile army of metaphors, metonyms, anthropomorphisms, in short, a sum of human relations that were poetically and rhetorically heightened, transferred, and adorned . . . " (TL 250/880; trans. adapted). But these two arguments, the one "extreme," the other (by now) "familiar," are not unconnected. For, Nietzsche adds, our metaphors, worn thin by overuse, have lost their sensory impact; they are *"sinnlich kraftlos geworden,"* "powerless" to be registered (again) at their original place of origin, the senses (TL 250/880; trans. adapted). One of Nietzsche's aims in his essay "On Truth and Lying" is to replenish the sensory dimensions of concepts and words—their palpability and their defining (negative) trait, their derivation out of that to which they universally stand opposed, sensation: concepts take on sensuous contours ("the concept, bony and eight-sided like a die, and equally susceptible of motion").[13] Words are made "mobile" again. And the relation that binds together the various "stages" in the pro-

---

12. Pagination refers to the facing German and English text and translation (frequently adapted) of the lectures on classical rhetoric (R) as printed in Gilman et al. 1989. Accompanying references to "Truth and Lying in an Extra-Moral Sense" (TL) will be to Blaire's translation in Gilman et al.1989 and to the German text in KSA vol. 1.

13. TL 251/882. Thought is ultimately in the realm of "appearances," and *eo ipso* enjoys a materiality; cf. KSA 7.208: "We behold thought as we do the body [*Wir schauen das Denken an wie den Leib*]"; 7. 130: "It is clear that all appearances are material."

cess leading "up" from sensation to concept-formation is reaffirmed, *à la* Friedrich Albert Lange (one of Nietzsche's major influences from 1866 on), as an "aesthetic" one:[14] "For between two absolutely different spheres such as subject and object there is no causality, no correctness, no expression, but at most an *aesthetic* behavior [*ein ästhetisches Verhalten*], I mean an allusive transference, a stammering translation into a completely foreign language" (TL 252/884). Nietzsche invites us to relive this aesthetic process in all its sensuous fragility and uncertainty.[15]

Nietzsche's premise is that language is derived from a series of discontinuities that are nonetheless translatable one into another, but at a price: contents are lost at each stage along the way. Language (for example, spoken sound) is materially heterogeneous [*ein Fremdes*] to sensation: "How can an act of the soul be presented by an aural image [*Tonbild*]?" Sensation is in turn a summation of nerve impulses, which are incommunicable (but can be felt), as are the sensations (whose contents can only be "copied"). What makes the process *rhetorical*, in addition to being aesthetic, is that, with causes beyond the reach of cognition, this sequence traces the effects of an effect, of a *Wirkung*, "that which makes an impression [*Eindruck*]" in the classical, Aristotelian sense of "rhetoric" (R 20/1). But additionally there is a selectivity to this process: We do not register every effect that makes an impact on us, but only certain kinds of effect; our perception of the world is partial (synecdochal) and even inverted (metonymical). We grasp parts as though they were wholes; we take effects for causes. Finally, if rhetoric, again classically, is whatever instills in us, not knowledge (*epistēmē*), but belief and opinion (*doxa*), then our entire relation to the world has to be described as irretrievably one of *doxa*. All language is in this sense figurative, which is to say, the result of figuration, understood in the broadest possible way.

Nietzsche is not reducing language to a figure of rhetoric. At the very least, he is overwriting, or rather complicating, one rhetoric through another—the rhetoric of the schools (the formal techniques of manipulating words through verbal substitutions) and the rhetoric of the body (the transpositions that occur between sensation and conception). *Prima facie*, his theory is physiological; and this physiology of rhetoric is not "grounded in the rhetorical structure of tropes," as some recent critics would have it,[16]

---

14. See Lange 1866.
15. Heidegger's response to this aspect of Nietzsche's aesthetics (its grounding, "physiological" aspect) is the obvious one, but it is far too literal-minded: "This is a chemical description, but scarcely a philosophical interpretation" (Heidegger 1961: 136).
16. de Man 1979: 123. De Man's views are for the most part typical of the French reception of Nietzsche in the 1970s and 1980s.

because it is not ultimately grounded in any way; rather, it is grounded in nothing but its own polemical and rhetorical purpose. Formally speaking, the theory must be a species of the *doxa* it describes; however, it is wrong to assume that the theory is exhausted by its own formal, self-decomposing logic. The sensualistic derivation of rhetoric remains polemically in place, whatever opinions about this process we may form, and it remains in place not least in the rendering *of* rhetoric (Nietzsche's own, for instance) into something sensual, not to say sensationalistic. If his theory is a piece of *doxa,* by the same token his language is now an extension of the processes it describes; you cannot take on board the premise without taking on its consequence too. There seems to be no exit from this vicious circle.

Nietzsche's theory of figuration represents, we might say, a material disfiguring of rhetoric, however we wish to conceive this last term. His object is not to build up a theory of persuasion, though he may be justifiably attributed with the opposite project: to foster in his readers a sense of *dissuasion* and disbelief, a certain skepticism towards language, and a defamiliarization with the very ideas of sensuousness and of rhetoric.[17] Beyond this, rhetoric can no longer be viewed in poststructuralist terms as the "possibility" of reversal in general;[18] it is just one more effect of a spectrum of indeterminacies, no more explicable than explicating. In dismantling systematically the generalizability of a category like rhetoric, Nietzsche comes down in favor of a much richer declension of specificities, in which the properties of sensation exist as much to undo as to support the properties of rhetoric. This is, after all, one of the lessons of "On Truth and Lying," namely, that categorical divisions, like all generalizations, are false. At this point, his rhetorical strategy becomes a *tactics*.

Nietzsche's earliest rhetorical theory tends towards a thoroughly aporetic stance on language, whose characteristics (rhetorical or other) can no longer be equated but only identified with the totality of their preconditions, and whose contingency lies precisely in this loss of control in the face of what exceeds either the properly linguistic, or else any final understandings of what this might amount to. We might compare his theory, as presented here, with de Man's reading of it: "The deconstruction of the metaphor of knowledge into the metonymy of sensation is a surface manifestation of a more inclusive deconstruction that reveals a metaleptic reversal of the categories of

---

17. Knowledge, Nietzsche knows, is by itself a form of "dissuasion" and a "self-critique." Nietzsche's task is simply to mime this feature of knowledge (GM III.25).

18. De Man defines the signal "property of language" as "the possibility of substituting binary polarities" (1979: 108).

anteriority and posteriority, of 'before' and 'after.'"[19] In contrast, Nietzsche's stance, from even before the lectures on rhetoric to the time of this fragment, is that "the material of the senses [is] adapted by the understanding, reduced to rough outlines, made similar, subsumed under related matters. Thus the fuzziness and chaos of sense impressions are, as it were, logicized" (1887; WP 569). Even if it is true that Nietzsche's claims are self-subverting, it is not because formal reversals can be said to have *replaced* the sensuous logic of Nietzsche's formulation. There is nothing in Nietzsche that would validate some final appeal to a "more inclusive" operation, or to a more powerful register (a deconstructive logic); to affirm the primacy of this logic is to repeat the argument that was to have been displaced, and to reinstate hegemonic categories all over again. Lange had helped Nietzsche formulate a position that would be subversive of its own presuppositions, often by drawing upon the force of sensation (its problematic, stigmatic character): the categories of logic (and *a fortiori* of rhetoric) are themselves sensations and the product of sensations. Causality is refuted, not because it collapses in a figurative metalepsis, but because it is, at bottom, a feeling or sensation to which we have become accustomed; it is "*das Gefühl der Kausalität*" (the feeling of causality) transposed onto the "source" of sensation, that gives the lie to the categorical, *a priori* status of causality.[20] But what is the *source* of this "feeling"? Pressed for an answer, Nietzsche no doubt would respond: it is in the "tone, strength, modulation, tempo with which a sequence of words [say, a proposition about causality] is spoken—in brief, the music behind the words, the passions behind the music . . . everything, in other words, that cannot be *written*." The answer leads us back to the totality of conditions that impinge on the logic of causation, its entire prehistory of symptoms and effects, even if we can never arrive in the end at its real origin or cause, although we can always, and always do, presuppose one after the fact (this is what de Man refers to as "metaleptic reversal"). We should ask ourselves whether we can simply attribute the whole of this process and its cause to language, when language itself figures as one of the *results* of the process ("language is the result of nothing but rhetorical arts").

Inveighing against the rubric-like generalizations which concepts are (and the concept of rhetoric, however it is conceived, is scarcely exempt from this either), Nietzsche returns us to the problem of particularities: "Every intuitional metaphor is individual and without equal, and thereby always escapes every attempt to put it under rubrics." Such resistances, we

---

19. de Man 1979: 124.
20. KSA 7.483; 7.469; R 58/59.

might say, are built into the chain of transcriptions across the spectrum of sensation and language. They do not bring us any closer to what is released in the process (meaning, force) or in the exchange of materialities, but they do make us mindful of these losses. Nietzsche's "aesthetics" of discourse, his "physiology of aesthetics," and his associated theory of rhetoric, is thus not an aesthetics of the body, but of *the body lost:*

> For what does man really know about himself? If only he could ever see himself perfectly, as if displayed in an illuminated showcase! Does not nature keep nearly everything secret from him, even about his own body, in order to hold him fast under the spell of a proud, delusory consciousness, unmindful of the windings of his intestines, the swift flow of his bloodstream, the intricate quivering of his tissues! She threw away the key: and woe to the fateful curiosity that would ever succeed in peering through a crack out of the room of consciousness and downward. . . . (TL 247/877)

By satisfying that curiosity in the very same essay and in the lectures on rhetoric (and indeed in this very passage) and by figuring language as the reflex of physiology, Nietzsche is bringing matter back into the picture, upsetting the bloodless abstractions of tropes and figures, and presenting their origins in a schematism that operates at a primary level of a first, and at first unconscious, "repression": the translation of physical stimuli into (subjective) sensations, in a language of signs that inaudibly gives our more familiar language its first determination. That determination is hopelessly lost to us, forever, but it is a loss that is nonetheless *felt*. It is a most poignant theory, and as a theory it would seem to be practically all in vain—were it not for historical precedents. Nietzsche is not reaching after the body, pure and simple. He is cultivating an image of the body that stems from classical antiquity itself.

III. Classical Rhetoric and Gustav Gerber's *Die Sprach als Kunst*

The physiological determination of language, of figures of speech and thought, and the consequent claim that all language is figured, is not something whimsically imposed from modernity and by Nietzsche upon the body in his lectures on classical rhetoric. It is a historically traceable component of classical rhetoric itself, even if it represents only a strand, and often a countertendency, within the classical tradition stamped by Plato and especially by Aristotle. The distinction between figured and unfigured discourse is commonly put into question in the eclectically constituted rhetorical tradition (e.g., by Dionysius of Halicarnassus, *Ars rhetorica* chap. 9 [λόγος ἀσχημάτιστος]; Quintilian, *Inst.* 9.1.12), but perhaps nowhere more dramatically than in a remarkable excerpt from the polemics of Alexander Numeniu, an obscure rhetor from the mid-first century C.E.

In this text devoted to a general classification of figures (*On Figures of Thought and Speech*),[21] Alexander must at the outset defend the difference between figured (rhetorical) and unfigured (lay) discourse against unnamed opponents: "*Some say that figures have no distinctive and proper feature* (οὐδὲν ἴδιον ἔχειν τὸ σχῆμα τῆς διανοίας), *for no unfigured discourse* (λόγον ἀσχημάτιστον) *can easily be found.*" The argument goes beyond the disproof that no unfigured language can be found, which is a large claim in itself. It is also grounded in empirical necessity, for the mind, being in constant motion and as that which gives language its forms, "takes on many shapes (lit.: "figurations," σχηματισμούς), e.g., when it defines, reproves, takes counsel, or does or experiences any one of the things which happens to it," while language, being a mere copy (μίμημα) of the mind cannot help but reflect these configurations in its own shape. The psychology on which this argument is based could easily be Stoic. But it is impossible to tell the provenience of the theory, which for all we know is an *ad hoc* invention of its author. No known Stoic, let alone Stoicizing, theory of rhetoric even comes close to matching it. All we have is this capsule formulation of the theory, which is endlessly fascinating regardless of its possible school affiliations.

Nietzsche would have had a first-hand acquaintance with this text through Spengel's edition of Greek rhetorical writings, *Rhetores Graeci* (1856), which he knew and used. But he would also have had access to it through Gustav Gerber's discussion of the passage in his work in two volumes, *Die Sprache als Kunst* (1871 and 1873),[22] a study that itself appears to be indebted in part to Lange or at least to be breathing in the same post-Kantian atmosphere, and a study from which Nietzsche is known to have borrowed some of his most radical and central formulations—the most famous being the statement, clearly congenial to Nietzsche's Langean persuasions, that all language is an aesthetic figuration, and the most intriguing being the discovery of "*die unbewußt schaffende Kunst*," "the unconsciously productive art" that is the essence of language (in Nietzsche's paraphrase, that which makes language

---

21. Spengel 1856: 11–13; translation from Russell 1981: 176–78.
22. Cf. Gerber 1873: 2.3, 11–12, 18–19.

"an unconscious art").²³ As the sequel will show, the extent of Nietzsche's borrowings in his reflections on rhetoric goes much deeper than has been suspected, and they take him far beyond Gerber—as well as beyond any interpretation of Nietzsche that reduces language to a formal tropology.²⁴

"*Eigentlich ist alles Figuration, was man gewöhnlich Rede nennt,*" "Everything that we usually call discourse is actually figuration" (R 24/5). Gerber's original words read, "That everything we usually call discourse is actually figuration is something into which the ancients had an abundant insight, as will be discussed below."²⁵ Far from being the mere product of a post-Humboldtian world, Gerber's most radical insights, like the bulk of his examples, are themselves in fact borrowed from ancient rhetorical handbooks and drawn from the materials of the Greek language. Instances were indeed abundantly in evidence in the ancient literature. In the passage from Alexander above, language follows the movements of the mind; all that is lacking is a theory of the mind's movements under a physiological description, but that connection was readily available from, say, the derivation in atomism of linguistic and perceptual conventions from natural events;²⁶ and Democritus, after all, was in Nietzsche's own words, "the Humboldt of the ancient world" (BAW 3, 364), a point that he went on to pursue at great length in his lectures and writings (both published and unpublished).²⁷ On this materialist psychology, there is a basic sense in which all language is a matter of figuration, literally a reconfiguration of the materials of sensation and an arrangement of atoms.²⁸ The logic of incommensurability, obtaining between external realities, subjective sensation, conceptualization and

---

23. Gerber 1873:1.392. Cf. 1.303 (critiquing Kant's divorce of sensuality and reason, based on Hamann's arguments to this effect). Gerber boasts himself to be mounting, in a phrase borrowed from Jacobi, "a critique of language."

24. For an unconvincing attempt to trace Nietzsche's ideas on the rhetoricity of language exclusively back to Gerber, see Meijers 1988 and Meijers and Stingelin 1988. A profitable lesson may be drawn from a comparison with Nietzsche's essay "The Dionysian Worldview," especially section 4, which anticipates many of Gerber's ideas on the intrinsically symbolic (in Gerber's terms "figurative") nature of language, the relative and positional value of sound (vis-à-vis its symbolic status) and even of meaning (vis-à-vis its context, *der Satz*). Nietzsche's view evolves partly in reaction to Hartmann. Cf. KSA 7.65 (3[18]); cf. 7.63–64 (3[15–16]), and esp. 60 (3[20]); the entries date back to 1869–70. Eduard Hanslick's ideas about the symbolic character of music in relation to language (e.g., Hanslick 1865: 21–23) are no doubt a further influence.

25. Gerber 1873: 1.391–92.

26. Lucretius, *De Rerum Natura* 4.35–36; Epicurus in Diogenes Laertius' *Lives of the Philosophers* 10.75–76. Both are cited in Gerber 1873: 1.168.

27. See Porter 2000, esp. chs. 1–2.

28. There are differences within this tradition. The Democritean impulse, present even in the Epicurean system, lies in this direction, as is shown by a series of Democritean fragments and Epicurus' *On Nature,* Bk. 28. (See David Sedley's edition of this text in Sedley 1973).

expression, is implied (we might say, rhetorically so) by the contrast that the atomistic view of language brings shockingly to the fore (language is analogous to atoms rearranged, sounds are but streaming atomic films). It is arguably the incommensurability between verbal concepts and things (to make this simplification) more than the specifics of any one mental psychology that is the most astonishing feature of all the conventionalist ancient accounts. (That reported by Alexander above, we might note, is not plainly naturalistic, since it is not clear whether or how the affections of the mind correspond to real objects in the world; at most, they might correspond to the impact of these objects on the mind, which is also the case in atomism.) The same insight, likewise clothed in an empirical psychology, is made into an excruciating aporia of logic in the fragments of Gorgias of Leontini, a flashy rhetorician who took up quarters in Athens around the time that Socrates and Democritus were flourishing.[29] Gorgias's thesis is particularly relevant because it turns on the paradox that if language communicates at all, it communicates not "things," external realities with which it has no measurable relation, but only itself. Words, on this view, are mere *Lautbilder*, or material images of sound.[30]

Both aspects—the physiological derivation of language's figures and the incommensurability of language to reality and vice versa—are present in Gerber's and Nietzsche's accounts; but it might be fair to say that in Gerber these two aspects coexist in peaceful harmony, whereas in Nietzsche they coexist in an unstable tension, as perhaps they should. For Gerber, language, once it is formed, ceases to be physiologically relevant. The material properties of language (euphony, alliteration, rhythm) receive at best perfunctory treatment in his study; they have no critical function and no contrastive purpose; they contain no threats, and they do not, in any case, go past the surface features of sound.[31] Sounds constituted in language may have the status of "things" in the world, but they are the peculiar product of human creativity, a "property of the soul," an appropriated reality—one that is unproblematically and comfortably anthropocentric.[32] This (neo-Kantian) insight into anthropocentrism, however inextricable the condition is held to be,[33] occasions no further probing, no doubts of any kind for Gerber, whose title spells out the exact borders of his study: language and art.

Finally, and most surprisingly of all, the striking claims about the fun-

---

29. See Gerber 1873:1.291, 337.
30. For discussion, see Porter 1993.
31. Gerber 1873: 1.425; vol. 2, sec. 2.3 (an uninspired and conventional treatment).
32. Gerber 1873: 1.169.
33. "aus dieser Welt kann [der Mensch] nicht heraus" (Gerber 1873: 1.160).

damentally tropic nature of language are subsequently watered down by the reintroduction of a "relative" contrast between so-called "aesthetic figures" (these are consciously applied enhancements of the materials of language) and "naive tropes" (unconscious figurations). Here, surprisingly, Gerber sides with Alexander Numeniu against his anonymous opponents, in holding to a proper, central meaning of "figure."[34] In the end, Gerber will deny outright that figures of thought have any meaningful existence,[35] while the unconscious figurative mechanisms of language are permitted to recede into relative unimportance. "The genesis [*Entstehung*] of verbal artworks cannot be explained by appealing to a mechanism that works unconsciously," he writes.[36] Stripped of explanatory or even diagnostic value, Gerber's thesis that "language is art" has lost its original and radical force. Perhaps the most striking sign of this trend, and of Nietzsche's distance from Gerber, is Gerber's insistence that the categories of the aesthetic and the rhetorical are fundamentally to be held apart and distinct: "aesthetic" figures have no rhetorical function "because they do not aim at rhetorical effects or the production [*Erregung*] of affect; rather, they spring from the formative impulse of fantasy . . . and they produce something *beautiful*."[37] This is nothing but aesthetic Kantianism.

Nietzsche, by contrast, appears to take Lange's *physiological* Kantianism to heart and *à la lettre*. Nietzsche's compression and selection of details in his lectures on rhetoric makes for a closer linkage than even Gerber would have liked to have seen between the initial stages of stimulus and sensation and the final stages of expression. That connection is even more prominent in the roughly contemporaneous essay "On Truth and Lying" (which was mentioned briefly above). Nietzsche's investigations into ancient rhythm had, moreover, already revealed the physiological imperatives of rhythm; these are developed along a parallel but somewhat different axis in the linguistic speculations of "The Dionysian Worldview" (1870). Applying these insights

---

34. Gerber 1873: 1.345, 358–59; 2.4–5, 21ff. (aesthetic/naïve); 2.15 (arguing "with" Alexander that "the concept of the figure is obliterated" when, for instance, emotional states are "uncritically" portrayed and reckoned as figures).

35. "Figuration of thought is in itself non-sense" (Gerber 1873: 2.19). Nietzsche would have been able to infer this conclusion from the first volume. (The relative dates of his lecture notes and of his acquaintance with Gerber's second volume are unclear, but this uncertainty is immaterial to my argument.)

36. Gerber 1873: 2.7.

37. Gerber 1873: 2.14; cf. 1.358–59. This difference is critically overlooked by Meijers, who is too keen to eliminate Lange from the picture and replace him with Gerber as the true source of Nietzsche's language theory. But Lange is not the immediate or sole inspiration either. Perhaps we should just allow Nietzsche to be what he for the most part is, a contrary spirit, who reads and interprets as he pleases.

to oratory was a logical step, particularly with respect to the rhetorical view of language as a material that awaits reshaping in the hands of the orator, whose art is that of rhythmical modulation. The orator "rhythms" his or her language, and his or her audience, by exercising a

> feeling for style [*das Stilgefühl*] that demands a modified expression in each case, roughly the way the same rhythm runs through a musical composition unimpaired, though within it the most delicate modifications are necessary. The characteristic style [*viz.*, style adapted to the circumstances and character of the situation at hand] is the proper domain of the art of the orator: here he practices a free *plastic* art; the language is his material lying ready to hand. (R 34/5; trans. adapted)

Language is gestural *because* it is figurative. This is the ancient rhetorical derivation of the meaning of *schēmata*, though one Nietzsche would hesitate to call its "proper" sense (R 66/7). His position is fundamentally that of Alexander Numeniu's opponents, and it reflects a more rigorous application of their principle: "*No* expression determines and delimits a movement of the soul with such rigidity that it could be regarded as the *actual* statement of the meaning" (R 66/7). In other words, if any motions of the soul are a figuration, then all such motions are only fluid, not proper, expressions of themselves. This line of argument has self-destructive implications, which will be discussed further below.

IV. "Hypocrisy"

The corporeal dimension of language and its use is the explicit topic of a subsequent section ("The Rhythm of Discourse," R 82/3), but it figures forth whenever attention is paid to the aural characteristics of discourse, written or spoken, or to oral and theatrical delivery, as in the section with which Nietzsche brings his lectures to a close, on the same note from which he set out:

> *Hypokrisis* [delivery]. According to Dionysius of Halicarnassus, it is divided into πάθη τῆς φωνῆς καὶ σχήματα τοῦ σώματος [modulations (affections) of the voice and gestures (figures) of the body]. The Romans called it *actio* or *pronuntiatio*: according to Cicero the eloquence of the body, *vocis et motus* (*gestus*), acting on the ear and eyes of the listener, is very important: a mediocre speech, recommended by a strong delivery, carries more

weight than the best one without any help. Demosthenes, when asked what was the most important aspect of the orator's profession, said (1) delivery; (2) delivery; (3) delivery. As for the voice, what matters most is its naturalness, and secondly, the way it is used. Range, strength and endurance, suppleness, and timbre [*Klangfarbe*].... A good, sonorous, smooth vocal apparatus [*Organ*] must provide variety by its mode of delivery, in order to avoid monotony.... Then gestures and physical posture [*Körperhaltung*]. The position of the head should be natural and erect. During the proof it is bowed somewhat forward together with the entire body. Gestures must never become pantomimes or living statues of body positions. A remarkable description [can be found] in Quintilian ([*Inst.*] 11.3). (R 164–66; trans. adapted)

"*A period in the classical sense is above all a physiological unit, insofar as it is held together by a single breath.*" (BGE 247; emphasis added). For Nietzsche, recuperating the physiological origins of language means, in ways that it does not for Gerber, retrieving them at every stage, offsetting the inevitable material losses of the medium (along the pathways of sensation leading to concept-formation) with newfound substitutes and a restored "good health" (R 38/9–40/1). The health is of the *body:* this is the kind of beauty–a robustly physiological one–that Nietzsche can oppose to Gerber's aestheticization of rhetoric. By replenishing language with what one might wish to call the "impurities" of its (debased and debasing) physical origins (for "in and of itself there is neither a pure nor an impure discourse," [R 26/7]), Nietzsche is in effect providing a genealogical framework for describing, in a deliciously critical way, the current state of the language. "Who knows how many barbarisms have worked in this way to develop the Roman language out of Latin? *And, it was through these barbarisms and solecisms that the good rule-bound French came about!*" (R 26/7; emphasis added). In reading into the present the preconditions of the linguistic "past," historically and physiologically speaking, Nietzsche is able to apply Gerber's logic more consequentially than Gerber had himself: "Thus, the popular tropes originated from embarrassment and stupidity, the rhetorical tropes from art and delight." With this last remark, Nietzsche captures the essence of Gerber's distinction between naive (*indoctae*) and aesthetic (*doctae*) figures. The sequel, however, tells decisively against Gerber, in the spirit of Gerber's own, more radical (but wavering) insight: "*This is an entirely false contrast*" (R 52/3; emphasis added).

In "On Truth and Language" Nietzsche holds the primary relation of language to reality to be an "aesthetic" one. And the "genealogy" proposed there is likewise calculated to vanish, or rather slowly fade away, in favor of a more embarrassing, because uncertain, question about the persistence of barbarisms in the current refinements of language. The pure essence of language, its *Wesen,* Nietzsche is suggesting, is already materially contaminated, and irretrievably so, with the phenomenality of appearances, and most symptomatically, with acoustic appearance (volume). It is this audibility (this is the full meaning of "rhetorical") or phenomenality (the full meaning of "aesthetic") embedded in language—even when it is written—which constitutes its nature or essence.

> Language is the result of nothing but rhetorical arts. The power [*Kraft*]— what Aristotle calls rhetoric—to discover and to make valid, with respect to everything, that which has an effect and makes an impression is at the same time the essence of language. Language is just as little related to truth, the *essence* of things, as is rhetoric; its object is not instruction, but conveying to others a subjective excitation [*Erregung*] and its acceptance. (R 20/1; trans. adapted)

The key terms are all translations from Greek, although their values have been shifted. Taking Aristotle's label for the *technē* of rhetoric, namely *dynamis* (faculty, capacity), and tying it more closely to a problematics of power and force (*Kraft*), Nietzsche is rewriting the classical definition of rhetoric and its conditions of possibility. In contesting these conditions, Nietzsche is also revisioning the history of classical rhetoric. The first of the lectures, "The Concept of Rhetoric," in fact, offers an interesting, because critical, overview of the historical progression of rhetoric. Passing from Plato's disparagement of rhetorical technique (it is recognized to be valuable only as strapped in the harness of philosophical truth [R 8/9]) to the promotion, by Aristotle, of rhetorical *dynamis* as a full-fledged *technē,* Nietzsche is clear about where his own interests lie—namely, in the common point of convergence between philosophy and rhetoric. For Plato and Aristotle, the rhetorical *dynamis* was neither a cognitive skill (*epistēmē*) nor a technique (*technē*) but rather a power that could be elevated to a *technē,* if not a cognition (R 8/9). At this early stage, Nietzsche has not yet explicitly refashioned the classical concept of *dynamis* into the essence of language's mechanisms, but his criticisms of Aristotle in particular are intelligible only in the light of subsequent arguments. They are also penetrating.

Despite improving on Plato's narrow acceptance of the oratorical art, Aristotle's rhetoric remained, Nietzsche sighs, *eine rein formale Kunst,* an art defined in purely formal terms, to the exclusion of what we might call its *material* conditions of possibility. "*Endlich wichtig das* θεωρῆσαι," "At bottom, theoretical knowledge is what counts [for Aristotle]" (R 10/11; trans. adapted). In Aristotle's view it suffices to know in theory, through a pure mental vision (a *theōrein*), "that which renders an argument plausible [the possible means of persuasion]," "*Es genügt* τὸ ἐνδεχόμενον πιθανόν *zu erkennen, zu schauen* [sc. θεωρῆσαι]." Quoting from Aristotle's definition of rhetoric (*Rhet.* 1.2, 1355b25–26), Nietzsche is also dilating upon its implications, starting with the rarefied duplication of "the possible": the faculty of persuasion, the *dynamis,* is knowing the possible means of persuasion, τὸ ἐνδεχόμενον πιθανόν (Nietzsche will later attack Kant on similar grounds, for justifying the "possibility" of *a priori* judgments by appealing tautologously to the "faculty" of reason for which such judgments are "possible" [*möglich*]; BGE 11). With Aristotle, *inventio* (the possibility, if you like, of discovering persuasive possibility) defines and *exhausts* the rhetorical *dynamis,* both as faculty and as object; together the two aspects of rhetoric, the "possible" as faculty and object, constitute its circular conditions of possibility. Meanwhile, Nietzsche ruefully observes, *elocutio, dispositio, memoria, pronuntiatio* are laid aside as secondary, even dispensable, items because now they only formally flow out of the definition that Aristotle gives to rhetoric.

In point of fact, Aristotle in his *Rhetoric* does slight these topics, which happen (as we saw) to be the subjects to which Nietzsche's own treatment will return at the close of his lectures, under the heading of "delivery" (*hypokrisis*). Nietzsche pursues the logic of his critique a step further:

> Aristotle probably wishes delivery to be viewed not as essential but only as accidental [to the essence of rhetoric; *als Accidens*]: for he views the rhetorical as one finds it in handbooks (*just as he also isolates in his mind the effect of drama as independent from the performance, and thus does not take up in its definition the question of physical presence* [*das sinnliche Erscheinung,* "sensuous appearance"] *on stage*). (R 10/11; trans. adapted)

Nietzsche's criticism strikes at a genuine vulnerability in Aristotle. The link with drama and the *Poetics* is doubly justified: for rhetoric comprises, among other things, the art of delivery, which is to say "acting" (*hypokritikē;* cf. R 34/5, where Nietzsche gives this a profound twist: the rhetor "speaks like an actor who plays a role unfamiliar to him or in an unfamiliar situation"; cf. KSA 7.312 (9[105])); and second, Aristotle's theories of rhetoric and poetics (drama) are founded on a common formalistic assumption, which scants the material and phenomenal dimensions (especially the performative aspects) of both speeches and plays. Compare an entry from 1869/70 (a fragment from the drafts towards *The Birth of Tragedy*): "*Against Aristotle,* who counts ὄψις [spectacle] and μέλος [music] only among the ἡδύσματα [pleasurable garnishing] of tragedy: and already here he sanctions the *Lesedrama*" (KSA 7.78). The physical embodiments of tragic drama, sight and sound, are last on Aristotle's list of tragic components; *lexis,* or linguistic expression, is likewise of lesser interest; and Aristotle does, after all, famously hold that *Oedipus Rex* read produces the same effects as does *Oedipus Rex* beheld on the stage. All of these factors are subordinated, like so many peripheral circumstances, to the formal structure of the play's action, which, at the limit, *needn't be performed at all.*[38] Nietzsche's critique extends along similar lines to rhetoric, because Aristotle's logic is the same here, too. The possibility of persuading, being "contained" already in the concept of the *pithanon* (the potentially plausible), needn't ever be actualized, once it is formally secured. "That is why every *artificial means* of *pronuntiatio* is to be made equally *dependent* upon this *pithanon,*" Nietzsche observes. "*Only the very act of speech [elocutio] is no longer necessary*" (*nur eben das* λέγειν *ist nicht nothwendig,*" R 10/11). And what is *rhetoric* without speech?

Here something quite remarkable stands out: Nietzsche's point is not just that rhetoric (or tragedy, for that matter) is not merely a conceptual, contemplative genre. It is that power and performance, and a certain materiality, must be incorporated into the very formal conditions of possibility of language (*das Wesen der Sprache*), at which point the clash that results destroys the very idea of "conditions of possibility" as a formal or transcendental concept: Either such conditions are a tautology (the possibility of their possibility), as above or in Kant (*vermöge eines Vermögens,* BGE 11); or they are a vanishing point of constitutional excessiveness, and as such indicate not a capacity, but an *incapacity.* "Not being able to contradict is proof of an incapacity [*Unvermögen*], not of 'truth'" (WP 515). Either way, reading these *conditiones sine quibus non* entails detailed cultural analysis and critique, not formal postulation: *there are no conditions of possibility in any pure sense.* Nietzsche's own theory of rhetoric will thus supplement and complete the tendencies of classical rhetoric. The cognitive activity of language is inextricable from the effects of the *dynamis* that it always was, and from the sensuous appearance (*sinnliches Erscheinen*) that Aristotle banned from the conditions of language. The historical progression towards a greater tolerance

---

38. On the extreme formalism of Aristotle, see Halliwell 1986, Appendices 3 and 4. If Aristotle seeks to separate text and performance, Nietzsche's view is that a text (like any thing) is equivalent only to its performances ([re]activations, effects, [mis]readings, viewings, and interpretations)—which are not its "realizations" in an Aristotelian sense. See Alexander Nehamas's discussion of the doctrine that "a thing is the sum of its effects" (Nehamas 1985, ch. 3, and, for example, p. 75, where the following is quoted from *Philosophy in the Tragic Age of the Greeks* 5: "The whole nature of reality lies wholly in its *acts* [*Wirken*]," a view that Nietzsche here associates with Heraclitus and with materialism).

of the technical dimensions of rhetoric, as traced by Nietzsche in his treatise, constitutes in fact a countermovement, which goes against the tide of ancient rhetorical speculation, and even constitutes a regression of sorts. "Theory," once it is exposed as a trope, returns to its physiological ground—as neural excitation (*Reiz*), lodged deeply in the unconscious layers of the body.

Rhetoric is "speech" through and through. *It is the performativity, and not just possibility, of discourse.* Nor can it be detached from the neural sensations that (somehow) entail it or that it entails (rather than causes). By an intriguing inversion, Nietzsche shows that form (the form of discourse) is merely the material limit of a body, while so-called formal conditions are despite themselves ultimately "about" the materializations that thrust form onto a limit. By forcing the phenomenal and material levels into the formal levels, he introduces a category mistake into Aristotle's notion of conditions of possibility, thereby eschewing their classical opposition. Of course, the combined gesture of bringing the body into rhetoric, into its conditions of possibility, and of bringing rhetoric into the center of language and thought is meant to be an impossible condition upon the nature of rhetoric and an affront to the classical tradition that it both contumaciously gainsays and hyperbolically extends.

Rhetoric is only one name for this multiple inversion, which is more than a formal reversal, because Nietzsche's strategy lies as much in his attack on the theoretical status of form (and hence, on various kinds of formalism) as it does in his putting into question the status of the figure and the nature of figuration (*schēma* as bodily gesture and linguistic trope). Rhetoric in the end is reducible not to a trope or figure, nor even to the generalizability of tropes, though its definition is, in effect, consequent upon a general collapsing of figuration, which can no longer support the classical system of figures, and not even its most recent poststructuralist rehabilitation. Hence the improbability of the claim put forward by one of the latter's exponents, namely, that "nonverbal acts, if such a thing were to be conceivable, are of no concern to [Nietzsche], since no act can ever be separated from the attempt at understanding, from the interpretation, that necessarily accompanies and falsifies it."[39] The logic here is incomplete. Because no act of understanding can be separated from the act it seeks to understand, nonverbal acts are very much a concern for Nietzsche, in particular those nonverbal acts which accompany utterance or writing and thereby falsify a purely verbal and formalized understanding of language, and especially those which define, metaphorically, the "language of the senses," or *Sinnensprache.* The senses are

---

39. de Man 1979: 127–28.

endowed, for Nietzsche, with a primitive interpretive function and an unconscious tropology, for "it is tropes, not unconscious inferences, on which our sensory perceptions rest [*Tropen sind's, nicht unbewußte Schlusse, auf denen unsre Sinneswahrnehmungen beruhn*]," and with which they are in fact identical (KSA 7.487; cf. 13.258–59). By this, Nietzsche means to challenge the commonest premises about both rhetoric and sensation (physiology). However, Nietzsche is not reducing sensation neatly to rhetoric. Rather, he is putting into question all valorizations and primacies, across a complex field of variable elements, each with multiple and contradictory associations (as, for instance, rhythm, language, sensation, representation, and rhetoric itself). There are no simple reversals in Nietzsche *because there are no pure elements to be reversed*. Rhetoric and the physiology with which it is inextricably bound up cannot be conceptualized with a "clear conscience": the theory of each of these is inseparable from Nietzsche's largest and ever ongoing polemics with various forms of reductionism. They are poses and postures, not positive doctrines. Indeed, they are the nemesis of any declarative understandings of their subject-matter.

> To study physiology with a clear conscience, one must insist that the sense organs are *not* phenomena [*Erscheinungen*] in the sense of idealistic philosophy; as such they could not be causes! Sensualism, therefore, at least as a regulative hypothesis, if not as a heuristic principle.
>
> What? And others even say that the external world is the work of our organs? But then our body, as a part of this external world, would be the work of our organs! But then our organs themselves would be—the work of our organs! It seems to me that this is a complete *reductio ad absurdum*, assuming that the concept of a *causa sui* is something fundamentally absurd. Consequently, the external world is *not* the work of our organs—? (BGE 15)

Nietzsche's hedging and unfinished thought are characteristic of his resistance to simple solutions. He probably means no more than to lay bare the difficult conjunction of ideas he has produced for us. The last question of this quote is therefore not quite rhetorical, because it has a rhetorical purpose, part of which is to unsettle any final certainties we may believe we have, and part of which serves to remind us that Nietzsche's writings often reflect a physiology conducted in *bad* conscience, hypocritically: physiology is less a *cause* than a *symptom* to be diagnosed; but neither is it eliminable as a factor. Nietzsche's earliest reflections on language and rhetoric are only one example of Nietzsche's *mauvais fois*.

V. Conclusion: *Caveat lector*

Above I mentioned that Nietzsche's borrowings and allusions in his lectures on rhetoric go beyond Gerber to unexpected sources. One of these sources is Kant. The formal resemblances that can be traced between Kant's "schematism," that "concealed art [*verborgene Kunst*]" to which Kant devotes a central chapter of the first *Critique* (B 176), and Nietzsche's own "unconscious art" (*unbewusste Kunst,* here taken from Gerber), which is hinted at and named throughout his entire *oeuvre,* are astonishingly close, but it will be impossible to examine these connections here. Were there time, one might also compare Nietzsche's parodic inversion of Kant's schematism in an early writing, presumably a draft of a never completed or included section to *The Birth of Tragedy* (it is placed by Mette among the papers to "Socrates and Greek Tragedy"), and formerly known under the heading, "On Word and Music" (KSA 7.359–69, written in the spring of 1871). The topic of this piece is the origins of language, which Nietzsche familiarly locates in an "indecipherable" region that nonetheless gives rise to tonality and then to gesture and finally to words. In an idiom that is indebted to Schopenhauer and that Nietzsche will never entirely reject, language (all discourse) is a translation and preservation, in another medium, of the "movement and appearance" of the "will"—its material embodiment. This commotion, rippling through words, emerges in a pulsating intermittence, be it in the form of a rhythmical tempo, of a tonal dynamic, of a harmonic or dissonant relation, or of logic itself ("The Dionysian Worldview," KSA 1.574–77). It makes no difference to Nietzsche that the source of this motion in language might itself be a projection, whether from within language (this is its idealizing tendency, especially in the face of its own essential incongruousness) or from without (by analogy to empirical motions), or, as is most probably the case, from a combination of the two.

Such Schopenhauerian moments in Nietzsche are always fraught with ambiguity. Schopenhauer gives Nietzsche one pretext to volatilize the concept of "language," but not the only pretext. What is language? We have already seen how Nietzsche takes pains, in "On Truth and Lying," to give us as alienating a reply to the question as the imagination, guided by scientific "rigor," is capable of offering. Schopenhauer suggests another: *language* is a most misleading word because it represents a halt in the rhythmical flow of the movements (of the will) that pulsate through the words we use (and so, too, is the word *language* itself made to tremble). But these are only two possibilities, and they crucially overlook a third: Nietzsche's own use of language. Provocatively, we might say that Nietzsche has no theory of "language" because such a concept is the very hypostasis that his own performative *practice* of language would call into question. The same can be said of his so-called "theory of rhetoric," which represents more than a radicalizing of then current rhetorical theory: it is best viewed as an extension of Nietzsche's ongoing use of classical philology as a mode of critiquing contemporary ("modern") culture.[40] A further observation on this practice, apropos of Schopenhauerian will, might be useful at this point.

What is essential in the pages on the origin of music and in "The Dionysian Worldview" essay, as well as in everything that Nietzsche wrote that smacks of Schopenhauerianism (from *The Birth of Tragedy* down to and including the notes on the so-called "will to power"), is the rhetorical duplicity with which he purveys the notion of "will." The word itself, far from alluding to an originary ground of representation, in fact, covers over its abyss—it is after all *nothing but a word* ("the one word 'will,'" BAW 3.353 [in "On Schopenhauer"]), and Nietzsche mimes this complication of origins with his own language, or rather with the rhetoric of his language, which hides what it borrows (by dint of homonymy, or by its *appearance* of critique) and thereby retracts what it offers at every turn. Nietzsche's writings reveal themselves as performances, as embodied paradoxes, which subtly undermine their polemical targets, the authors and texts on which his own language is manifestly parasitical (and hence, often indistinguishably different from that of his "interlocutors"). Critique, once it has been so vitiated, is put into place again on a different register, in a drama that is rhetorically played out between Nietzsche and his antagonists (who are pressed into the service of interlocution), or between Nietzsche and his readers (who all too readily assume identificatory postures with respect to the appearances of Nietzsche's own text). There is no space left to illustrate this ventriloquism here, but our reading of Nietzsche's rhetoric would be incomplete were we to forget that the performative value of his writings *is* their rhetorical value, even when rhetoric is no longer the explicit theme.

One of the main points of this animation and dramatization of voices (or *voicings*) in Nietzsche's writings (a phenomenon that is more subtle—it transpires, after all, *sotto voce*—than his assumption of "masks," which voices also are) is, I take it, that language is uncontrollably historical, overlaid with inheritances, fraught with entanglements and contradictions that are of its nature only to the extent that it has no autonomous nature, but only a history. That history (its "genealogy," in Nietzsche's much misused term) is composed, variously, of memory traces and forgetfulnesses, conscious or

---

40. This notion of philology as cultural critique in Nietzsche is the subject of Porter 2000.

otherwise.[41] Nietzsche's rhetorical artfulness consists in the attempt to activate as many of these registers as possible at any given time, to awaken their memory, and to implicate both himself and the reader in them. Reading Nietzsche, then, is like a perilous balancing act: one is forever in want of ground on which to stand. For this reason, he makes a singularly poor conceptual ally, although this doesn't seem to have diminished his appeal in any way. Nietzsche's theory of tropes, of figures of speech and thought, turns out to be quite alien to our own formal theorization of these things. To follow Nietzsche's writing, one has perhaps to read Barthes, whose suspectly "retrograde" celebration of voice and of textual pleasure is in fact part of a critique of meaning: "*Writing aloud* is not expressive . . . it belongs to the geno-text. What it searches for . . . are the pulsional incidents, the patina of consonants . . . : the articulation of the body, of the tongue [*langue*], not that of meaning, of language [*langage*]. . . . [I]t granulates, it crackles, it caresses, it grates, it cuts, it comes."[42] Or one has to take pleasure in the perilous rhythms of Nietzsche's texts: "The dangerous delight of the quivering, over-sharp blade that desires to bite, hiss, cut" (BGE 246). Nietzsche's writings deserve, and in fact need, to be "read aloud." Only so can a reader's participation in them become *public* (cf. BGE 247).[43] And as for rhetoric—that science which of late has grown so "short of breath"? Nietzsche's writings contain an implicit program for this, too. If our present-day ideas about difference, figure, and even sense can be made to tremble a little, in the light of the vast tradition that underlies them and that in a sense also gives the lie to them, they shall have been done a minimum of justice.

---

41. On genealogy, see Porter 2010.
42. Barthes 1975: 66–67 (trans. adapted).
43. Cf. KSA 10.23: "It is impolite and imprudent to preempt the reader in the easier objections. It is very polite and very prudent [*klug*] to leave it to the reader to express [*selber auszusprechen*, lit. "to say out loud"] the ultimate quintessence of our wisdom himself."

CHAPTER 8

The Philosophy of Philology and the Crisis of Reading

Schlegel, Benjamin, deMan

Ian Balfour

> Philology is now more desirable than ever before . . . it is the highest attraction and incitement in an age of "work"; that is to say, of haste, of unseemly and immoderate hurrying, which is intent upon "getting things done," at once, even every book, whether old or new. Philology itself, perhaps, will not "get things done" so hurriedly: it teaches how to read well, that is, slowly, profoundly, attentively, prudently, with inner thoughts, with the mental doors ajar, with delicate fingers and eyes.
>
> —Nietzsche, *Morgenröte*

How should one think about philology? Is it a subject that lends itself to or even demands philosophical treatment? And how do the general (and thus perhaps philosophical) matters about philology relate to the knotty singularities of reading a given or not-so-given text? Almost as long as the existence of the modern notion of philology there has been a discontinuous tradition of what we could call, after Friedrich Schlegel, "philosophy of philology," some of whose figures would include: Vico, Schlegel, Schleiermacher, Nietzsche, and Walter Benjamin. Each of these figures in their way saw the need for taking a step back from or beyond the workaday protocols of philology to think in a serious, sometimes rigorous way about what philology can and should do. Sooner or later they came to think that not only should one philosophize about philology, but that it may be that a certain philosophy or philosophizing has to be built into philology if it is to live up to what Schlegel calls the "ideal" of philology. I shall try to trace some threads of this tradition in the not wholly arbitrarily chosen trio of Friedrich Schlegel, Walter Benjamin, and Paul de Man.

NUMEROUS THINGS contributed to the sense in the 1790s in Western Europe and particularly in "Germany" (which did not yet exist as such) that the foundations of traditional understanding had been shaken to the core: the French Revolution (according to Schlegel, famously, one of the three great "tendencies" of the age along with the seemingly less earth-shattering "events" of Goethe's *Wilhelm Meister* and Johann Gottlieb Fichte's *Wissenschaftlehre*) was at once the symptom and the cause of many upheavals in social practices, with massive consequences for the rethinking of a whole spectrum of theoretical and political assumptions; Winckelmann's *History of Ancient Art* had effected something of a revolution of its own in its spectacular three-pronged attempt to do justice to the history, theory, and experience of ancient art (Egyptian, Etruscan, Roman but mainly Greek); and in the republic of letters in Enlightenment Europe, the effects of the "Quarrel of the Ancients and Moderns" had deepened, such that the stakes were no longer simply deciding who was better, the Ancients or Moderns, or whether or not or how to imitate one's ancient predecessors. Now it seemed necessary to narrate the immense trajectory or trajectories of history from the beginning of recorded history to now—and to make sense of them. For his part, Schlegel will appear to rethink just about everything regarding texts and history, from "minor" issues (Schlegel asks himself "what exactly is a syllable?") to the most fundamental matters of literature and philosophy ("But what actually is reading?").[1] Many of the possibly eternal verities no longer seemed so veritable: taken together the French Revolution and the Kantian critical philosophy (a new "Copernican revolution," as Kant phrased it) combined to create something of a *tabula rasa* for the subject of the subject: epistemologically, politically, and just about every other way, all bets were off.[2] It would be surprising if there were not manifold consequences for the rethinking of language, texts, and their historical understanding. Is it an accident that philosophical hermeneutics comes into its own as a discipline just at this time?

Friedrich Schlegel writes at a peculiarly fertile, perhaps even tumultuous moment in the history of philology, broadly understood, on the cusp of what would soon be acknowledged as "scientific philology" in the sense

---

1. References to the fragments grouped as "On Philology" ("Zur Philologie") are from Schlegel 1981, henceforth KFSA. References will be given by volume, page and fragment number. "Was ist wohl eine Sylbe ?—Versuch einer Dedukzion derselben" (KFSA 16.34, #148); "Aber was ist denn überhaupt Lesen? Offenbar etwas Philologisches" (KFSA 16.67, #74).

2. And then there was also the matter of writers writing for a new strange thing called the "reading public" (Coleridge called it a "monster"), with which the Schlegel brothers (Friedrich and the less flashy but deeply learned August Wilhelm) had to reckon in their efforts as intellectual "journalists" and translators.

of *Wissenschaft* (organized, systematic, methodology-based knowledge). Depending on how exactly one dates it, this once new philology becomes consolidated just before, during, or just after Schlegel's time. Some would track its inception to the likes, at least in Germany, of Wolf (as Nietzsche does) or Eichhorn; others would hold off on calling it "scientific" philology until the era of Jakob Grimm and Bopp.[3] The premier objects of this emergent philology were the texts of Greco-Roman antiquity, the Bible, and to a lesser extent—as for William Jones, as well as for Friedrich Schlegel and "company," sometimes literally the East India company—the newly discovered (for the modern West) texts of ancient India.

Schlegel often writes in fragmentary fashion, deliberately so, it being a credo of his that the alternatives of being systematic and not systematic are equally deadly. The texture of his thinking oscillates between the totalizing fantasies of a Coleridge and the gnomic pithiness of a Nietzsche. What he writes often has the character of a hypothesis or an experiment or an improvisation, a series of tentative investigations tried out in private and even in public, even if this or that fragment can sound like the most absolute pronouncement, as if fixed in stone.[4] It is not for nothing that one of the best recent readings of Schlegel thinks through his writing on poetry and chemistry in the same, protracted breath.[5]

Most of Schlegel's explicit thoughts on philology, clustered around 1797, remain in sketchy form, in what appear to be notes for an unfinished essay. One of the working titles for the project was "Philosophy of Philology."[6]

---

3. On the history of philology in this period, see for an analysis that is more wide-ranging and international than its title suggests, Aarsleff 1983. Aarsleff (154ff.) discusses Schlegel and his text *Über die Sprache und Weisheit der Indier*. (He is sharply critical of Schlegel's text and its largely uncritical reception. Indeed, the text seems more admirable for venturing into the territory of Sanskrit and ancient Indian culture than for its philological achievements.) In the account of language in Foucault's *Les mots et les choses*, the watershed between epistemes comes sometime in Schlegel's time, say, between Rousseau and Bopp. Schlegel himself ascribes the beginning of "progressive" (modern?) philology to Winckelmann, understanding philology in a typically broad sense. Schlegel studied briefly in Göttingen, a relative "hotbed" for philological practice at the time.

In the matter of dating the beginning of philology, one usually tries to distinguish between more or less learned antiquarianism and "scientific (*wissenschaftlich*)" textual studies and usually philology is reserved for the latter. There is some consensus that for the modern West, it begins in Germany at the end of the eighteenth or beginning of the nineteenth century. For a somewhat different account, see Pfeiffer 1976 on the rich history of philology/proto-philology before the late eighteenth century.

4. See *Athenaeum* Fragment 403: "A real review should be the solution of a critical equation, the result and description of a philological experiment and a literary investigation."

5. Chaouli 2002.

6. Among the few analyses of this text by Schlegel (fortunately, helpful ones) are Patsch 1966 and Michel 1982, especially Chapter II, section 2: 35–42. The pioneering edition and brief study of these fragments is the still useful Körner 1928.

Interpreting this text about interpretation is no easy matter, because it is not so clear what sort of weight Schlegel gives to each of these lapidary notes. Very little appears in the form of an argument: the text, if it even is one, consists of sometimes linked, sometimes disjunctive assertions, together with questions to himself (or us?), as well as notes whose status is hard to ascertain. Some of the claims registered in these notes co-exist uneasily with others and some are downright contradictory when confronted with theses expressed elsewhere in this same cluster. One thing will be asserted in one fragment and the next, distinct fragment will begin "*Nein!*" Or within one and the same fragment an assertion will be ventured, only to have it qualified or contradicted by an "or rather . . . " as if part of what is important is the process or sequence of thinking one thing and then another.

Moreover, and perhaps most tellingly, it is almost as if the formulations regarding the relations of the key terms "philology," "hermeneutics," "critique," and "philosophy" are manipulated like a Rubik's cube to see what permutations and combinations work best, to see what "clicks." Some of these are literally or otherwise in the form of equations or along the lines of "X is nothing other than Y" and "Y is nothing other than Z," "X is Z," and so on. Thus Schlegel will say:

> "Philology is itself nothing other than critique."[7]
>
> or
>
> "Is hermeneutics not also a kind of critique?"[8]
>
> or
>
> "Philology is philosophy."[9]

This last formula or equation (Schlegel often uses mathematical symbols and indices, as unusual in such non-"scientific" texts about philology as they are in psychoanalytic writing other than Lacan's) is listed as one of the "five" "paradoxa." But we are alas only told what some of the other four are, left to wonder for ourselves and not helped out by the fact that so many of Schlegel's dicta have the ring of paradox. Schlegel revels in writing that is in keeping with the root sense of paradox, something apart from the *doxa*, the common or received opinions on states of affairs. He is nothing if not provocative.

The Schlegelian philologist, as becomes clear from these fragments and elsewhere, is in league with both the poet and the philosopher. Schlegel

---

7. "Die Philologie ist selbst nichts andres als die Kritik" (KFSA 16.72, #53).
8. "Ist die Hermeneutik nicht auch eine Art der Kritik?" (KFSA 16.62, #35).
9. Körner 1928: 37.

sometimes appeals to philology as the discourse of the love of words (one thing its etymology possibly suggests) and as such there is no particular difference between the poet and the philologist.[10] Schlegel will sometimes even use the word philology as if it simply refers to what he calls ancient literature, reserving the word "*Literatur*" for something closer to what we might call *modern* literature.[11] This seems to confuse, retroactively, a kind of study of texts with the (literary or nonanalytic) texts themselves; but what seems paramount for Schlegel, in some lights, is the *relation* to words and texts rather than the genre of text one is writing in or about.

With equal plausibility, for Schlegel, the *logos* of philology could mean "reason" as much as "word," "story" or "discourse," and perhaps it is the sense of reason that intimates to Schlegel the proximity, even the identity, of philology and philosophy. As we have seen, in one of his characteristic propositions, Schlegel says in so few words: "Philology is philosophy," one of the five "paradoxa" that seem to be (among) the organizing principles or at least central pronouncements of the essay that was to come. Alternately Schlegel would say (I translate from his shorthand): "Philosophy minus philology equals nothing" ("φσ—φλ = 0").[12] Even if one has a rather lofty idea of philology, it's a very strong claim to say that philosophy without philology is nothing, and thus not even the philosophy it pretends to be.[13] Does Schlegel mean philosophy without the love of words is nothing? Or that philosophy without a certain self-consciousness is nothing, without, that is, reflection in and on the language of philosophy? Likely, it is both: Schlegel tends to assume a subjective enthusiasm for the reader if the text is really to be understood, which he then wants supplemented by some reflection on the process of understanding itself.

These fragments come from a period in which Schlegel had been much taken with Fichte's philosophy, with its commitment to (and faith in) the virtually self-guaranteeing activity of self-positing that characterizes the (free) subject. (One might understand Schlegel's only somewhat later preoccupation with the self-reflexive dynamics of irony as a version, with a twist, of this project.) It seems clear that for philosophy a turn inward to

---

10. See also *Athenaeum* Fragment 404, which reads as something of a digest of many of the points made in the fragments on philology from 1797.

11. On the massive importance and complicated character of Schlegel's distinction between ancient and modern, see, among others, Jauss 1970.

12. KFSA 16.72, #124.

13. Schlegel is hardly the only one to have a sense of the affinity of philology and philosophy. His fellow "Romantic" Novalis could say in so few words: "Philology and philosophy are one" (Novalis 1993: 165).

think about its own procedures, its language in a strict and broad sense, should be an integral protocol, not something that may or may not take place. The very first of the *Athenaeum* fragments (which rarely garners much consideration) reads as follows: "About no object do they philosophize less than about philosophy."[14] Strikingly, the "they" is not specified here: does Schlegel mean philosophers or anyone who thinks philosophically? In any event, Schlegel's inaugural *Athenaeum* fragment laments the conspicuous absence of philosophy's philosophizing about itself, its lack of self-reflection.

If philosophy without philology is nothing, something like the symmetrical reverse is true because the "philologist must be a philosopher."[15] Why might this be so? Because philology, in Schlegel's eyes, not only has to think (doesn't every intellectual discourse?), it has to be reflexive and self-conscious.[16] Schlegel often refers to his own ruminations in these notes on the subject as "philology of philology," philology to the second power. Not every actual work of philology need be reflexive in quite this way—certainly not all of Schlegel's philological essays are so "meta-philological"[17]—but it does to need to be reflective and self-conscious and to this extent is it like the discourse of philosophy (self-conscious, if it is to earn its salt as philosophy) as well the discourse of literature or what Schlegel sometimes calls *Poesie*. For Schlegel, the work of art too is also, at least to judge from its paradigmatic instances, self-conscious. When Schlegel comes to theorize about criticism or critique (*Kritik*) most pointedly, Goethe's *Wilhelm Meister* surfaces as the privileged text: " . . . it turns out to be one of those books which carries its own judgment within it, and spares the critic his labor. Indeed not only does it judge itself, it also describes itself."[18] To be sure, not every novel (much less, every work of art) is so explicitly self-reflexive as Goethe's *Wilhelm Meister*, with all of its manifest theatricality, from puppet plays to a sustained engagement with *Hamlet*. These meta-artistic moments are said to be "not so much criticism as high poetry," thus dissolving the putative

---

14. KFSA 2.3, #1.
15. KFSA 16.35, #8.
16. Schlegel will become one of the premier theorists—and practitioners—of irony, a process that is potentially relentlessly self-reflexive, more so in his hands than some others. For an authoritative general account of irony in Schlegel, see Behler 1993, especially 141–153. For a more pointed but searching essay on the pervasive idea and ramifications of irony in Schlegel, see de Man 1996. Schlegel defines irony as a "permanent parabasis," a paradoxical formulation that makes of interruption, usually by definition occasional and punctual, a constant feature or at least a constant threat.
17. Thus Schlegel's contemporaneous (1797) *On the Study of Greek Poetry* (*Über das Studium der griechischen Poesie*) is by no means as self-reflective as the notes toward the "Philosophy of Philology," though even the title already indicates that it is *about* the study of Greek poetry, not just "a" study of that poetry.
18. "On Goethe's Meister" in Bernstein 2003: 275.

difference between the reflective (analytical?) and the poetic. Philology can be of a piece with its object of study.

And if the philologist, as Schlegel says, "should as such philosophize," this is partly because the literary work that is his or her object is always already philosophical—or at least proto-philosophical—and critical from the outset. It is, as Benjamin phrases it in his extended study of Schlegel, a "medium of reflection."[19] That the philologist needs to be something of a philosopher in the face of the proto-philosophical work of art can be a humbling prospect for the would-be or wannabe philologist, even before we face the prospect of Schlegel's claim in the *Athenaeum* fragments that "one has to be born for philology, just as for poetry or philosophy." Who short of a Curtius or an Auerbach would have the temerity to claim that? We usually think of philology as a rather more artisanal, pragmatic undertaking than is poetry or philosophy.

If, however, born to it or not, one were to become a philologist, one would never be, as it were, out of a job or, more precisely, at a loss for work. Schlegel tells us that the "completed, absolute Philology would cease to be philology": it would "annihilate itself." The odds of this happening—of philology annihilating itself by completing itself—are slim to nil since we are also assured by Schlegel and his contemporaries and friends, such as Schleiermacher, that interpretation, as well as translation in the broad and narrow senses, is an "infinite task." Schlegel invokes just this term to characterize what is entailed in translation: "Every interpretation is an indeterminate, infinite task" (*Jede Uebersetzung* [sic] *ist eine unbestimmte unendliche Aufgabe*).[20] To make matters worse, Schlegel remarks, "Whether translations are *possible:* no one has concerned themselves with that." (*Ob Uebersetzungen möglich seyn darum hat sich niemand bekümmert*).[21] The very status and possibility of translation is thrown into question, even as elsewhere in this same series of remarks Schlegel "knows" that his era is a "true epoch in the art of translation" (KFSA 5.64) for which his brother's translations of Shakespeare are a primary example.[22]

A good deal of the polemical animus in Schlegel's inchoate essay on philology is directed against Kant and Kantians: aspects of this attack hit the target, others glance off. Schlegel maintains, for example: "It strikes one immediately how ridiculous is would be if a real Kantian were to seize on philology. There needs to be much greater insistence on the historicism that

---

19. Benjamin 1973. English: *The Concept of Criticism in German Romanticism* in Benjamin 1996. See especially part, 2 section 1.
20. KFSA 5.16 #18.
21. KFSA 5.60, #18.
22. KFSA 16.64, #50.

is necessary for philology. On the spirit, against the letter."²³ Schlegel seems to presume that the real Kantian would be the Kant(ian) of the critical and/or transcendental philosophy, overlooking, if understandably, given the prominence of the three *Critiques,* the fact that Kant in his early work, in his miscellaneous essays, and in dozens of his lectures, could be as empirical as the next intellectual. Still, there is a powerful insistence in Kant on timeless truths, even when it comes to hermeneutic matters. Thus what counts in the reading of the Bible is not what the human or even divine authors would have meant in their time; rather, Kant simply reads the text for what might correspond to the (timeless) truths arrived at by reason. This too is a matter of spirit over letter, though Schlegel's appeal to spirit goes under the banner of historicism, insofar as what is entailed in historical understanding often means not taking the text at face value, or what appears to a later reader as its literal sense.

One of Schlegel's isolated aphorisms in these notes towards a philosophy of philology reads: "There is a hermeneutic imperative" (*Es giebt einen hermeneutischen Imperativ*).²⁴ This sounds vaguely like some dictum Kant might have uttered—a categorical imperative if there ever was one—but did not. In contrast to the hypothetical Kantian philologist, Schlegel argues for a rigorously and relentlessly historicized understanding. "Everything must be subordinated to history," Schlegel proclaims. After all, the impetus for philology seems to emerge, in the first instance, from a need to understand texts from a time and place decidedly different from that of the interpreter, most notably across the chasm between ancient and modern, a gulf that has to be bridged and may not be able to be bridged.²⁵

Thus the philologist has to be philosopher, critic, and historian. And every reader has to be something of a philologist because the simple act of reading demands something along the lines of what would be philology in the formal, more organized sense. That reading and philology in principle lead or should lead to philosophy, history (or historicizing), and critique (or criticism) means that the process is relentless, as infinite as it is inexorable. That is: if reading is to be reading, if philology is to be philology.

---

23. "Es fällt in die Augen, wie lächerlich es seyn würde, wenn ein eigentl.[icher] Kantianer s.[ich] über die Philolog.[ie] hermachen wollte.—Weit mehr muß insistirt werden auf den Historismus, der zur Philol.[ogie] nothwendig. Auf Geist, gegen den Buchstaben." KFSA 5.35.

24. KFSA 16.68, #10.

25. Numerous fragments posit, by turns, the necessity and impossibility of bridging this gulf. Moreover, the study of the ancients is no mere hermeneutic task, since *being* modern is partly predicated on understanding the ancient Greeks. It goes without saying that in addition to the historical chasm between ancient and modern, one also often has to cross linguistic and national or geographic boundaries.

IN TURNING FROM Schlegel to Benjamin, we are hardly turning at all, since the line from Schlegel to Walter Benjamin could scarcely be more direct. At a decisive moment in his early thinking, when he was embarking on his dissertation (the doctoral dissertation, not the later, failed *Habilitation* on the German Baroque *Trauerspiel*), Benjamin began to explore the parameters of philology in relation to aesthetics, trying to take account of and respond to the various challenges of what he designated as the domains of commentary and critique. He begins this with his early essay on Hölderlin of 1916 or so, an essay never published in his lifetime, and the preoccupation continued through the great essay on Goethe's *Elective Affinities* composed between 1919 and 1922. Philology as a topic and even as a vocation emerges explicitly in some letters to Gershom Scholem in 1921. Here Benjamin notes, in rather unusual terms, how he has "given some thought to philology" and how he "was always aware of its seductive side."[26] He goes on to circumscribe what he means by philology, a discipline one might think of as already rather circumscribed:

> I define philology, not as the science or history of language, but as the *history of terminology* at its deepest level. In doing this, a most puzzling concept of time and very puzzling phenomena must surely be taken in to consideration. If I am not mistaken, I have an idea of what you are getting at, without being able to elaborate on it, when you suggest that philology is close to history viewed as a chronicle. The chronicle is fundamentally interpolated history. Philological interpolation in chronicles simply reveals in its form the intention of its content, since its content interpolates history. (176; emphasis in original)

The apparent delimitation—a history only of terminology—seems very quickly, for Benjamin, to lead to history much more broadly conceived and various of its narrative modes, by virtue of the fact that one would have to come to terms with terms over time. Those who know Benjamin's enigmatic, powerful "Theses on the Philosophy of History" will recognize here some of the key categories of that work (especially that of the "chronicle") drafted some two decades earlier, and thus long before the *soi-disant* conversion to a certain or uncertain Marxism. (Some of these same categories are crucial to other works of the 1930s such as "The Storyteller" essay about Leskov and the long essay on the historical materialism of Eduard Fuchs.) The form of the chronicle preoccupies Benjamin because it stands as a mode that tends

---

26. Benjamin 1994: 175.

not to distinguish between great and small, recording all manner of things, significant or insignificant, for its deferred reading and even redemption at a later day, at some small or ultimate version of the Last Judgment.

This insistence on the desirability of philology is never really left behind, not even in what turned out to be the last years of his life. When Benjamin, in the 1930s, was devoting a good deal of his energy to fighting fascism, he saw his massive, unfinished (perhaps unfinishable) book on Baudelaire and the Arcades as at least indirectly related to that struggle, and part and parcel of his political thinking. But the status of philology in all this was rather fraught, as became clear in the exchanges between Benjamin and Adorno about the former's work on Baudelaire. Having eagerly awaited Benjamin's long-in-the-works work, Adorno, on first reading it, could not conceal his disappointment with what Benjamin had produced, charging it especially with an inattention to *mediation* in its shuttling, perhaps lurching, from the macro- and micro-economic to the sphere of cultural production as it was exemplified in Baudelaire's poems. In responding to and sometimes countering Adorno's various charges, Benjamin wrote back the following on December 9, 1938:

> When you speak of a "wide-eyed presentation of the bare facts," you are characterizing the genuinely philological stance. This had to be embedded in the construction as such and not only for the sake of results. The nondifferentiation between magic and positivism must in fact be liquidated, as you so aptly formulated it. In other words, the author's philological interpretation must be *sublated* in Hegelian fashion by dialectical materialists; that is to say, negated, preserved and raised to a higher level. Philology is the examination of a text, which, proceeding on the basis of details, magically fixates the reader on the text. What Faust took home in black on white is closely related to Grimm's reverence for small things. They have in common that magical element which is reserved for philosophy to exorcise, reserved here for the concluding part.

The allusion to Goethe's *Faust* conjures up the episode where a student says, "Denn was man schwarz auf weiss besitzt, kann man getrost nach Hause tragen" ("What one has in black on white, one can take home with confidence [literally, 'consoled']"), a saying that, when spoken in the presence of Mephistopheles, comes across as distinctly naïve. But this taking-the-text-at-its-word seems to be part of the necessary wide-eyedness of philology, even if it constitutes only one aspect of the philological posture. The other reference to the great philologist Jakob Grimm is perhaps apocryphal; nonetheless, he invokes it at least twice; one other place he does so is in his essay "Rigorous Study of Art" where he praises this attention to (even) insignificant things as "the spirit of true philology."[27] Nothing, in principle, escapes philology and in this it resembles, once again, the chronicle, a mode of history that avoids weighing matters in a balance of great and small. Everything remains to be read, and to be read again, later, differently.

In his response to Adorno, what Benjamin summons up with one hand—the magic of philology's fixation on the text—is spirited away with the other, the more or less tight fist of dialectical materialism. Yet we might not be wrong in thinking Benjamin wants to have it both ways, especially if we understand the emphasis on "sublated" (*aufgehoben*) as indicating preservation. In any event, Benjamin goes on to assuage Adorno on the score of a certain (kind of) philology's eventual disappearance:

> The appearance of closed facticity which attaches to a philosophical investigation and places the investigator under its spell, fades to the extent that the object is construed in an historical perspective. The base lines of this construction converge in our own historical experience.

Benjamin's rejoinder is perhaps somewhat disingenuous, momentarily overstating philology's disappearance to appease Adorno. Indeed, the strong emphasis on the constructive character of what counts as historical knowledge in the present, namely, that it has as much to do with the present moment as with given moments of the past, should be compatible with a permanent need for philology to respond to the demands of two historical moments, one past and one present. Philology's "infinite task" is hardly lessened, much less done away with, by the requirements of this newly conceived historical materialism.

We witness in Benjamin's letters to Adorno the linkage of philology to the outlines of Benjamin's now familiar but still challenging theory of historical understanding. If there is still any lingering doubt about the import of philology for Benjamin's (especially later) thinking, one should pause over this remarkable, lapidary pronouncement in the drafts to his "Theses on the Philosophy of History," which is also to say the theoretical underpinnings of the *Arcades* project, namely: "The historical method is a philological one."[28] Such a resonant and not-so-self-evident dictum virtually requires us to inquire into what is at stake, in Benjamin's hands, in this thing called

---

27. Benjamin 2003: 442. On the origin of the phrase, see Thomas Y. Levin's helpful footnote (n11, p. 448).

28. Benjamin 1972: 1.3, 1238.

philology. The larger passage from which Benjamin's pronouncement comes clarifies what is at stake in his claim and why he might make it:

> If one wants to consider history as a text, then what a recent author says of literary texts would apply to it. The past has deposited in it images, which one could compare to those captured by a light-sensitive plate. "Only the future has developer at its disposal which is strong enough to allow the image to appear in all its details. Some pages of Marivaux or Rousseau suggest a secret sense, which the contemporary reader could not have deciphered completely." The historical method is a philological one, whose foundation is the book of the world. "Read what was never written," says Hofmannsthal. The reader to be thought of here is the true historian.[29]

If for Schlegel and a good many philologists one of the principal tasks is to cross the gulf to the past from the present, Benjamin posits a rather different model whereby the very movement of history can make a text more legible at a date long removed from the moment of its inscription or first publication. This is not an overt or covert argument for "presentism" (as is abundantly clear from the attention to historical detail in the Arcades project especially). That historical knowledge (including most of what is commonly understood as philology) necessarily involves and is only rendered possible in and through the conjunction of two moments, past and present, is spelled out in one of the passages proximate to the "Theses on the Concept of History":

> Historical articulation of the past means: to recognize in the past that which comes together in the constellation of one and the same moment. Historical knowledge is uniquely and solely possible in the historical moment. Cognition in the historical moment, however, is always cognition of a moment. Insofar as the past gathers itself together in a moment—in a dialectical image—it enters into the involuntary memory of mankind.[30]

Historical knowledge occurs only as a relation of one moment to another (and not to some large or small, more or less causally articulated "chain of events"), which is one reason why the models of reading and citation come to be paradigmatic for Benjamin's understanding of history. The French revolutionaries *cite* the Roman revolution (Thesis XIV); they do not tell a grand, continuous narrative that connects them to their forebears.

---

29. Benjamin 1972: 1.3, 1238.
30. Benjamin 1972: 1.3, 1233.

It is not just that our knowledge of history is mediated by reading and citation: it is *structured* as they are, as the encounter of a (more or less) determinate present with a (more or less) determinate past, or of one act of language with another, or of an act of language with something other than language. To speak of historical method as philological risks having it sound academic or antiquarian or worse, rather as if speaking of history in terms of reading and citation might risk "reducing" history to a text. Charges like these pose no particular challenge to or for Benjamin, since there could be no trivialization or reduction involved when language and text are the models, since both for Benjamin are historical through and through, and must be addressed with all due attention, not least in political terms. There is in actuality no such thing as pure language, even if now and then Benjamin explicitly invokes such a model to think about language and history.

This history which demands a philological reading is, to take Benjamin's scattered writings as a (quasi-)whole, structured in the same way as critique, language, and translation. Each, as Benjamin elaborates them, is structured in terms of a relation between two moments, the earlier of which somehow calls for the latter, entailing a logic and a rhetoric of fulfillment, of which Benjamin's "weak messianic power" that inhabits each moment of the past is only the most celebrated and extreme version.

Still, it is striking that philology is proposed as the general model for all historical investigation, given what is entailed, for Benjamin, in the twin guises of history (as *historia rerum gestarum* or historiography and as *res gestae* or action): history's paradigmatic event is the revolution, when things come to a standstill, typically, in a citation of a past revolutionary moment and with an opening to a radically uncertain future, as Benjamin proposes, following closely the opening pages of Marx's *Eighteenth Brumaire*. Benjamin can imagine philology as the model for history because, for him, reading is always a matter of the confrontation of one moment to another. Long before Lyotard's account of postmodernism, Benjamin argued vehemently against the regime of totalizing grand narratives, especially those of inexorable freedom and progress, to focus rather on the moments of knowing and known, reading and what is read.

In the early, great and still not well-enough-known essay on Goethe's *Elective Affinities*, Benjamin spells out one reason why the demands of reading and thus philology are always changing:

> Critique seeks the truth content of a work of art; commentary, its material content. The relation between the two is determined by that basic law of literature according to which the more significant the work, the more

inconspicuously and intimately its truth content is bound up with its material content. If, therefore, the works that prove enduring are precisely those whose truth is most deeply sunken in their material content, then in the course of this duration, the concrete realities rise up before the eyes of the beholder all the more distinctly the more they die out in the world. With this, however, to judge by appearances, the material content and the truth content, united at the beginning of the work's history, set themselves apart from each other in the course of its duration, because the truth content always remains to the same extent hidden as the material content comes to the fore. More and more, therefore, the interpretation of what is striking and curious—that is, the material content—becomes a prerequisite for any later critic. One may compare him to a paleographer in front of a parchment whose faded text is covered by the lineaments of a more powerful script which refers to that text. As the paleographer would have to begin by reading the latter script, the critic would have to begin with commentary. And with one stroke, an invaluable criterion of judgment springs out for him; only now can he raise the basic critical question of whether the semblance/luster [*Schein*] of the truth content is due to the material content, or the life of the material content to the truth content. For as they set themselves apart from each other in the work, they decide on its immortality. In this sense the history of works prepares for their critique, and thus historical distance increases their power. If, to use a simile, one views the growing work as a burning funeral pyre, then the commentator stands before it like a chemist, the critic like an alchemist. Whereas for the former, wood and ashes remain the sole objects of his analysis, for the latter only the flame itself preserves an enigma: that of what is alive. Thus, the critic inquires into the truth, whose living flame continues to burn over the heavy logs of what is past and the light ashes of what has been experienced.[31]

One would not normally think it is the task of philology to determine the truth content of a literary text. Usually it takes the form of a commentary that "simply" tries to establish what the text is saying and to provide explanations for anything that is not clear on the surface of the text (allusions, quotations, references, relation to a pertinent context). In the *Elective Affinities* essay Benjamin provides what he calls critique in what looks like commentary. That is partly because of the peculiar and (over time) changing relation between the truth content and material. Necessarily conjoined at the moment of a work of art's production, the two become disarticulated

---

31. Benjamin 1996: 298.

with passing time. The progressive rendering strange—or stranger—of the *realia* of the subject matter (or *Sachgehalt*) means that the re-articulation of the material content with the truth content is constantly changing and thus the demands of reading are always different. Reading and thus philology is in a kind of permanent crisis, if that is not too oxymoronic a way to phrase it. Or at least it has to reinvent the actual task of reading at every given historical moment.

The ever-changing task of reading, for Benjamin, entails what he calls critique, a notion worked out in the most elaborate fashion in his dissertation, *Der Begriff der Kunstkritik in der deutschen Romantik* (translated as *The Concept of Criticism in German Romanticism*).[32] There Benjamin drew on Friedrich Schlegel's exemplary reading of Goethe's *Wilhelm Meister* to formulate a far-reaching theory of the work of art as both entailing its own critique (in advance, so to speak) and necessitating a critique external to the work, a strangely necessary supplement to what seems like the autonomous work of art. Benjamin extended Schlegel's notion of critique by conceiving of the work as that which gazes at the reader or spectator and in turn demands that its gaze be met. This already means that it makes little or no sense to consign a work of art simply to the moment of its production, as Adorno would later underscore. The reflection that is critique is required again and again of and by the work, in principle, and simply is not able to be limited to one and only one historical moment. Critique, then, is nothing if not historical, a kind of intellectual event that responds partly to the demands of the moment; but it is perhaps not historical in the same sense as implied by the conceptual framework of "historicism," about which the historically-minded Benjamin had nothing good to say. Philology has to be sublated but by a historical materialism that not only takes its cue from philology but does to and for history what philology does to and for the text.

AT THE CHRONOLOGICAL end of the announced trajectory we come across the perhaps surprising programmatic invocation of the term "philology" by Paul de Man in his short polemical piece from 1982 entitled "The Return to Philology."[33] The most immediate provocation to his text was a short essay by Walter Jackson Bate, then still an influential professor at Harvard, lamenting the decline of literary studies in the American (or perhaps North American) academy. The fault was laid at the door of what was then and now

---

32. Benjamin 1973.
33. de Man 1982 (cited henceforth from de Man 1986).

loosely called "theory"—and theory, from this point of view, was nothing if not loose. "Theory" in these contexts almost always meant the (post) structuralist thought of the likes of Foucault, Lacan, Derrida and Deleuze—and even worse, their progeny. The main perpetrator of "theory" in Bate's piece was Jacques Derrida, called by Bate a "puckish Parisian," it being no accident that the source of theory was foreign and, as a kind of bonus, French, as if Bates were rehearsing Edmund Burke's diatribe against what he—Burke—called "upstart theory" emanating from the French revolutionaries a little over two hundred years ago.[34]

De Man replied by suggesting that the discomfort felt by Bate and legions of like-minded critics could be not be traced—or not simply, only traced—to the newly demonized thing called "theory" but rather—or at least also—to what he perhaps oddly termed *philology*—by which he meant a kind of analysis that focuses in the first instance on "the *way* meaning is conveyed rather than the meaning itself" (my emphasis).[35] This distinction corresponds to the division, in de Man's lexicon but not only his, between the two relatively autonomous practices of poetics and hermeneutics. That the two are in some sense and at the end of the day inextricable does not mean there are not important differences in principle and in practice between the two, especially if hermeneutics proceeds as if poetics were neither necessary nor crucial. The relation between poetics and hermeneutics is hardly straightforward and however inextricable they are, they are not necessarily compatible.

But one thing is clear for de Man: poetics comes *first*. The attention to *how* meaning is conveyed is granted a methodological and even a conceptual priority. One must, in the first instance, try to read the text as a text, which means at least provisionally bracketing questions of meaning as such. De Man glosses his polemical point by tracing his own genealogy and that of numerous more or less prominent literary critics in America to one locus of origin in Harvard's legendary HUM 6 course (and thus as close to home as could be for Walter Jackson Bate) and most particularly to one of its renowned instructors: Reuben Brower. Brower's fastidious, close readings, which took poetry as their main object and tended to read prose and drama in a manner more usually associated with poetry, could well seem a far cry from the variously extravagant or virulent strains of imported poststructuralism but for de Man they do something at least potentially radical and disruptive simply by attending to what texts actually say and do.[36]

---

34. On the relation to French theory in Burke's thought, see Chandler 1984 and Simpson 1993.
35. de Man 1986.
36. A sense of the Brower "school" (not actually a school) can be gleaned from the excellent col-

De Man describes the parameters of teaching and learning with Brower at Harvard as follows:

> Students, as they began to write on the writings of others, were not to say anything that was not derived from the text they were considering. They were not to make any statements that they could not support by a specific use of language that actually occurred in the text. They were asked, in other words, to begin by reading texts closely as texts and not to move at once into the general context of human experience or history. Much more humbly or modestly, they were to start out from the bafflement that such *singular* turns of tone, phrase, and figure were bound to produce in readers attentive enough to notice them and honest enough not to hide their non-understanding behind the screen of received ideas that often passes, in literary instruction, for humanistic knowledge.[37]

The note of singularity sounded here is a recurrent one in de Man's late work.[38] It is importantly elaborated on in the essay entitled "The Resistance to Theory," where one thing that resists theory is the stubborn singularity of the literary text, despite the way the text is traversed by any number of not-so-singular things: grammar, genre and its conventions, figures of speech, and the like. Literary theory, unlike theoretical work in the natural sciences (but, interestingly, like political theory, according to de Man) is characterized by its inexorable ties to the example, an example that in its singularity or quasi-singularity is at the same time counterexemplary because not fully generalizable. For most scientific purposes, any and every leaf from any maple tree could be equally "good" as an example of a maple leaf. Even literary *theory*, to say nothing of literary criticism, has to dwell with and in the example, the example that turns out to be something less or other than fully exemplary, that is, not able to stand in for all other pertinent examples: a certain singularity abides, even if in some respects it can indeed also function as an example. (One thing teaching literature teaches is that not every example is equally "good.")

If de Man, contrary to popular belief, tended to practice philology (as he would insist—though sometimes he will call it "rhetorical reading"), what does this philology look like? At some charged moments, the task of phi-

---

lection of essays, Brower and Poirier 1962. The volume contains a preface by Brower and early essays by Paul de Man, Neil Hertz, Stephen Orgel, and others.

37. de Man 1986: 23; my emphasis.

38. I explore this matter as it appears in Derrida and in Enlightenment/Romantic thinking in Balfour 2007.

lology (or reading, which amounts to virtually the same thing) consists in figuring out what, in the most literal way, the text is saying. De Man will several times, in his reading of Kant, Hegel, Hölderlin, or Rousseau, at some preliminary point in his analyses pause to ask in what he somewhat coyly calls "the most naïve," the "most literal fashion" what the text says. This might seem like a rather humble, straightforward task, nothing really to write home about. Yet determining just what the text says often entails a lot of (difficult) things, starting with reading through a thicket of misapprehensions, varyingly institutionalized, by benighted or misguided critics of the best and less than the best intentions. Sometimes the filter is the "screen of received ideas" invoked in the passage on Brower above, sometimes bad periodization, or an unwarranted notion of the homogeneity of a period or an author's corpus—which produces nothing but pseudo-historicism in the guise of history. (Often a critic or student will begin with a certain reductive notion of "Romanticism," say, then submit a putatively "Romantic" poem to analysis only to find—*quelle surprise*—that it is indeed "Romantic.") A number of de Man's analyses, especially the late essays collected in the volume *Aesthetic Ideology*, read Hegel and Kant against the grain of their readers, Hegelians and Kantians. A good many of them could also be called Schillerians, Schiller having crystallized better than anyone, in de Man's view, the unquestioned and unquestioning ideology of the aesthetic (in Schiller's case: the aesthetic as the locus of resolution for social and political tensions). The tangled web of mediations entailed in reading Kant and Hegel gets in the way of our comprehending just what is being said even when it appears, on the face of it, to be perfectly straightforward.[39] Thus, for example, when Kant in his third Critique says apropos the possible sublimity of oceans: " . . . one must consider the ocean merely as the poets do [*wie die Dichter es tun*], in accordance with what its appearance shows [*was der Augeschein zeigt*], for instance, when it is considered in periods of calm, as a clear watery mirror bounded only by the heavens, but also when it is turbulent, an abyss threatening to devour everything, and yet still be able to find it sublime." The phrase de Man seizes on is one that is indeed easy to skip over perhaps because it seems to go so directly against what has become common sense. If the model for poetic here is "*was der Augenschein zeigt*"—how it strikes the eye or how it appears—that seems to run counter to our collective sense of the poet as creative and his or her productions as vitally metaphorical or fresh in their perceptions—not just in registering in a flat, literal way what

---

39. It is not as though de Man's or anyone else's readings are somehow unmediated; rather, some ungrounded mediations can be exposed to lack textual evidence.

appears to the eye. What could be less creative, what could be less imaginative? And yet generations of critics of Kant will enlist him in paeans to the creative imagination, without pausing over a passage that is plainly there in the text and, on the face of it, posing no hermeneutic problem. A certain set of received notions or an ideology of the aesthetic seems to get in the way of our registering just what Kant is saying, as here, that the proposed model for poetry is one of automatic perception.

On the other hand, when the text seems to demand it, allegorical reading, not simple citation of a passage to be understood literally, is the order of the day.[40] Thus in his reading of Hegel's *Aesthetics,* when de Man confronts a seemingly pedestrian statement by Hegel: "*Im Sklaven fängt die Prosa an*" ("Prose begins in the slave,") his sense of the Hegelian corpus seems to require or at least suggest that the proposition that what appears to say something as simple as "Aesop was the first prose writer" turns out, on reflection, to be linked with the permanent potential of the slave to become master of the master (because, as outlined in the famous master–slave dialectic from Hegel's *Phenomenology of Spirit,* the seemingly autonomous master turns out to be dependent on the slave for his identity as master), which is also to say, of the subordinate to overcome the dominant. Prose, which seems, in aesthetic terms, initially so subordinate to poetry, turns out to be the very discursive mode that poetry must give way to, as art in its highest determination—and poetry for Hegel is the highest of the arts—has to give way in the end to philosophical prose, to the discourse in which the logos recognizes itself in the medium most commensurate with it.[41]

Whether flatly literal or sweepingly allegorical, the text says and does what it says and does: the task of reading is to figure that out by first attending to how meaning means, by attention especially to the poetics of the text, the mechanisms and machinations of the rhetorical movements or performance of the text, which includes but is not at all limited to what J. L. Austin terms performative language. Attending to what happens in a text sometimes means recognizing that the movements and meanings of a text can scarcely all be chalked up to or understood in terms of authorial intention.[42] Thus in de Man's reading of Kleist's essay "On the Marionette Theater," a text about

---

40. And yet simple citation is not necessarily so simple. De Man said in one of his last seminars: "Penser, c'est trouver la bonne citation." ("Thinking is finding a good quotation.")

41. Raymond Geuss, in his response in *Critical Inquiry* to de Man's essay on Hegel (Geuss 1983), protested de Man's allegorical reading of Hegel as un-Hegelian, though one could easily understand Hegel's relentlessly spiritualizing discourse as demanding allegorical interpretation, rather as the Pauline letters promote the spirit over the letter.

42. That Hegel's overt statements about allegory express a rather dim, dismissive view of it is beside the point when one can show how the text makes (good) sense allegorically.

the perils and even the possible paralysis of self-consciousness when trying to perform, as, say, to dance gracefully (a text that ends up with one character suggesting that the only way to get back to paradise is to eat of the apple again, i.e., to heighten self-consciousness), de Man shows how the use of the word or even the syllable *Fall* ("*Fall*" in German partly overlaps with "fall" in English) in its various configurations (as *Sündenfall, Rückenfall, Einfall* and *Beifall*) has a subsemantic life of its own that exceeds and disrupts the presumed intention of the author, even in so precise and sovereign a writer as Kleist.

What happens in the text is an event, though a text, especially a text that is a work of art, is an odd kind of event, one that repeats itself, repeatedly, like "a broken record."[43] To attend to the movements and machinations of the text is necessarily to attend to something historical, even if the critic is not so concerned to link (as in some of de Man's readings) what happens in the text to what happens outside it. The repetitive event of the literary text both dates and un-dates itself: it marks itself as historical—no text is written in some timeless and universal language—but by the same token it cannot be contained by its putative moment of production, even if we thought we could isolate it. This stance of de Man's, more implicit than not, seems to me close to the spirit of Adorno's thinking on the historicity of the work of art:

> The relation to the art of the past, as well as the barriers to its apperception, have their locus in the contemporary condition of consciousness as positively or negatively transcended; the rest is nothing more than empty erudition.... The opposite of a genuine relation to the historical substance of artworks—their essential content—is their rash subsumption to history, their assignment to a historical moment.[44]

Adorno's claims in the larger passage from which I am quoting are derived in no small measure from Walter Benjamin, whose mark on Adorno's and de Man's thinking is profound. Both Adorno and Benjamin are generally thought, and not without reason, to do more justice to the demands of history than is de Man. Doubtless the texture of Benjamin's and Adorno's writings is more infused with history than is de Man's; but the gulf between them is narrower than is normally acknowledged. Even if de Man can set out some theoretical principles about the (philological) understanding and

---

43. See de Man 1984.
44. Adorno 1997: 194.

analysis of literature—such as the priority of poetics—the priority of attending to how meaning is conveyed in advance of its interpretation proper, the singular and thus historical event of the text entails the reinvention of philology over and over again.

It is in response to the historical and not-simply-historical event of the text that the somewhat disparate figures of Schlegel, Benjamin, and de Man turn to philology and beyond that to philosophical reflection on philology to ground their readings in and on the uncertain ground of language. They respond to the "seductive side of philology" for its promise and the possibility to help resolve what cannot quite be resolved ultimately, confronting, paradoxically, a kind of permanent crisis, yet not without having achieved along the way any number of local advances in interpretation as well as an acute sense of the stakes of reading. Seduced but not abandoned.

WORKS CITED

Aarsleff, Hans. 1983. *The Study of Language in England 1780–1860.* 2nd ed. Minneapolis: University of Minnesota Press.
Abad, Francisco. 1990. "Positivismo e idealismo en la 'escuela española' de Filología." In *Homenaje al profesor Lapesa: XI curso de lingüística textual, Murcia 25–29 abril 1988.* Ed. José Munò Garrigós, 15–29. Murcia: Universidad de Murcia.
Adorno, Theodor W. 1973. *Negative Dialectics.* Trans. E. B. Ashton. New York: Seabury Press.
———. 1997. *Aesthetic Theory.* Ed. Gretel Adorno and Rolf Tiedemann. Trans. Robert Hullot-Kentor. Minneapolis: University of Minnesota Press.
Adorno, Theodor W., and Walter Benjamin. 1999. *The Complete Correspondence, 1928–1940.* Ed. Henri Lonitz. Trans. Nicholas Walker. Cambridge, MA: Harvard University Press.
Albrektson, Bertil. 1963. *Studies in the Text and Theology of the Book of Lamentations.* Lund: Gleerup.
Allen, Michael J. B. 1998. *Synoptic Art: Marsilio Ficino on the History of Platonic Interpretation.* Florence: Olschki.
Altschul, Nadia. 2003. "Difracción, *collatio externa* y diasistemas: De la cultura del manuscrito y la crítica textual." *Corónica* 32: 187–204.
———. 2005. *La literatura, el autor y la crítica textual.* Madrid: Pliegos.
———. 2006. "The Genealogy of Scribal Versions: A 'Fourth Way' for Medieval Editorial Theory." *Textual Cultures* 1: 114–36.
Arellano, Ignacio. 2003. *El auto sacramental.* Ed. J. Enrique Duarte. Madrid: Laberinto.
Assmann, Jan. 1994. "Ancient Egypt and the Materiality of the Sign." In *Materialities of Communication.* Ed. Hans Ulrich Gumbrecht and Karl Ludwig Pfeiffer. Trans. William Whobrey, 15–31. Stanford: Stanford University Press.
Auerbach, Erich. 1949. *Introduction aux études de philologie romane.* Frankfurt am Main: Vittorio Klostermann.
———. 1965. *Literary Language and its Public in Late Latin Antiquity and the Middle Ages.* Trans. Ralph Manheim. New York: Bollingen.
———. 1969. "Philology and *Weltliteratur.*" Trans. Edward and Maire Said. *The Centennial Review* 13: 1–17.

Austin, Colin, ed. 1973. *Comicorum Graecorum Fragmenta in Papyris Reperta.* Berlin: de Gruyter.

Baldassarri, Stefano Ugo. 1998. "Lodi medicee in un dimenticato best seller del Quattrocento fiorentino: Il *Driadeo* di Luca Pulci." *Forum Italicum* 32: 375–402.

Balfour, Ian. 2007. "Singularities: On a Motif in Derrida and Romantic Thought (Kant's Aesthetics, Rousseau's Autobiography)." *Studies in Romanticism* 46: 337–60.

Barbi, Michele. 1938. *La Nuova Filologia e l'edizione dei nostri scrittori: Da Dante al Manzoni.* Florence: Sansóni.

Barkan, Leonard. 1999. *Unearthing the Past: Archaeology and Aesthetics in the Making of Renaissance Culture.* New Haven: Yale University Press.

Bartalucci, A., E. Castorina, E. Cecchini, I. Lana, and V. Tandoi. 1975. "Il nuovo Rutilio Namaziano." *Maia* 27: 3–26.

Barthes, Roland. 1975. *The Pleasure of the Text.* Trans. Richard Miller. New York: Hill and Wang.

———. 1977. "The Death of the Author." In *Image, Music, Text.* Trans. Stephen Heath, 142–48. New York: Hill and Wang.

———. 1985. *The Responsibility of Forms: Critical Essays on Music, Art, and Representation.* Trans. Richard Howard. New York: Hill and Wang.

Bausi, Francesco. 1996. *Nec rhetor neque philosophus: Fonti, lingua e stile nelle prime opere latine di Giovanni Pico della Mirandola (1484–87).* Florence: Olschki.

———. 2003. Introduction to Poliziano 2003. Rome: Salerno.

Bédier, Joseph. 1913. Introduction to *Le lai de l'ombre,* by Jean Renart. Paris: Firmin-Didot.

———. 1928. "La tradition manuscrite du 'Lai de l'ombre.' Réflexions sur l'art d'éditer les anciens textes." *Romania* 54: 161–96, 321–56.

Behler, Ernst. 1993. *German Romantic Literary Theory.* Cambridge: Cambridge University Press.

Bell, Catherine. 1992. *Ritual Theory, Ritual Practice.* Oxford: Oxford University Press.

Benjamin, Walter. 1972. *Gesammelte Schriften.* Ed. R. Tiedemann and H. Schrenppenhäuser. Frankfurt am Main: Suhrkamp.

———. 1973. *Der Begriff der Kunstkritik in der deutschen Romantik.* Frankfurt am Main: Suhrkamp.

———. 1977. *The Origin of German Tragic Drama.* Trans. John Osborne. London: NLB.

———. 1994. *The Correspondence of Walter Benjamin, 1910–1940.* Ed. Gershom G. Scholem and Theodor W. Adorno. Trans. Manfred R. Jacobson and Evelyn M. Jacobson. Chicago and London: University of Chicago Press.

———. 1996. *Selected Writings I (1913–1926).* Ed. Michael W. Jennings and Marcus Bullock. Trans. Ian Balfour et al. Cambridge, MA: The Belknap Press of Harvard University Press.

———. 2003. "Toward a Rigorous Study of Art (1931)." In *The Vienna School Reader: Politics and Art Historical Method in the 1930s.* Ed. Christopher S. Wood, 105–32. New York: Zone.

———. 2006. *Selected Writings IV (1938–1940).* Ed. Howard Eiland and Michael W. Jennings. Trans. Edmund Jephcott *et al.* Cambridge, MA: Harvard University Press.

Bernstein, J. M., ed. 2003. *Classic and Romantic German Aesthetics.* Cambridge: Cambridge University Press.

Bertotti, T. 1969. "Rutiliana." In *Contributi a tre poeti latini.* Ed. R. Nordera et al., 93–134. Bologna: Pàtron.

Blanchard, W. S. 1995. *Scholars' Bedlam: Menippean Satire in the Renaissance.* Lewisburg, PA: Bucknell University Press.
Blecua, Alberto. 1983. *Manual de crítica textual.* Madrid: Castalia.
———. 1991. "Los textos medievales castellanos y sus ediciones." *Romance Philology* 45: 73–88.
———. 1995. "Medieval Castilian Texts and Their Editions." Trans. Stephen B. Raulston. In *Scholarly Editing: A Guide to Research.* Ed. David C. Greetham, 459–85. New York: MLA.
Bloch, Howard. 1990. "New Philology and Old French." *Speculum* 65: 38–58.
Bolling, George Melville. 1929. "Linguistics and Philology." *Language* 5: 27–32.
Borja, Juan de. 1981 [1680]. *Empresas morales.* Ed. Carmen Bravo-Villasante. Madrid: Fundación Universitaria Española.
Bourdieu, Pierre. 1977. *Outline of a Theory of Practice.* Trans. Richard Nice. Cambridge: Cambridge University Press.
Bowers, Fredson. 1978. "Greg's 'Rational of Copy-Text' Revisited." *Studies in Bibliography* 31: 90–161.
Bravo, Benedetto. 2006. "*Critice* in the Sixteenth and Seventeenth Centuries and the Rise of the Notion of Historical Criticism." In *History of Scholarship: A Selection of Papers from the Seminar on the History of Scholarship held Annually at the Warburg Institute.* Ed. C. Ligota and J.-L. Quantin, 135–95. Oxford: Clarendon Press.
Brink, C. O. 1986. *English Classical Scholarship: Historical Reflections on Bentley, Porson, and Housman.* Oxford: Oxford University Press.
Brower, Reuben A., and Richard Poirier, eds. 1962. *In Defense of Reading: A Reader's Approach to Literary Criticism.* New York: Dutton.
Buonincontri, Lorenzo. 1999. *De rebus naturalibus et divinis.* Ed. with introduction by Stephan Heilen. Stuttgart and Leipzig: Teubner.
Buridan, John. 1983. *Quaestiones in Praedicamenta.* Ed. Johannes Schneider. München: Verlag der Bayerischen Akademie der Wissenschaften.
Burkert, Walter. 1960. "Platon oder Pythagoras? Zum Ursprung des Wortes 'Philosophie.'" *Hermes* 88: 159–77.
———. 1972. *Lore and Science in Ancient Pythagoreanism.* Trans. Edwin L. Minar, Jr. Cambridge, MA: Harvard University Press.
Calderón de la Barca, Pedro. 2003. *El gran mercado del mundo.* Vol. 39, *Autos sacramentales completos.* Ed. Ana Suárez. Pamplona: Universidad de Navarra.
Cameron, Alan. 1967. "Rutilus Namatianus, St. Augustine, and the Date of the *De Reditu.*" *Journal of Roman Studies* 57: 31–39.
———. 2004. *Greek Mythography in the Roman World.* American Classical Studies, 48. New York: Oxford University Press.
Campanelli, M. 1994. "L'*oratio* e il 'genere' delle orazioni inaugurali dell'anno accademico." In Lorenzo Valla, *Orazione per l'inaugurazione dell'anno accademico 1455–1456: Atti di un seminario di filologia umanistica.* Ed. S. Rizzo, 25–26. Rome: Roma nel Rinascimento.
Cancik, Huber. 1995. "Der Einfluss Friedrich Nietzsches auf klassische Philologen in Deutschland bis 1945: Philologen am Nietzsche-Archiv (I)." In *Altertumswissenschaft in den 20er Jahren: Neue Fragen und Impulse.* Ed. Hellmut Flashar and Sabine Vogt, 381–402. Stuttgart: F. Steiner.
Canfora, Luciano. 1989. *The Vanished Library.* Trans. Martin Ryle. Berkeley: University of California Press.

Capponi, Filippo. 1986. "Il venatus di Rutilio Namaziano." *Koinonia* 10: 81–87.
Carcopino, Jérôme. 1963. "La date et le sens du voyage de Rutilius Namatianus." In *Rencontres de l'histoire et de la littérature romaines*, 233–70. Paris: Flammarion.
Cardini, Roberto. 1973. *La critica del Landino*. Florence: Sansoni.
Carrai, Stefano. 1985. *Le Muse del Pulci*. Naples: Guida.
Castillo, David R. 2001. *(A)wry Views: Anamorphosis, Cervantes, and the Early Picaresque*. West Lafayette: Purdue University Press.
Catana, Leo. 2005 "The Concept 'System of Philosophy:' The Case of Jacob Brucker's Historiography of Philosophy." *History and Theory* 44: 72–90.
———. 2008. *The Historiographical Concept 'System of Philosophy:' Its Origin, Nature, and Legitimacy*. Leiden: Brill.
Cavalca, Domenico. 1837. *Il pungilingua*. Ed. Giovanni Bottari. Milan: Giovanni Silvestri.
Celenza, Christopher S. 1999. "Pythagoras in the Renaissance: The Case of Marsilio Ficino." *Renaissance Quarterly* 52: 667–711.
———. 2001. *Piety and Pythagoras in Renaissance Florence: The Symbolum Nesianum*. Leiden: Brill.
———. 2002. "Late Antiquity and Florentine Platonism." In *Marsilio Ficino: His Theology, his Philosophy, his Legacy*. Ed. M. J. B. Allen and V. R. Rees, with Martin Davies. Leiden: Brill: 71–98.
———. 2004. *The Lost Italian Renaissance: Humanists, Historians, and Latin's Legacy*. Baltimore: Johns Hopkins University Press.
———. 2005. "Lorenzo Valla and the Traditions and Transmissions of Philosophy." *Journal of the History of Ideas* 66: 483–506.
———. 2007. "The Platonic Revival." In *The Cambridge Companion to Renaissance Philosophy*. Ed. James Hankins, 72–96. Cambridge: Cambridge University Press.
———. 2010. *Angelo Poliziano's Lamia: Text, Translation, and Introductory Studies*. Leiden: Brill.
Cerquiglini, Bernard. 1989. *Éloge de la variante: Histoire critique de la philologie*. Paris: Seuil.
———. 1999. *In Praise of the Variant: A Critical History of Philology*. Trans. Betsy Wing. Baltimore: Johns Hopkins University Press.
Cervantes, Miguel de. 1978. *El ingenioso hidalgo don Quijote de la Mancha II*. Ed. Luis Andrés Murillo. Madrid: Clásicos Castalia.
Champier, Symphorien. 1537. . . . . *Libri VIII de dialectica, rhetorica, geometria, arithmetica, astronomia, musica, philosophia naturali, medicina et theologia, et de legibus et republica eaque parte philosophiae quae de moribus tractat.* . . . Basel: Henricus Petri.
Chandler, James K. 1984. *Wordsworth's Second Nature: A Study of the Poetry and Poetics*. Chicago: University of Chicago Press.
Chaouli, Michel. 2002. *The Laboratory of Poetry: Chemistry and Poetics in the Work of Friedrich Schlegel*. Baltimore: Johns Hopkins University Press.
Chaucer, Geoffrey. 1926. *Troilus and Criseyde*. Ed. R. K. Root. Princeton: Princeton University Press.
Childers, William. 2006. *Transnational Cervantes*. Toronto: University of Toronto Press.
Clark, William. 2006. *Academic Charisma and the Origins of the Research University*. Chicago: Chicago University Press.
Clarke, Samuel, ed. 1743. *Homer: Opera omnia quae extant. Tomus prior sive Ilias Graece et Latine*. Amsterdam: J. Wetstenium.

Collinet, Paul. 1925. *Histoire de l'école de droit de Beyrouth*. Paris: Sirey.
Constantine, David. 1984. *Early Greek Travellers and the Hellenic Ideal*. Cambridge: Cambridge University Press.
Contini, Gianfranco. 1939. "Ricordo di Joseph Bédier." *Letteratura* 3: 145–52.
———. 1986. *Breviario di ecdotica*. Milano: Riccardo Ricciardi.
Contreras, Jaime. 1991. "Family Patronage: The Judeo-Converso Minority in Spain." In *Cultural Encounters: The Impact of the Inquisition in Spain and the New World*. Ed. Anne J. Cruz and Mary Elizabeth Perr, 127–45. Berkeley: University of California Press.
Corsaro, Francesco. 1981. *Studi rutiliani*. Bologna: Pàtron.
Cortés, Manuel Muñoz. 1956–57. "El humanismo de Menzéndez Pelayo desde la perspectiva de la filología moderna." *Anales de la Universidad de Murcia: Filosofía y Letras* 15: 493–519.
Cribiore, Raffaella. 2001. *Gymnastics of the Mind: Greek Education in Hellenistic and Roman Egypt*. Princeton: Princeton University Press.
———. 2007. *The School of Libanius*. Princeton: Princeton University Press.
Curtius, Ernst Robert. 1953. *European Literature and the Latin Middle Ages*. Trans. Willard R. Trask. New York: Bollingen.
Dain, Alphonse. 1964. *Les Manuscrits*. Rev. ed. Paris: Les Belles Lettres.
Daly, Peter M. 1979a. *Emblem Theory: Recent German Contributions to the Characterization of the Emblem Genre*. Nendeln: KTO.
———. 1979b. *Literature in Light of the Emblem: Structural Parallels between the Emblem and Literature in the Sixteenth and Seventeenth Centuries*. Toronto: University of Toronto Press.
Daston, L., and P. Galison. 2007. *Objectivity*. New York: Zone.
De Man, Paul. 1979. *Allegories of Reading: Figural Language in Rousseau, Nietzche, Rilke, and Proust*. New Haven: Yale University Press.
———. 1982. "The Return to Philology." *Times Literary Supplement*, December 10.
———. 1984. *The Rhetoric of Romanticism*. New York: Columbia University Press.
———. 1986. *The Resistance to Theory*. Minneapolis: University of Minnesota Press.
———. 1996. "The Concept of Irony." In *Aesthetic Ideology*. Ed. Andrew Warminski, 163–84. Minneapolis: University of Minnesota Press.
Doblhofer, Ernst, ed. 1972. *Rutilius Claudius Namatianus, De reditu suo sive Iter Gallicum*. Vol. 1. Heidelberg: Winter.
Duff, J. Wright, ed. 1934. *Minor Latin Poets*. Trans. J. Wright Duff and Arnold M. Duff. Cambridge, MA: Harvard University Press.
During, Simon. 2005. *Cultural Studies: A Critical Introduction*. London: Routledge.
Ebbesen, Sten, Karin Fredborg, and Lauge Nielsen, eds. 1983. "Compendium logicae Porretanum." *Cahiers de l'Institut du Moyen Age grec et latin* 46: 1–113.
Erbse, Hartmut, ed. 1969–88. *Scholia Graeca in Homeri Iliadem*. Berlin: de Gruyter.
Fabian, Bernhard. 1976. Bibliographical note in *An Essay on the Original Genius of Homer (1769 and 1775)* by Robert Wood. Hildesheim: Georg Olms Verlag.
Farmer, Stephen A. 1998. *Syncretism in the West: Pico's 900 Theses (1486): The Evolution of Traditional Religious and Philosophical Systems*. Tempe, Arizona: MRTS.
Fera, Vincenzo, and Mario Martelli, eds. 1998. *Agnolo Poliziano; Poeta, scrittore, filologo: Atti del convegno internazionale di studi, Montepulciano 3–6 novembre 1994*. Florence: Le Lettere.

Ferrari, Mirella. 1970. "Le scoperte a Bobbio nel 1493: Vicende di codici e fortuna di testi." *Italia medioevale e umanistica* 13: 139–80.

———. 1973. "Spigolature bobbiesi." *Italia medioevale e umanistica* 16: 1–41.

Ficino, Marsilio. 2000a. *Opera Omnia*. Basel: Henricus Petri, 1576. Reprint with intro. by S. Toussaint, Paris: Phénix Éditions.

———. 2000b. *The Philebus Commentary*. Ed. and tr. M.J.B. Allen. Tempe: MRTS (Reprint of 1975 University of California Press edition).

Field, Arthur. 1988. *The Origins of the Platonic Academy of Florence*. Princeton: Princeton University Press.

Fink, Robert Orwill, James Frank Gilliam, and Charles Bradford Welles, eds. 1959. *The Excavation at Dura-Europos Conducted by Yale University and the French Academy of Inscriptions and Letters*. Final Report V, Part I, *The Parchments and Papyri*. New Haven: Yale University Press.

Fleischman, Suzanne. 1990. "Philology, Linguistics, and the Discourse of the Medieval Text." *Speculum* 65: 19–37.

———. 1996. "Medieval Vernaculars and the Myth of Monoglossia: A Conspiracy of Linguistics and Philology." In *Literary History and the Challenge of Philology: The Legacy of Erich Auerbach*. Ed. Seth Lerer, 92–106. Stanford: Stanford University Press.

Fo, Alessandro, ed. 1992. *Claudius Rutilius Namazianus: Il Retorno*. Turin: G. Einaudi.

Frassinetti, P., trans. 1980. "I nuovi frammenti di Rutilio Namaziano." *Studi e ricerche dell'Istituto di Latino* 3: 51–58.

Funes, Leonardo, and Felipe Tenenbaum, eds. 2004. *Mocedades de Rodrigo: Estudio y edición de los tres estados del texto*. Woodbridge, Suffolk: Tamesis.

Gaisser, Julia H. 2007. "Some Thoughts on Philology." *Transactions of the American Philological Association* 137: 477–81.

Gammersbach, Suitbert. 1959. *Gilbert von Poitiers und seine Prozesse im Urteil der Zeitgenossen*. Köln: Böhlau Verlag.

Ganz, Peter F. 1968. "Lachmann as an Editor of Middle High German Texts." In *Probleme mittelalterlicher Überlieferung und Textkritik: Oxforder Colloquium 1966*. Ed. Peter F. Ganz and Werner Schröder, 13–20. Berlin: Erich Schmidt Verlag.

Garcìa, Elisa R. 1985. "Crítica textual. Edición de textos." In *Métodos de estudio de la obra literaria*. Ed. José María Díez Borque, 67–120. Madrid: Taurus.

Garfagnini, Gian Carlo, ed. 1997. *Giovanni Pico della Mirandola, 1494–1994: Convegno internazionale*, 2 vols. Florence: Olschki.

Garin, Eugenio, ed. 1952. *Prosatori latini del Quattrocento*. Milan: Ricciardi.

———. 1979. *La Cultura filosofica de rinascimento Italiano: Richerche e documente*. Florence: Sansoni.

Gentile, Sebastiano. 1990. "Sulle prime traduzioni dal greco di Marsilio Ficino." *Rinascimento*, 2nd series, 30: 57–104.

———. 2002. "Il ritorno di Platone, dei platonici e del 'corpus ermetico.' Filosofia, teologica e astrologica nell' opera di Marsilio Ficino." In *Le filosofie del Rinascimento*. Ed. C. Vasoli, 193–228. Milan: Mondadori.

Gerber, Gustav. 1873. *Die Sprache als Kunst*. 2 vols. Bromberg: Mittler'sche Buchhandlung.

Gesner, Conrad. 1548. *Pandectarum sive partitionum universalium Conradi Gesneri Tigurini . . . libri XXI*. Zürich: Christophorus Froschoverus.

Geuss, Raymond. 1983. "A Response to Paul de Man." *Critical Inquiry* 10: 375–82.

Gibson, Roy K., and Christina Shuttleworth Kraus, eds. 2002. *The Classical Commentary: Histories, Practices, Theory.* Leiden: Brill.

Gildenhard, Ingo, and Martin Ruehl, eds. 2003. *Out of Arcadia: Classics and Politics in Germany in the Age of Burckhardt, Nietzsche and Wilamowitz.* London: University of London.

Gilman, Sander L., Carole Blair and David J. Parent, eds. and trans. 1989. *Friedrich Nietzsche on Rhetoric and Language.* New York: Oxford University Press.

Grabes, Herbert. 2002. "The Cultural Turn of Philology." In *Changing Philologies: Contributions to the Redefinition of Foreign Language Studies in the Age of Globalisation.* Ed. Hans L. Hansen, 51–62. Copenhagen: Museum Tusculanum.

Grafton, Anthony. 1983. *Joseph Scaliger: A Study in the History of Classical Scholarship.* Oxford: Oxford University Press.

———. 1988. "Quattrocento Humanism and Classical Scholarship." In *Renaissance Humanism: Foundations, Forms, and Legacy.* Vol. 3. Ed. Albert Rabil, 23–66. Philadelphia: University of Pennsylvania Press.

———. 1991. *Defenders of the Text: The Traditions of Scholarship in an Age of Science, 1450–1800.* Cambridge, MA: Harvard University Press.

———. 1997. *Commerce with the Classics: Ancient Books and Renaissance Readers.* Ann Arbor: University of Michigan Press.

Granada, M. A. 2002. "Giovanni Pico e il mito della Concordia. La riflessione di Pico dopo il 1488 e la sua polemica antiastrologica." In *Le filosofie del Rinascimento.* Ed. C. Vasoli, 229–46. Milan: Mondadori.

Greetham, David C. 1992. "Textual Scholarship." In *Introduction to Scholarship in Modern Languages and Literatures.* 2nd ed. Ed. Joseph Gibaldi, 103–37. New York: MLA.

———. 1994. *Textual Scholarship: An Introduction.* New York: Garland.

———. 1997. "The Resistance to Philology." In *The Margins of the Text.* Ed. David Greetham, 9–24. Ann Arbor: University of Michigan Press.

Greg, Walter W. 1950–51. "The Rationale of the Copy-Text." *Studies in Bibliography* 3: 19–36.

Gumbrecht, Hans Ulrich. 2003. *The Powers of Philology: Dynamics of Textual Scholarship.* Urbana: University of Illinois Press.

———. 2004. *Production of Presence: What Meaning Cannot Convey.* Stanford: Stanford University Press.

Gurd, Sean A. 2005. *Iphigenias at Aulis: Textual Multiplicity, Radical Philology.* Ithaca: Cornell University Press.

Hadot, Pierre. 1998. *The Inner Citadel: The Meditations of Marcus Aurelius.* Trans. Michael Chase. Cambridge, MA: Harvard University Press.

———. 2002. *What Is Ancient Philosophy?* Trans. Michael Chase. Cambridge, MA: Harvard University Press.

Hahn, Thomas, ed. 2001. *Race and Ethnicity in the Middle Ages.* Special issue of the *Journal of Medieval and Early Modern Studies* 31.1.

Halliwell, Stephen. 1986. *Aristotle's Poetics.* Chapel Hill: University of North Carolina Press.

Hankins, James. 1990. *Plato in the Italian Renaissance.* 2 vols. Leiden: Brill.

———. 2003–4. *Humanism and Platonism in the Italian Renaissance.* 2 vols. Rome: Edizioni di Storia e Letteratura.

Hansen, Hans Lauge. 2004. "Towards a New Philology of Culture." In *The Object of Study in the Humanities: Proceedings from the Seminar at the University of Copenhagen, September 2001.* Ed. Julio Hans Casado Jensen, 113–26. Copenhagen: Museum Tusculanum.

Hanslick, Eduard. 1865. *Vom Musikalisch-Schönen: Ein Beitrag zur Revision der Ästhetik in der Tonkunst.* 3rd ed. Leipzig: Weigel.

Havelock, Eric A. 1963. *Preface to Plato.* Cambridge, MA: The Belknap Press of Harvard University Press.

Heidegger, Martin. 1961. *Nietzsche.* Vol. 1. Pfullingen: Neske.

———. 1977. *The Question Concerning Technology, and Other Essays.* Trans. William Lovitt. New York: Harper and Row.

Henderson, John. 2006. *'Oxford Reds:' Classic Commentaries on Latin Classics.* London: Duckworth.

Heysse, Albanus, ed. 1953. *Liber de sex principiis Gilberto Porretae ascriptus.* Münster: Aschendorff.

Hitchens, Christopher. 2009. "A Home for the Marbles." *The New York Times,* June 18.

Hornblower, Simon, and Anthony Spawforth, eds. 2003. *The Oxford Classical Dictionary.* 3rd ed. Oxford: Oxford University Press.

Housman, A. E. 1961 [1925]. "The Application of Thought to Textual Criticism." In *A. E. Housman, Selected Prose.* Ed. John Carter, 131–50. Cambridge: Cambridge University Press.

Hummel, Pascale. 2000. *Histoire de l'histoire de la philologie: Étude d'un genre épistémologique et bibliographique.* Geneva: Droz.

Hunt, Jonathan. 1995. *Politian and Scholastic Logic: An Unknown Dialogue by a Dominican Friar.* Florence: Olschki.

Hutton, C. A. 1927. "The Travels of 'Palmyra' Wood in 1750–51." *The Journal of Hellenic Studies* 47: 102–28.

Jackson, H. J. 2001. *Marginalia: Readers Writing in Books.* New Haven: Yale University Press.

Jauss, Hans Robert. 1970. "Schlegel und Schillers Replik auf 'die Querelle des Anciens et des Modernes.'" In *Literaturgeschichte als Provokation.* Frankfurt am Main: Suhrkamp, 67–106.

Jordan, Constance. 1986. *Pulci's* Morgante*: Poetry and History in Fifteenth-Century Florence.* Washington, DC: Folger.

Kallendorf, Craig. 1994. "Philology, the Reader, and the *Nachleben* of Classical Texts." *Modern Philology* 92: 137–56.

Keene, Charles H., ed. 1907. *Rutilii Claudii Namatiani De reditu suo libri duo: The homecoming of Rutilius Claudius Namatius from Rome to Gaul in the year 416 A. D.* London: Bell.

Kenney, Edward J. 1974. *The Classical Text: Aspects of Editing in the Age of the Printed Book.* Berkeley: University of California Press.

Konstandaras, Nikos. 2009. "Majestic in Exile." *New York Times,* June 18.

Körner, Josef. 1928. "Friedrich Schlegel's 'Philosophie der Philologie.'" *Logos* 18: 1–72.

Kouremenos, Theokritos, George M. Parássoglou, and Kyriakos Tsantsanoglou, eds. 2006. *The Derveni Papyrus.* Florence: Olschki.

Kraye, Jill. 2002. "Ficino in the Firing Line: A Renaissance Neoplatonist and his Critics." In *Marsilio Ficino: His Theology, his Philosophy, his Legacy.* Ed. Michael J. B. Allen and Valero Rees, 377–98. Leiden: Brill.

Kuhn, Thomas S. 1996. *The Structure of Scientific Revolutions*. 3rd ed. Chicago: University of Chicago Press.
Lana, Italo, ed. 1961. *Rutilio Namaziano*. Turin: Giappichelli.
Lange, Friedrich A. 1866. *Geschichte des Materialismus und Kritik seiner Bedeutung in der Gegenwart*. Iserlohn: Baedeker.
Lees, Clare A. and Gillian R. Overing, eds. 2004. *Gender and Empire*. Special issue of the *Journal of Medieval and Early Modern Studies* 34.1.
Lerer, Seth, ed. 1996. *Literary History and the Challenge of Philology: The Legacy of Erich Auerbach*. Stanford: Stanford University Press.
Levine, Joseph M. 1987. *Humanism and History: Origins of Modern English Historiography.* Ithaca: Cornell University Press.
Liddel, H. G., R. Scott, and H. R. Jones. 1996. *A Greek-English Lexicon*. 9th ed. Oxford: Oxford University Press.
Lines, David A. 2001. "Ethics as Philology: A Developing Approach to Aristotle's *Nicomachean Ethics* in Florentine Humanism." In *Renaissance Readings of the Corpus Aristotelicum*. Ed. M. Pade, 27–42. Copenhagen: Museum Tusculanum.
———. 2002. *Aristotle's Ethics in the Italian Renaissance (ca. 1300–1650): The Universities and the Problem of Moral Education*. Leiden: Brill.
———. 2006. "Humanism and the Italian Universities." In *Humanism and Creativity in the Italian Renaissance: Essays in Honor of Ronald G. Witt*. Ed. Christopher S. Celenza and Kenneth Gouwens, 327–46. Leiden: Brill.
Lloyd-Jones, Hugh. 2004. Review of Gildenhard 2003. *Bryn Mawr Classical Review*, February 23. http://ccat.sas.upenn.edu/bmcr/2004/2004-02-43.html.
Lloyd-Jones, Hugh and P. Parsons, eds. 1983. *Supplementum Hellenisticum*. Berlin: de Gruyter.
Lobel, Edgar and Denys L. Page, eds. 1963. *Poetarum Lesbiorum fragmenta*. Oxford: Clarendon Press.
Logan, Marie-Rose. 2003. "Gulielmus Budaeus' Philological Imagination." *Modern Language Notes* 118: 1140–51.
Lohr, Charles H. 1990. *Latin Aristotle Commentaries*. 3 vols. Florence: Olschki.
López, Sagrario S. 1999. Introduction to *Empresas políticas*, by Diego de Saavedra Fajardo. Madrid: Cátedra.
Lowe, E. A. 1972 [1964]. "*Codices Rescripti:* a List of the Oldest Latin Palimpsests with Stray Observations on their Origin." In *Palaeographical Papers 1907–1965*. Ed. Ludwig Bieler, 480–519. Oxford: Clarendon Press.
Maas, Paul. 1927. *Textkritik*. Leipzig: Teubner.
———. 1963. *Textual Criticism*. Trans. Barbara Flower. Oxford: Clarendon Press.
Maaz, W. 1988. "Poetisch-mythologische Realität in De Reditu Suo des Rutilius Namatianus." In *Roma Renascens: Beiträge zur Spätantike und Rezeptiongeschichte*. Ed. Michael Wissemann, 235–56. Frankfurt am Main: Peter Lang.
Maestro, Jesús G. 2004. *El mito de la interpretación literaria*. Madrid: Iberoamericana.
Mahíques, Rafael García. 1998. Introduction to *Empresas morales de Juan de Borja: Imagen y palabra para una iconología*. Ed. García Mahíques, 17–51. Valencia: Ajuntament de Valencia.
Maïer, I. 1965. *Les manuscrits d'Ange Politien*. Geneva: Droz.
Mandosio, J.-M. 1996. "Filosofia, arti e scienze: L'enciclopedismo di Angelo Poliziano," in *Agnolo Poliziano nel suo tempo*. Ed. L. Secchi Tarugi, 135–64. Florence: F. Cesati.

———. 1997. "Les sources antiques de la classification de sciences et des arts à la Renaissance." In *Les Voies de la science grecque*. Ed. Danielle Jacquart, 331–90. Geneva: Droz.
Maravall, José Antonio. 1972. "La literatura de emblemas en el contexto de la sociedad barroca." In *Teatro y literatura en la sociedad barroca*, 149–88. Madrid: Seminarios y ediciones.
Martinelli, L. Cesarini. 1996. "Poliziano professore allo studio fiorentino," in *La Toscana al tempo di Lorenzo il Magnifico*, multi-authored, 3 vols, 2: 463–81. Pisa: Pacini.
McGann, Jerome J. 1983. *A Critique of Modern Textual Criticism*. Chicago: University of Chicago Press.
McNamee, Kathleen. 1992. *Sigla and Select Marginalia in Greek Literary Papyri*. Brussels: Fondation Égyptologique Reine Élisabeth.
———. 1994. "School Notes." In *Proceedings of the 20th International Congress of Papyrologists, Copenhagen 23–29 August 1992*. Ed. Adam Bülow-Jacobsen, 177–84. Copenhagen: Museum Tusculanum.
———. 1995. "Missing Links in the Development of Scholia." *Greek, Roman, and Byzantine Studies* 36: 399–414.
———. 1998. "Another Chapter in the History of Scholia." *Classical Quarterly* 48: 269–88.
———. 2007. *Annotations in Greek and Latin Texts from Egypt*. American Studies in Papyrology, 45. Oakville, CT: Oxbow Books.
Meijers, Anthonie. 1988. "Gustav Gerber und Friedrich Nietzsche." *Nietzsche-Studien* 17: 369–90.
Meijers, Anthonie, and Martin Stingelin. 1988. "Konkordanz zu den wörtlichen Abschriften und Übernahmen von Beispielen und Zitaten aus Gustav Gerber." *Nietzsche-Studien* 17: 350–68.
Merone, Emilio, ed. 1959. *Rutilio Ellenizzante*. Naples: Loffredo.
Michel, Willy. 1982. *Ästhetische Hermeneutik und frühromantische Kritik: Friedrich Schlegels fragmentarische Entwürfe, Rezensionen, Charakteristiken und Kritiken (1795–1801)*. Göttingen: Vandenhoeck & Ruprecht.
Miller, Peter N. 2000. *Peiresc's Europe: Learning and Virtue in the Seventeenth Century*. New Haven: Yale University Press.
Minio-Paluello, Lorenzo. 1957. "A Latin Commentary (Translated by Boethius?) on the Prior Analytics, and its Greek Sources." *The Journal of Hellenic Studies* 77: 93–102.
Momigliano, Arnaldo. 1966. "Ancient History and the Antiquarian." In *Studies in Historiography*. Trans. Judith Wardman, 1–39. London: Weidenfeld & Nicolson.
———. 1994. *A. D. Momigliano: Studies on Modern Scholarship*. Ed. G. W Bowersock and Tim J. Cornell. Trans. Tim J. Cornell. Berkeley: University of California Press.
Müller-Sievers, Helmut. 2006. "Reading without Interpreting: German Textual Criticism and the Case of Georg Büchner." *Modern Philology* 103: 498–518.
Müllner, Karl. 1899. *Reden und Briefe italienischer Humanisten*. Vienna: Hölder. Reprint with introduction and bibliography by B. Gerl. Munich: Fink, 1970.
Munroe, D. B., and T. W. Allen, eds. 1920. *Homer: Opera*. Oxford: Clarendon.
Myerson, Joel. 1995. "Colonial and Nineteenth-Century American Literature." In *Scholarly Editing: A Guide to Research*. Ed. D. C. Greetham, 351–64. New York: MLA.
Naoumides, N. 1969. "The Fragments of Greek Lexicography in the Papyri." In *Classical Studies Presented to Ben Edwin Perry by his Students and Colleagues at the University of Illinois (1924–60)*, 181–202. Urbana: University of Illinois Press.
Nauta, Lodi. 2009. *In Defense of Common Sense: Lorenzo Valla's Humanist Critique of Scholastic Philosophy*. Cambridge, MA: Harvard University Press.

Nehamas, Alexander. 1985. *Nietzsche: Life as Literature.* Cambridge, MA: Harvard University Press.
Nelson, B. 2005. "From Hieroglyphic Presence to Emblematic Sign: the Ritual Motivation of Bias in the Auto Sacramental." In *Hispanic Baroques: Reading Cultures in Context.* Ed. Nicholas Spadaccini and Luis Martín-Estudillo, 107–36. *Hispanic Issues* 31. Nashville: Vanderbilt University Press.
Nichols, Stephen G. 1990a. "Philology in a Manuscript Culture." *Speculum* 65: 1–10.
———. 1990b. *The New Philology.* Special issue of *Speculum* 65: 1.
———. 1994. "Philology and Its Discontents." In *The Future of the Middle Ages: Medieval Literature in the 1990s.* Ed. William D. Paden, 113–44. Gainesville: University Press of Florida.
Nietzsche, Friedrich Wilhelm. 1933–42. *Historisch-Kritische Gesamtausgabe: Werke.* Ed. Hans Joachim Mette and K. Schleechta. 5 vols. Munich: Beck.
———. 1966. *Beyond Good and Evil: Prelude to a Philosophy of the Future.* Trans. Walter Kaufmann. New York: Vintage.
———. 1967a. *On the Genealogy of Morals and Ecce Homo.* Trans. Walter Kaufmann and R. J. Hollingdale. New York: Vintage.
———. 1967b. *The Birth of Tragedy and The Case of Wagner.* Trans. Walter Kaufmann. New York: Vintage.
———. 1967c. *The Will to Power.* Ed. Walter Kaufmann. Trans. Walter Kaufmann and R. J. Hollingdale. New York: Random House.
———. 1988. *Sämtliche Werke: Kritische Studienausgabe in 15 Einzelbänden.* 2nd ed. Ed. Giorgio Colli and Mazzino Montinari. 15 vols. Berlin: de Gruyter.
Novalis. 1993. *Das Allgemeine Brouillon: Materialien zur Enzyklopädistik 1798/99.* Hamburg: F. Meiner.
Obbink, Dirk. 2007. "Readers and Intellectuals." In *Oxyrhynchus: A City and Its Texts.* Ed. A. Bowman, R. A. Cole, et al., 271–82. Oxford: Egypt Exploration Society.
Ong, Walter J. 1982. *Orality and Literacy: The Technologizing of the Word.* New York: Methuen.
Orduna, Germán. 1991. "Ecdótica hispánica y el valor estemático de la historia del texto." *Romance Philology* 45: 89–101.
———. 1995. "Hispanic Textual Criticism and the Stemmatic Value of the History of the Text." In *Scholarly Editing: A Guide to Research.* Ed. D. C. Greetham, 486–503. New York: MLA.
Paden, William D., ed. 1994. *The Future of the Middle Ages: Medieval Literature in the 1990s.* Gainesville: University Press of Florida.
Page, Denys L. 1951. *Alcman: The Partheneion.* Oxford: Oxford University Press.
———, ed. 1962. *Poetae Melici Graeci.* Oxford: Oxford University Press.
Parry, Adam. 1971. "Introduction." In *The Making of Homeric Verse: The Collected Papers of Milman Parry.* Ed. Adam Parry, x–xxi. Oxford: Clarendon Press.
Pasquali, Giorgio. 1929. Review of Maas 1927. *Gnomon* 5: 417–35, 498–521.
———. 1934. *Storia della tradizione e critica del testo.* Florence: Le Monnier.
———. 1952. *Storia della tradizione e critica del testo.* 2nd ed. Florence: Le Monnier.
Patsch, Hermann. 1966. "Friedrich Schlegels 'Philosophie der Philologie' und Schleiermachers Frühe Entwürfe zur Hermeneutik: Zur Frühgeschichte der romantischen Hermeneutik." *Zeitschrift für Theologie und Kirche* 63: 434–72.
Patterson, Lee. 1987. *Negotiating the Past: The Historical Understanding of Literature.* Madison: University of Wisconsin Press.

———. 1990. "On the Margin: Postmodernism, Ironic History, and Medieval Studies." *Speculum* 65: 87–108.
———. 1994. "The Return to Philology." In *The Past and Future of Medieval Studies*. Ed. John V. Engen, 231–44. Notre Dame, IN: University of Notre Dame Press.
Pfeiffer, Rudolf, ed. 1949–53. *Callimachus*. 2 vols. Oxford: Oxford University Press.
———. 1968. *History of Classical Scholarship from the Beginnings to the End of the Hellenistic Age*. Oxford: Clarendon Press.
———. 1976. *History of Classical Scholarship from 1300 to 1850*. Oxford: Clarendon Press.
Piggott, Stuart. 1976. *Ruins in a Landscape: Essays in Antiquarianism*. Edinburgh: Edinburgh University Press.
Poliziano, Angelo. 1498. *Opera Omnia*. Venice: Aldus Manutius.
———. 1986. *Lamia: Praelectio in priora Aristotelis analytica*. Ed. Ari Wesseling. Leiden: Brill.
———. 1996. *Silvae*. Ed. Francesco Bausi. Florence: Olschki.
———. 2003. *Due poemetti latini*. Ed. Francesco Bausi. Rome: Salerno.
———. 2004. *Silvae*. Ed. and trans. Charles Fantazzi. Cambridge, MA: Harvard University Press.
Polizzotto, Lorenzo. 1994. *The Elect Nation: The Savonarolan Movement in Florence, 1494–1545*. Oxford: Clarendon Press.
Pope, Alexander. 1967. *The Odyssey of Homer: Books I-XII*. Vol. 9 of *The Poems of Alexander Pope*. Ed. Maynard Mack. New Haven: Yale University Press.
Porphyry. 1998. *Isagoge: Texte grec, translatio Boetii*. Ed. and trans. A. de Libera and A.-P. Segonds. Paris: Vrin.
Porter, James I. 1993. "The Seductions of Gorgias." *Classical Antiquity* 12: 267–99.
———. 2000. *Nietzsche and the Philology of the Future*. Stanford: Stanford University Press.
———. 2004. "Homer: The History of an Idea." In *The Cambridge Companion to Homer*. Ed. Robert Fowler, 324–43. Cambridge: Cambridge University Press.
———, ed. 2006. *Classical Pasts: The Classical Traditions of Greece and Rome*. Princeton: Princeton University Press.
———. 2010. "Theater of the Absurd: Nietzsche's Genealogy as Cultural Critique." *American Catholic Philosophical Quarterly* 84.2: 313–36.
Portolés, José. 1986. *Medio siglo de filología española (1896–1952): Positivismo e idealismo*. Madrid: Cátedra.
Prins, Yopie. 1999. *Victorian Sappho*. Princeton: Princeton University Press.
Pugliatti, Paola. 1998. "Textual Perspectives in Italy: From Pasquali's Historicism to the Challenge of 'Variantistica' (and Beyond)." *Text* 11: 155–88.
Pulci, Luca. 1916. *Il Driadeo d'Amore*. Ed. P. Giudici. Lanciano: Carabba.
Quentin, Henri. 1926. *Essais de critique textuelle (ecdotique)*. Paris: Picard.
R. de la Flor, Fernando. 1995. *Emblemas: Lecturas de la imagen simbólica*. Madrid: Alianza Editorial.
———. 2000. "La sombra del *Eclesiastés* es alargada. «Vanitas» y deconstrucción de la idea de mundo en la emblemática española hacia 1580." In *Emblemata aurea. La emblemática en el arte y la literatura del siglo de oro*. Ed. R. Zafra and J. J. Azanza, 337–52. Madrid: Ediciones Akal.
———. 2002. *Barroco: Representación e ideología en el mundo hispánico (1580–1680)*. Madrid: Cátedra.

Rawles, Stephen. 2001. "Layout, Typography and Chronology in Chrétien Wechel's Editions of Alciato." In *An Interregnum of the Sign: The Emblematic Age in France: Essays in Honour of Daniel S. Russell.* Ed. David Graham, 49–71. Glasgow: Glasgow Emblem Studies.
Real Academia Española. 2001. *Diccionario de la lengua española.* 22nd ed. Madrid: Editorial Espasa Calpe.
Reynolds, Leighton D., and Nigel G. Wilson. 1991. *Scribes and Scholars: A Guide to the Transmission of Greek and Latin Literature.* 3rd ed. Oxford: Clarendon Press.
Rodríguez, Juan Carlos. 2003. *El escritor que compró su propio libro: Para leer el* Quijote. Barcelona: Debate.
Rousseau, Jean-Jacques. 1997. "Essay on the Origins of Languages." In *The Discourses and Other Early Political Writings.* Ed. Victor Gourevitch, 247–99. Cambridge: Cambridge University Press.
Rovighi, S. Vanni. 1956. "La filosofia di Gilberto Porretano." *Miscellanea del Centro di studi medievali* 1: 1–64.
Ruiz, Elisa. 1985. "Crítica textual. Edición de textos." *Métodos de estudio de la obra literaria.* Ed. José María Díez Borque, 67–120. Madrid: Taurus.
Russell, D. A. 1981. *Criticism in Antiquity.* Berkeley: University of California Press.
Russell, Daniel S. 1995. *Emblematic Structures in Renaissance French Culture.* Toronto: University of Toronto Press.
Rutherford, Ian. 2001. *Pindar's Paeans: A Reading of the Fragments with a Survey of the Genre.* Oxford: Oxford University Press.
Said, Edward W. 1978. *Orientalism.* New York: Pantheon Books.
———. 2004. *Humanism and Democratic Criticism.* New York: Columbia University Press.
Said, Edward, and Maire Said. 1969. Introduction to Auerbach 1969.
Sánchez Prieto-Borja, Pedro. 1996. "Problemas lingüísticos en la edición de textos medievales (la relación entre crítica textual e historia de la lengua)." *Incipit* 16: 19–54.
Sandys, John E. 1964. *A History of Classical Scholarship.* 3 vols. New York: Hafner.
Santoro, M. 1952. "La polemica Poliziano-Merula." *Giornale italiano di filologia.* 5: 212–33.
Saussure, Ferdinand de. 1916. *Cours de linguistique générale.* Ed. Charles Bally, Albert Sechehaye, and Albert Reidlinger. Paris: Payot.
———. 1986. *Course in General Linguistics.* Ed. Charles Bally, Albert Sechehaye, and Albert Sechehage. Trans. Roy Harris. La Salle, IL: Open Court.
Schiller, Friedrich. 1995. *Letters on the Aesthetic Education of Man,* in *Essays.* Ed. Walter Hinderer and Daniel O. Dahlstrom. New York: Continuum.
Schlegel, Friedrich A. 1981. *Kritische-Friedrich-Schlegel-Ausgabe.* Vol. 16. Ed. Hans Eichner. Paderborn, Munich and Vienna: Ferdinand Schöningh.
Schmidt, P. L. 1988. "Lachmann's Method: On the History of a Misunderstanding." In *The Uses of Greek and Latin: Historical Essays.* Ed. A. C. Dionisotti, Anthony Grafton and Jill Kraye, 227–36. London: Warburg Institute Surveys and Texts.
Sedley, David N. 1973. "Epicurus, On Nature, Book XXVIII." *Cronache Ercolanesi* 3: 5–83.
Selig, Karl-Ludwig. 1990. *Studies on Alciato in Spain.* New York: Garland.
Shillingsburg, Peter L. 1997. *Resisting Texts: Authority and Submission in Constructions of Meaning.* Ann Arbor: University of Michigan Press.

Sider, David. 2005. *The Library of the Villa dei Papiri at Herculaneum.* Los Angeles: J. Paul Getty Museum.
Silverman, Joseph. 1991. "On Knowing Other People's Lives, Inquisitorially and Artistically." In *Cultural Encounters: the Impact of the Inquisition in Spain and the New World.* Ed. Anne J. Cruz and Mary Elizabeth Perry, 157–75. Berkeley: University of California Press.
Simpson, David. 1993. *Romanticism, Nationalism, and the Revolt against Theory.* Chicago: University of Chicago Press.
Snell, Bruno, Richard Kannicht, and S. L. Radt, eds. 1971–2004. *Tragicorum Graecorum fragmenta.* 5 vols. Göttingen: Vandenhoeck & Ruprecht.
Speer, Mary B. 1979. "In Defense of Philology: Two New Guides to Textual Criticism [review of *L'edizione critica dei testi volgari,* by Franca Brambilla Ageno; *Medieval Manuscripts and Textual Criticism,* ed. Christopher Kleinhenz]." *Romance Philology* 32: 335–44.
Spencer, T. J. B. 1957. "Robert Wood and the Problem of Troy in the Eighteenth Century." *Journal of the Warburg and Courtauld Institutes* 20: 75–10.
Spengel, Leonhard von, ed. 1856. *Rhetores Graeci.* Vol. 3. Leipzig: Teubner.
Spitzer, Leo. 1948. *Linguistics and Literary History; Essays in Stylistics.* Princeton: Princeton University Press.
Suárez, Ana E., ed. 2003. *Pedro Calderón de la Barca: El gran mercado del mundo.* Pamplona: Universidad de Navarra.
Sweet, Rosemary. 2001. "Antiquaries and Antiquities in Eighteenth-Century England." *Eighteenth-Century Studies* 34: 181–206.
Szondi, Peter. 1962. "Über philologische Erkenntnis." *Die Neue Rundschau* 73: 146–65.
———. 1986. *On Textual Understanding, and Other Essays.* Trans. Harvey Mendelsohn. Minneapolis: University of Minnesota Press.
Tanselle, G. Tomas. 1981. "The Society for Textual Scholarship." *Text: Transactions of the Society for Textual Scholarship* 1: 1–9.
———. 1990. *Textual Criticism and Scholarly Editing.* Charlottesville: University of Virginia Press.
———. 1996. "Textual Instability and Editorial Idealism." *Studies in Bibliography* 49: 1–60.
Tarugi, Luisa R. S., ed. 1996. *Poliziano nel suo tempo.* Florence: Cesati.
Tavernati, Andrea. 1985. "Appunti sulla diffusione quattrocentesca de 'Il Driadeo' di Luca Pulci." *La bibliofilia* 87: 267–79.
Timpanaro, Sebastiano. 1981. *La genesi del metodo del Lachmann.* Rev. ed. Padua: Liviana.
———. 2005. *The Genesis of Lachmann's Method.* Ed. and trans. Glen W. Most. Chicago: University of Chicago Press.
Tissol, Garth E. 2002. "Ovid and the Exilic Journey of Rutilius Namatianus." *Arethusa* 35: 435–46.
Trumpener, Katie. 1997. *Bardic Nationalism: The Romantic Novel and the British Empire.* Princeton: Princeton University Press.
Turner, Eric G. 1952. "Roman Oxyrhynchus." *Journal of Egyptian Archaeology* 39: 78–93.
———. 1956. "Scribes and Scholars of Oxyrhynchus." In *Akten des VIII Internationalen Kongress für Papyrologie, Wien 1955 (29 August–3 September),* 141–46. Vienna: Rohrer.
———. 1980. *Greek Papyri: An Introduction.* 2nd ed. Oxford: Oxford University Press.
Uhlig, Gustav, ed. 1883. *Dionysii Thracis Ars Grammatica (Grammatici Graeci vol 1).* Leipzig: Teubner.

Uitti, Karl D. 1982. Introduction to *Language and Philology in Romance*. Vol. 3 of *Trends in Romance Linguistics and Philology.* Ed. Rebecca Porner and John N. Green. The Hague: Mouton.
Valla, Lorenzo. 1982. *Repastinatio dialectice et philosophie*. 2 vols. Ed. Gianni Zippel. Padua: Antenore.
Van Engen, John H., ed. 1994. *The Past and Future of Medieval Studies*. Notre Dame, IN: University of Notre Dame Press.
Vasoli, Cesare. 1968. *La dialettica e la retorica dell'Umanesimo: 'Invenzione' e 'metodo' nella cultura del XV e XVI secolo*. Milan: Feltrinelli.
———, ed. 2002. *Le filosofie del Rinascimento*. Milan: Mondadori.
Verde, Armando F. 1973–94. *Lo studio fiorentino, 1473–1503: Ricerche e documenti*. 5 vols. Florence: Olschki.
Vermeule, Emily D. T. 1996. "Archaeology and Philology: The Dirt and the Word." *Transactions of the American Philological Association* 126: 1–10.
Verrycken, Koenraad, and Charles H. Lohr, eds. 1994. *Joannis Grammatici Alexandrei cognomento Philoponi in libros Priorum resolutivorum Aristotelis commentariae annotationes ex colloquiis Ammonii cum quibusdam propriis meditationibus*. Stuttgart-Bad Cannstatt: Frommann-Holzboog.
Vico, Giambattista. 2001. *New Science: Principles of the New Science Concerning the Common Nature of Nations*. 3rd ed. Trans. David Marsh. New York: Penguin.
Voigt, E. M. 1971. *Sappho et Alcaeus*. Amsterdam: Polak & Van Gennep.
Vuilleumier, Florence Laurens. 2000. *La Raison des figures symboliques à la Renaissance et à l'âge classique: Études sur les fondements philosophiques, théologiques et rhétoriques de l'image*. Geneva: Droz.
Weinstein, Donald. 1970. *Savonarola and Florence: Prophecy and Patriotism in the Renaissance*. Princeton: Princeton University Press.
Wellek, René, and Austin Warren. 1956. *Theory of Literature*. 3rd ed. New York: Harcourt. Orig. pub. 1942.
Wesseling, Ari. 1986. Introduction to *Lamia: Praelectio in priora Aristotelis analytica*. Ed. Ari Wesseling, xiii–xxxviii. Leiden: Brill.
———. 2002. "Dutch Proverbs and Expressions in Erasmus' *Adages, Colloquies,* and *Letters*." *Renaissance Quarterly* 55: 81–147.
West, Martin L. 1973. *Textual Criticism and Editorial Technique Applicable to Greek and Latin Texts*. Stuttgart: Teubner.
Wieland, Georg. 1982. "The Reception and Interpretation of Aristotle's *Ethics*." In *The Cambridge History of Later Medieval Philosophy*. Ed. Norman Kretzmann, Anthony Kenny, and Jan Pinborg, 657–72. Cambridge: Cambridge University Press.
Wilamowitz-Moellendorff, Ulrich. 1982. *History of Classical Scholarship*. Ed. Hugh Lloyd-Jones. Trans. Alan Harris. London: Duckworth.
Williams, Raymond. 1977. *Marxism and Literature*. Oxford: Oxford University Press.
Wilson, Nigel G. 1967. "A Chapter in the History of Scholia." *Classical Quarterly* 17: 244–56.
———. 2007. "Scholiasts and Commentators." *Greek Roman and Byzantine Studies* 47: 39–70.
Wittgenstein, Ludwig. 1963. *Philosophical Investigations: The German Text, with a Revised English Translation*. Trans. G. E. M. Anscrombe. 3rd ed. Oxford: Blackwell.
Wolf, Friedrich A. 1985. *Prolegomena to Homer, 1795*. Trans. Anthony Grafton, Glenn W. Most, and James E. G. Zetzel. Princeton: Princeton University Press.

Wood, Robert. 1753. *The Ruins of Palmyra, Otherwise Tedmor, in the Desart.* London (n.p).
———. 1775. *An Essay on the Original Genius and Writings of Homer.* London: T. Payne and P. Elmsley.
———. Collection. Joint Library of Hellenic and Roman Societies, Senate House, London.
Zini, F. Mariani. 1996. "Poliziano, allievo degli antichi, maestro dei moderni." In *Poliziano nel suo tempo.* Ed. L. Secchi Tarugi, 165–91. Florence: Franco Cesati.
———. 1999. "Ange Politien: la grammaire philologique entre poésie et philosophie," *Chroniques italiennes* 58/59: 157–72.
Ziolkowski, Jan M., ed. 1990a. *On Philology.* University Park: Pennsylvania State University Press.
———, ed. 1990b. *On Philology.* Special issue of *Comparative Literature Studies*, 27.1.
Žižek, Slavoj. 1991a. *Looking Awry: An Introduction to Jacques Lacan through Popular Culture.* Cambridge, MA: MIT Press.
———. 1991b. *For They Know not What They Do: Enjoyment as a Political Factor.* New York: Verso.
Zumthor, Paul. 1970. "La Chanson de Bele Aiglentine." *Travaux de Linguistique et de Littérature* 8: 325–37.
———. 1972. *Essai de poétique médiévale.* Paris: Seuil.
———. 1981. "Intertextualité et mouvance." *Littérature* 41: 8–16.
Zuntz, Günther. 1975. *Die Aristophanes-Scholien der Papyri.* 2nd ed. Berlin: Seitz.

CONTRIBUTORS

NADIA ALTSCHUL (Johns Hopkins University) is the author of *La literatura, el autor y la crítica textual* (Madrid: Pliegos, 2005) and numerous articles on editorial theory and medieval studies. She has previously engaged with technologies of communication, the development of copyright and modern authorship, and comparative philological histories of Spain, France, and Germany.

IAN BALFOUR (York University) is the author of *Northrop Frye* (Twayne Publishers, 1988), *The Rhetoric of Romantic Prophecy* (Stanford: Stanford University Press, 2002) and essays on the Romantics (Wordsworth, Blake, Godwin, Inchbald), Walter Benjamin, Paul de Man, and topics in popular culture (music, TV, film). He co-edited (with Atom Egoyan) *Subtitles: On the Foreignness of Film,* and (with Eduardo Cadava) *And Justice For All?: The Claims of Human Rights* (SAQ), and is the sole editor of a collection called *Late Derrida* (SAQ). He has taught at Cornell, Stanford, the Johann Wolfgang Goethe University in Frankfurt, and Williams College.

CHRISTOPHER S. CELENZA (Johns Hopkins University) is the author of *The Lost Italian Renaissance: Humanists, Historians, and Latin's Legacy* (Baltimore and London: The Johns Hopkins University Press, 2004), which won the Renaissance Society of America's 2005 Phyllis Goodhart Gordan Prize and was selected as a CHOICE Outstanding Academic Title in 2006; *Piety and Pythagoras in Renaissance Florence: The Symbolum Nesianum,* Studies in the History of Christian Thought, 101 (Leiden, Boston, and Cologne: Brill, 2001), and *Renaissance Humanism and the Papal Curia: Lapo da Castiglionchio the Younger's De curiae commodis,* Papers and Monographs of the American Academy in Rome, 31 (Ann Arbor: University of Michigan Press, 1999).

SEAN ALEXANDER GURD (Concordia University) is the author of *Iphigenias at Aulis: Textual Multiplicity, Radical Philology* (Ithaca: Cornell University Press, 2006) and articles on Greek and Latin literature and their scholarly reception.

KATHLEEN McNAMEE (Wayne State University) is the author of *Annotations in Greek and Latin Papyri from Egypt* (New Haven: American Society of Papyrologists, 2007), *Sigla and Select Marginalia in Greek Literary Papyri, Papyrologica Bruxellensia* 26 (Brussels: 1992), and *Abbreviations in Greek Literary Papyri and Ostraca* (Chico, California 1981). She has published many articles on ancient papyri and the history of scholarship in antiquity.

CRAIG MAYNES (Memorial University of Newfoundland) works on Latin literature and textual criticism. His dissertation concerned the *De Reditu Suo* of Rutilius Namatianus.

BRADLEY J. NELSON (Concordia University) is the author of many articles on Spanish Golden Age literature, including "*Los trabajos de Persiles y Sigismunda:* Una crítica cervantina de la alegoresis emblemática," *Cervantes* 24.2 (2004): 43–69 and "The Marriage of Art and Honor: Anamorphosis and Control in Calderón's *La dama duende*." *Bulletin of the Comediantes* 54.2 (2002): 407–42. A monograph, *The Persistence of Presence: Emblem and Ritual in Early Modern Spain,* is forthcoming with the University of Toronto Press (2010).

JAMES I. PORTER (University of California at Irvine) is the author of *The Invention of Dionysus: An Essay on The Birth of Tragedy* (Stanford: Stanford University Press, 2000), *Nietzsche and the Philology of the Future* (Stanford: Stanford University Press, 2000), and many articles on ancient literature and its reception. He has also edited *Constructions of the Classical Body (*Ann Arbor: University of Michigan Press 1999), *Before Subjectivity? Lacan and the Classics* (with Mark Buchan), special double issue of *Helios,* Summer 2004, and *Classical Pasts: The Classical Traditions of Greece and Rome* (Princeton: Princeton University Press, 2006).

JONATHAN SACHS (Concordia University) is the author of *Romantic Antiquity: Rome in the Romantic Imagination, 1789–1832* (Oxford University Press, 2010) and articles on the intersections of literary, political, and historical writing in the Romantic Period.

INDEX

Adorno, Theodor Wiesengrund, 9–10, 169–70, 171, 201–2, 211
Aeschines, 29
Aeschylus, 28, 34, 35
Aesop, 94, 210
Alcaeus, 31, 34, 35, 39, 40, 41
Alexander Numeniu, 178, 181–82
Alexandria, 22, 23, 27
Alciato, Andrea, 109–11
Alcman, 31, 33, 34
allegory, 22, 22n5, 121, 210
Alexander of Aphrodisias, 81
Anacreon, 37
annotation. *See* marginalia
antiquarianism, 128, 143
Ammonius of Alexandria, 81
Apuleius, 84
Aratus, 34, 92n67
Argyropoulos, Johannes, 76
Aristophanes, 30, 34, 35
Aristotle, 15, 22n5, 76, 78, 79, 80, 83, 97, 100, 103, 184–85
Auerbach, Erich, 151, 161
author, 47
authorial intention, 58, 110, 111, 124
auto sacramental, 116–19

Bacchylides, 29
Bakhtin, Mikhail, 122, 125
Barbaro, Ermolao, 82–83, 94

Barthes, Roland, 124, 166, 191
Bate, Walter Jackson, 206–7
Bédier, Joseph, 155–58
Benjamin, Walter, 9–10, 19, 121, 192, 198, 200–6, 211
Bobbio, 65
body, 167, 169, 170, 174, 177, 182, 187
Boethius, 103
Bononi, Filippino, 66
Borja, Juan de, 107, 120
Borra, Giovanni, 130
Bourdieu, Pierre, 117
Bouverie, John, 130
Bowers, Fredson, 156
Brower, Reuben, 207
Brukner, Johann Jacob, 92
Budé, Guillaume, 149
Burke, Edmund, 207
Burley, Walter, 81, 104
Burney, Charles, 140

Cage, John, 166
Calderón de la Barca, Pedro, 107, 116–19, 120, 121
Callimachus, 30, 31, 35, 39, 40, 42
Callistus, Andronicus, 76
Cervantes, Miguel de, 120–21, 123–24, 125
Chaucer, 81
Cicero, 64, 91, 129

231

codicology, 48, 127
commentary, 25, 30, 33, 81, 205
correction, 20, 28–29
Corinna, 31, 35
critical apparatus, 52–54, 56
Crucianus, Ioannes Andreas, 68, 70, 71
cultural studies, 18, 159–63

Dawkins, James, 130, 131, 138
deconstruction, 19
Democritus, 179, 180
Demosthenes, 183
Dionysius of Halicarnassus, 182
Dionysius Thrax, 37, 42–43
di Tommaso, Francesco, 76

ecdotics, 18, 153, 154–58
editorial intention, 56–58
Egypt, 22, 137
emblem, 16, 107, 108–11
emblematic mode of representation, 111–12
Epicharmus, 37
Epictetus, 100, 103
Epicurus, 77
Epimenides, 39
Erasmus, 91
Eratosthenes, 15, 41
etymology, 22, 115, 162
Euphorion, 41

Fichte, Johann Gottlieb, 193, 196
Ficino, Marsilio, 76, 90, 94, 94n73
Fonzio, Bartolomeo, 76
Foucault, Michel, 108

Galbiato, Giorgio, 65
geno-song, 167
geno-text, 167, 191
Gerber, Gustav, 18, 178–79, 180, 181, 183
Gilbert of Poitiers, 81, 103–4
glosses, 30, 31–32

Goethe, Johann Wolfgang von, 131, 193, 197, 201, 204–5, 206
Gorgias of Leontini, 180
grammatike, 37, 42–43. See also Dionysius Thrax.
grammaticus, 15, 17, 24, 83, 101–3
Grattius, 66
Greg, Walter, 156
Gumbrecht, Hans Ulrich, 16, 17, 108, 112, 124, 126, 127–28, 129, 133, 143, 151

Havelock, Eric, 129
Heidegger, Martin, 4, 124
Herder, Johann Gottfried, 131
Hesiod, 77
Heyne, Christian Gottlob, 131
Heytesbury, William, 81
hieroglyph, 113, 115, 120
Hipponax, 34
history, 4, 7, 203–4; and philology, 7
Hellanicus, 39
Hervaeus Natalis, 81
Homer, 28, 30, 33, 34, 38, 42, 76, 77, 128, 129, 131–38
Horace, 75, 84

Ibycus, 31
Iamblichus, 90, 92, 93, 95, 97
Inghirami, Tommaso (AKA Fedro), 52, 66
interpretation, 1, 4, 13, 14, 135
Isocrates, 30, 31, 32

Josephus, 129
Juvenal, 95

Kant, Immanuel, 15, 186, 189, 193, 198–99
Kuhn, Thomas, 99

Lachmann, Karl, 3, 3n6, 42, 155, 158
Lange, Friedrich, 18, 174, 176, 178, 181

language, as gesture, 172
Libanius, 31
literature, 1, 5
locative hermeneutics, 17, 134
Lucretius, 77
Lycophron, 31

Maas, Paul, 42
de Man, Paul, 19, 127, 148, 159, 175–76, 192, 206–12
marketplace, 92, 117, 123, 125–26
materialism, 13, 18, 177, 202. *See also* body.
materiality: of communication, 126; of the letter, 127; of literature, 7, 14–15, 16, 205; of rhetoric, 186
marginalia, 12, 13, 17, 20–46, 138–42. *See also* corrections; scholarly notes; scholia; variants
Merula, Giorgio, 65
Marxism, 200, 204
Menander, 34
modernity, 113
mythology, 37–39

Namatianus, Rutilius Claudius, 14–15, 47–74.
neo-Lachmannism, 154, 157, 158. See also *nuova filologia*
new philology, 155–57
Nietzsche, Friedrich, 18, 19, 95, 127, 149, 164–91, 192, 194
nuova filologia, 154, 156, 158. *See also* neo-Lachmannism

Ong, Walter, 129
Ovid, 72
pseudo-Ovid, 66
Oxyrhynchus, 23, 24, 43

paleography, 48, 127, 205
palimpsests, 63–64
papyri, 13–14, 20–46

papyrology, 127
Parry, Adam, 129
Parry, Milman, 129
Parthenius, 35, 38
Pergamum, 22
philology: absolute, 198; identical with ancient literature, 196; and authorial process, 71; characteristic of, 8; and the chronicle, 200; and contingency, 10–11; and culture, 18, 158, 165, 190; definition, 1, 47, 149–51; and emblem, 112, 119, 126; and Eratosthenes, 15; etymology of, 47n1; and *Geistesgeschichte*, 152; and history of terminology, 200; and historicism, 17, 161n49, 172; 198–99, 202; history of, 4, 5, 6–7, 8, 10, 14, 48; and *Kulturgeschichte*, 152, 158; is infinite, 199; and linguistics, 151, 151n14, 152; and literature, 124; and medieval studies, 148; multiple modes of, 48; name of, 17–18; and its object of study, 198; in a permanent crisis, 206, 212; and philosophy, 12, 15, 19, 75–106, *esp.* 105, 192, 195–97; and presence, 124; a regulative discipline, 102, 106; revivals, 2; and rhetoric, 164–91; seductive side of, 200, 212; must be sublated by historical materialism, 206; and textual recycling, 63–64; and textual criticism, 18, 150, 152, 153, 154–58; and self-critique, 8, 10, 164, 197; temporalities of, 12, 202. See also *grammatike; grammaticus;* materiality; slow reading
Philoponus, 81
philosophers, compared to bloodsucking witches with removable eyes, 85–87
philosophy, 87–100; and philology, 12, 15, 19, 75–106, *esp.* 105, 192, 195–97
Pisistratus, 129
Pico della Mirandola, Giovanni, 76, 81–83, 90, 94, 95
Pindar, 30, 31, 34, 38, 39, 40
Pio, Giambattista, 67–68, 70, 71

place, experience of, 130. *See also* locative hermeneutics
Plato, 34, 91, 93, 95, 97, 184
Plutarch, 86
Poliziano, Angelo, 2, 3, 15, 18, 65, 75–106
Porphyry, 90, 103
presence, 16, 107, 108, 112, 113, 117, 128, 133, 147, 185
Pythagoras, 84, 88–91

Quintilian, 31, 39, 101, 183
Quintin, Dom Henri, 154–55, 155n27

Revette, Nicholas, 130
revisors, 21. *See also* textual criticism; variants
rhythm, 167, 172–73, 181–82, 189
Rousseau, Jean-Jacques, 146

Said, Edward, 11, 161
Sannazaro, Jacopo, 66, 70
Sappho, 31
de Saussure, Ferdinand, 2n2
Savonarola, Girolamo, 90
Schlegel, Friedrich, 19, 192, 194–99, 203, 206
Schiller, Friedrich, 145–46, 209
scholarly notes, 32–34. *See also* marginalia
scholia, 13n18, 22. *See also* marginalia
Schopenhauer, Arthur, 189
Simonides, 31
Simplicius, 81
slow reading, 10–12, 192; and textual criticism, 12
Socrates, 94, 95, 180
Solon, 129
Sophocles, 30, 34
Sophron, 31
Spitzer, Leo, 11
Statius, 31
stemmatic recension, 53, 127, 154
Stesichorus, 31

Strode, Ralph, 81
Stuart, James, 130
style, 168–169
Suetonius, 101

Tanselle, Thomas, 156
Tertullian, 84
textual criticism, 1, 3, 4, 5, 7, 8, 12, 21, 22, 42, 48, 49n2, 54–55, 150–51, 154–58, 159, 160n42; and the history of philology, 14; and slow reading, 12. *See also* ecdotics; revisors; variants
textual history, 6, 49
textual scholarship, 159–60
Theocritus, 30, 34, 42
Theophrastus, 81
theory, 9, 208
Thucydidies, 31
Timpanaro, Sebastiano, 2–4, 5, 6
travel, 130, 134, 135, 141, 142, 147. *See also* locative hermeneutics

university, German, 1

Valla, Lorenzo, 104
variants, 29–31. *See also* textual criticism; revisors
Vico, Giambattista, 129, 131–32, 136, 144, 192
Virgil, 72–74, 77, 78

wannabe philologists, 198
William of Ockham, 81
Winckelmann, Johann Joachim, 193
Wittgenstein, Ludwig, 96
Wolf, Friedrich August, 2, 3, 128, 129, 131, 147, 194
Wood, Robert, 17, 127–47

Zeno, 100
Zenodotus, 42

CLASSICAL MEMORIES/MODERN IDENTITIES
Paul Allen Miller and Richard H. Armstrong, Series Editors

This series consistently explores how the classical world has been variously interpreted, transformed, and appropriated to forge a usable past and a livable present. Books published in this series will detail both the positive and negative aspects of classical reception and will take an expansive view of the topic. Therefore, it will include works that examine the function of translations, adaptations, invocations, and classical scholarship in the formation of personal, cultural, national, sexual, and racial identities. This series's expansive view and theoretial focus thus separate cultural reception from the category of mere *Nachleben*.

Paul Allen Miller
Postmodern Spiritual Practices: The Construction of the Subject and the Reception of Plato in Lacan, Derrida, and Foucault

www.ingramcontent.com/pod-product-compliance
Lightning Source LLC
Chambersburg PA
CBHW032004220426
43664CB00005B/133